The Black Book
and the Mob

The Black Book and the Mob

The Untold Story of the Control of Nevada's Casinos

Ronald A. Farrell

and

Carole Case

The University of Wisconsin Press

The University of Wisconsin Press
1930 Monroe Street
Madison, Wisconsin 53711

3 Henrietta Street
London WC2E 8LU, England

Library of Congress Cataloging-in-Publication Data
Farrell, Ronald A.
The black book and the mob: the untold story of the control of
Nevada's casinos / Ronald A. Farrell and Carole Case.
300 p.   cm.
Includes bibliographical references and index.
ISBN 0-299-14750-9   ISBN 0-299-14754-1 (pbk.)
1. Casinos—Nevada.   2. Organized crime—Nevada.   3. Gambling—
Nevada.   I. Case, Carole, 1942–   . II. Title.
HV6711.F37   1995
364.1'06'09793—dc20   95-12293

Surely, gentlemen, this is not what the American way is all about.
—Gary Logan, attorney for James Tamer,
before the Nevada Gaming
Commission, August 16, 1978

Contents

Contents

Part 4. DENUNCIATION AND INEQUALITY

Illustrations

Preface

With the spread of casino gambling in the United States, there has been increased concern with issues of its regulation. Of persistent preoccupation is its potential infiltration by organized crime. For direction in addressing these concerns, others embarking on casino gambling have looked to "the Nevada experience." An important aspect of that experience is a regulatory procedure that involves what has come to be known as the Black Book. The Black Book is a list of persons who are to be excluded from casinos in the state because of their perceived threat to the public image of gaming. Most of those listed are reputed to be associates of organized crime, and the majority are Italian.

We knew little about the Black Book and its importance to Nevada before undertaking our study. As sociologists, however, we quickly became intrigued with this regulatory procedure and its meaning for social control. We were especially struck by the dramaturgical quality of newspaper accounts about those listed or to be entered in the book, and wondered what such a drama must mean for the image of the industry and its regulatory body. Just what functions were being served? Surely some of them must be symbolic, we thought, given the small number of individuals entered relative to the size of the industry. And what about the so-called notorious and unsavory characters who were listed? Were they really as bad as they had been depicted? The whole notion of some sinister mafia* has been suspect for some time, and this regulatory procedure seems to be grounded in

*We have deliberately made the term *mafia* lowercase throughout this work, because capitalizing it, which is the conventional treatment, would give credence to the objective reality of the mafia's existence.

such an assumption. Then, there was the question of whether those listed in the Black Book were the real culprits or the losers in attempts to gain control in the industry. If the latter, then who were the winners?

With these questions in mind, we set out in our study of the Black Book. Our conceptual framework was derived from sociological theories of deviance and its control, particularly from a blending of neofunctionalist and labeling explanations. We recognized from the outset that some sociologists would be uncomfortable with this conceptual integration, given that these theories traditionally have been viewed as having disparate and competing assumptions. For them, it will be a task of this work to demonstrate otherwise. Others may feel that our theoretical interpretations get in the way of more important practical concerns. Here, we would argue that meaningful social policy can best be achieved through conceptual understanding, an approach that is too often missing in contemporary analyses of crime and its control.

Some may also be disturbed by our interpretations, viewing them as unduly analytical or as treading on "sacred grounds." But this is precisely what sociology is about. Our role is not to validate established institutions. Nor does it require that we protect the interests of particular groups or organizations. Indeed, most of the groups that we deal with in this book appear to be quite adept at protecting their own interests.

Additionally we are without policy recommendations for our findings. Our intent is to present as accurate a picture of the Black Book as possible, and to offer explanations consistent with our observations. The relevance of these findings and explanations to future regulatory action, legislation, and legal decisions is, from our perspective, the purview of the regulators, policy makers, and the courts, not that of the social scientist.

While we have sought to approach the Black Book with as much objectivity as possible, the controversial nature of the regulatory procedure has not always made that an easy task. In an effort to circumvent some of this controversy, we limited our analysis to official documents, public hearings, and media accounts. We had originally considered complementing these sources with interviews of regulators and government officials, as well as with excluded persons themselves, that is, those entered in the book.

But, as the study progressed, we felt that the potential problems connected with the interviews would outweigh any appreciable advantages. In particular we did not want our research to be publicized and become part of the controversy, or to be seen as supporting one or the other side of the issue. Also, the richness of the public records seemed more than sufficient to address the kinds of questions that we had about the Black Book.

When we were presented with opportunities to join the faculty at the University of Nevada, Las Vegas, we thought, "What an ideal place for the study of organized crime." Indeed, this became an important factor in our decision. At the time, we asked if others on the faculty had been doing research in the area. Surprisingly, the answer was no. What about the Black Book itself; had anyone done research on it? Apart from a law review article on the constitutionality of the procedure, we learned that there had been no other investigations of this fascinating issue, either inside or outside the university. Why hadn't the related issues of the Black Book and organized crime received more social scientific attention? Aside from the possibility that little social significance is accorded the issues, they seem to us to enjoy a kind of protective sanctity. It is a sanctity that appears to be based on a fear of organized crime as mythically constructed. When we told others of our intent to undertake this study, the response of many was implicit with suggested caution, if not outright concern for our well-being. These expressions were by no means limited to those in Nevada. It seemed as though virtually everyone with whom we talked about the study questioned whether there were dangers associated with the research or expressed concerns for our safety. Though some of this was obviously in jest, it nonetheless conveys the potency of the imagery of violence that accompanies the mafia stereotype. This imagery becomes all the more salient when placed within the context of Las Vegas—for many, the organized crime capital of the United States. Thus, when you talk about a study of this sort in Las Vegas, it carries a special meaning, one that is very real in light of the images that people have of the city. This became for us another reason for studying the Black Book.

Many have contributed to the research and its final product. The University of Nevada, Las Vegas, contributed substantially toward the costs of photocopying the regulatory transcripts and provided us with time away from teaching to pursue the study. Several colleagues and individuals in various state positions in Nevada were also helpful, though they are in no way responsible for our findings. The records department of the Gaming Control Board provided access to the hearing transcripts and space at its Las Vegas offices for us to review materials on a regular basis. Additionally, staff members at the Nevada State Library and Archives in Carson City and at the Nevada Historical Society in Reno were helpful in providing biographical information on the regulators and other regulatory documents. Faculty colleagues in criminal justice offered suggestions and assistance on various issues. Thanks are especially due Joseph Albini, John Crank, and, most notably, Leonard Gilbert. We also wish to thank the book's reviewers for their comments and suggestions: Professors John Galliher of the University of Missouri; Richard Hawkins of Southern Methodist University; Pat Lauderdale of Arizona State University; and Allen Liska of the State University of New York at Albany. And Robin Whitaker did a superb job of copyediting the manuscript. Finally, Rosalie M. Robertson, editor at the University of Wisconsin Press, deserves tremendous gratitude for her support and the careful attention that she has given our work.

The Black Book
and the Mob

1

Denunciation and the Illusion of Social Control

This is a story about good and evil. The setting is Las Vegas, and the plot involves the control of legalized gambling. The good in our story is theoretically the law and those responsible for the protection of state interests; the evil is organized crime, which is seen as presenting a threat to those interests. We say "theoretically" because our analysis does not always bear out such clear distinctions; the law does not always look good, and there is much about the alleged criminals that does not appear to be evil. The perception of the social context itself as essentially evil makes the task of the law to render it good highly provocative at least.

The story begins in the gambling halls of the silver mining towns of territorial Nevada and continues through to the present. It chronicles the development of casino gambling and the competition among underworld entrepreneurs for its control. The backdrop is the conflict that emerged between organized crime interests in Las Vegas, the widespread publicity that accompanied the conflict, and the attempts of the state to address the problem. The focus is on state efforts to exclude individuals who are said to pose a threat to the industry and on the ritualized denunciation process integral to that exclusion. This process involves the "Black Book," a list of persons banned for life from all licensed gambling establishments in the state.

Started in 1960 and kept current, the Black Book (officially referred to as the List of Excluded Persons) has, over the years,

3

listed 38 notorious and unsavory persons, most of whom are reputed to be associated with organized crime. The book, which includes pictures and background information on those listed, is distributed to all casinos with instructions to exclude or eject such persons or otherwise risk loss of their license. Should the banned individuals enter a casino, they have committed a "gross misdemeanor." To the extent that the regulators are thought to have driven mob interests out of Las Vegas, good would appear to have won out in the battle with evil.

However, the struggle to control legalized gambling has involved more than conflicts between the state and its regulators on the one hand and some monolithic organized crime entity on the other. Our story traces a pattern of exclusion that suggests that certain competing criminal interests have been winners in part because they established themselves as legitimate and were licensed preferentially by the regulators. Thus, the Black Book blacklisted only certain organized crime figures and forbade them from entering casinos. While no more criminal than many of their more businesslike counterparts in the industry, those whose names have been placed in the book tend to be caricatures of the mafia stereotype. The stereotype that organized crime is the exclusive domain of Italians has been particularly seductive to the moral orientations of the regulators. Thus, the forces of good appear as pawns in the struggle, favoring certain groups over others.

The framework for our story derives from several suppositions about deviance and its control, suppositions drawn in large part from the neofunctionalist and labeling perspectives of sociology. We argue that the origin and use of the Black Book are responses to perceived threats to the gaming industry, a particularly fragile entity, or to its regulatory body. During times of threat, regulators demonstrate their ability to control the industry by designating certain individuals as disreputable types who are joined in opposition to the industry's service of public and state interests. This process of designation and denunciation of deviance often proceeds with much drama; the more drama is involved, the more control is seen to be effected. The images of disreputability are drawn largely from those that are publicly accepted and promulgated by the media. Threats to gambling are most often seen as emanating from forces alien both to estab-

4

lished groups and to those designated responsible for effecting control. The selection of individuals for the Black Book thus reflects stereotypes of evil, cultural conflicts, and the differential ability of groups to institutionalize their interests. Institutional legitimacy and dominant group superiority become affirmed through this denunciation process.

The story is told in the words of the regulators, the notorious and unsavory individuals themselves, and those who have sought to defend these individuals against entry into the Black Book. The words are from the transcripts of regulatory hearings dating back to 1959.* These transcripts are alive with drama, pathos, and humor on the backgrounds, illicit activities, and personalities of the excluded persons, as well as with the moralism and mentality of those who regulate gambling. They also reveal the influences and motivations that impel decisions to exclude certain individuals. The rich and detailed dialogue and arguments are scripts of the events, thoughts, and emotions surrounding gambling and organized crime in Las Vegas. These scripts are viewed against the backdrop of local and national newspaper accounts, observations of recent regulatory meetings, and the relevant literatures of deviance and organized crime.

THE REGULATORY PROCEDURE

Those to be excluded from licensed gambling establishments in Nevada are selected by the state's gaming regulators. The regulators are gubernatorial appointees and serve full-time on the Gaming Control Board and part-time on the Nevada Gaming Commission. The board serves primarily as an investigative and enforcement body for the commission, and recommends to the commission those who should be entered into the Black Book.

---

*The official record of all meetings of the Gaming Control Board (1955–present) and the Nevada Gaming Commission (1959—present) was nearly complete, although there were differences in the quality and detail of the records over time. Board minutes prior to the 1960s were not recorded verbatim. Over the 35-year period of the study, there were also a few instances in which the minutes of board and commission meetings could not be located or were not transcribed in their entirety. In these instances, we relied on the detailed summaries of meetings available on microfiche, summaries that included the regulatory decisions and their rationales.

The regulators come from the fields of law, business, government, and law enforcement.*

The Black Book is officially said to have been established as a means of excluding persons who are seen as a threat to the gaming industry. Although the book is said to have derived its name from its initial binding in a black cover,[1] it is dubious that the name evolved independently of the similarities that the regulatory procedure has to the now generally unacceptable practice of blacklisting. Although now officially referred to as the List of Excluded Persons and currently bound in a silver cover that bears the state seal, the term *Black Book* remains the popular designation and is used in regulatory hearings as well as in media accounts of the procedure. Upholding the constitutionality and lawfulness of the procedure, the Nevada Supreme Court has ruled that the list is designed to "protect the interests of [the] State and the licensed gaming industry by avoiding any potentially significant criminal or corruptive taint and thus maintaining public confidence and trust in the gaming industry."[2] Since its inception in 1960, the Black Book has been directed principally toward those reputed to be associated with organized crime.

While instituted without apparent formal proceedings or legislative approval, the Black Book was authorized by law in 1967 as part of the legislative revisions of the Nevada Gaming Control Act. These revisions, in addition, provided for notice, hearing, and judicial review of the administrative hearing, as well as for specific sanctions for casinos that failed to exclude or eject the designated persons.[3] Thereafter, casinos could be fined and their licenses limited, conditioned, or even suspended for failure to comply with the new law. Not until 1972, however, did the Nevada Gaming Commission adopt a regulation specifically delineating the characteristics of those eligible for exclusion. And not until 1978 did the regulators hold hearings for those to be nominated and entered into the Black Book.

In the Black Book's 35-year history, the criteria for determining an individual's threat to the gaming industry have evolved

*It is now required that the board be composed of members with particular professional backgrounds. The chair is to be from the field of business or public administration. Another member is to have experience in the gaming industry or fields of law or law enforcement. A third is to be an accountant.

from the unique circumstances surrounding the specific cases. Partly on the basis of the accumulated circumstances of these cases, the conditions have come to include: (1) a prior felony conviction or conviction of a crime involving moral turpitude; (2) violation of or conspiracy to violate gaming law; (3) a "notorious or unsavory reputation which would adversely affect public confidence and trust that the gaming industry is free from criminal and corruptive elements"; and (4) previous exclusion from licensed gaming activities of other states.[4] As recently as November 1991, the Nevada Supreme Court ruled that any one of these conditions is a sufficient basis for an individual's inclusion in the book. The state also made it clear in 1989 that "race, color, creed, national origin or ancestry, or sex" must not be a basis for entry.[5]

The due process requirements of notice and hearing also have evolved from the specific cases and subsequent legal challenges and, therefore, have been only gradually implemented. Presently, the names of persons considered for entry are submitted to the Gaming Control Board by either the Las Vegas Metropolitan Police Department or by members of the regulatory body itself. (It is interesting to note that the Nevada Gaming Control Board materials that we reviewed make no mention of names being submitted to the board by city police departments other than Las Vegas.) Upon receipt of the names, the board conducts an investigation into each individual's background, often drawing upon materials provided by the police department. When the investigation is completed, the case is prepared and the issue is placed on the agenda of a board meeting whose time and itinerary are announced publicly. At this meeting, the state's deputy attorney general for gaming presents the board's case supporting inclusion of the person in the Black Book. The meeting is held publicly, and a court reporter transcribes the proceeding. Seldom is the "candidate" or his attorney present at this stage of the regulatory process.

Following the board's action, the candidate must be formally notified of his nomination, and, within 20 days, is entitled to a "bill of particulars" listing the grounds for his proposed entry. He is also entitled to a hearing before the commission, which, if requested, is to take place within 60 days of his nomination. It is a "show cause" hearing, in that it is the responsibility of the nomi-

Table 1.1. Nevada's Black Book nominees and entries

	Nominated	Entered	Removed
1. John Louis Battaglia	6/13/60	6/13/60	1/23/75
2. Marshal Caifano	6/13/60	6/13/60	
3. Carl James Civella[a]	6/13/60	6/13/60	
4. Nicholas Civella	6/13/60	6/13/60	6/1/83
5. Michael Coppola	6/13/60	6/13/60	1/23/75
6. Louis Tom Dragna	6/13/60	6/13/60	
7. Robert L. Garcia	6/13/60	6/13/60	10/16/86
8. Sam Giancana	6/13/60	6/13/60	12/19/75
9. Motel Grzebienacy	6/13/60	6/13/60	1/23/75
10. Murray Llewellyn Humphreys	6/13/60	6/13/60	1/23/75
11. Joseph Sica	6/13/60	6/13/60	
12. Ruby Kolod	4/65	4/65	5/65
13. Felix Alderisio	4/65	4/65	1965
14. William Alderman	4/65	4/65	5/65
15. Alvin George Kaohu	1/23/75	1/23/75	
16. Wilford Kalaauala Pulawa	1/23/75	1/23/75	
17. Anthony Giordano	3/4/75		4/20/76
18. Michael Santo Polizzi	8/29/75		4/15/76
19. Anthony Joseph Zerilli	9/12/75		4/15/76
20. Anthony Joseph Spilotro	10/13/78	12/2/78	10/16/86
21. Carl Angelo DeLuna	6/26/79		12/21/89
22. Joseph Agosto	6/29/79		6/28/84
23. John Joseph Vaccaro, Jr.	3/21/86	6/19/86	
24. Sandra Kay Vaccaro	10/2/86	4/16/87	
25. Chris George Petti	10/2/86	5/21/87	
26. Michael Anthony Rizzitello	3/31/88	7/28/88	
27. William Gene Land	7/21/88	9/21/88	
28. James Tamer	10/2/86	9/22/88	
29. Frank Joseph Masterana	7/21/88	10/19/88	
30. Frank Larry Rosenthal	3/31/88	11/30/88	
31. Harold Travis Lyons	12/8/88	3/23/89	
32. Gaspare Anedetto Speciale	12/8/88	3/23/89	4/23/92
33. Joseph Vincent Cusumano	12/7/89	6/21/90	
34. Carl Wesley Thomas	3/21/86	6/21/90	2/22/94
35. Douglas Joseph Barr, Jr.	6/7/90	11/29/90	
36. Timothy John Childs	7/21/90	2/27/91	
37. Francis Citro, Jr.	12/6/90	11/21/91	
38. Richard Mark Perry	4/9/92	10/28/92	
39. Albert Anthony Corbo	4/14/93	7/29/94	
40. Dominic Spinale	5/6/93		
41. Samuel Filippo Manarite	5/6/93		11/5/93
42. Anthony Michael St. Laurent, Sr.	5/6/93	9/23/93	
43. Edward Lawrence DeLeo	5/6/93	12/16/93	
44. Douglas William Barr	10/7/93	3/24/94	
45. Brent Eli Morris	12/2/93	2/24/94	

[a]Carl James Civella died on October 2, 1994, but as of this writing his name has not yet been removed from the Black Book.

nee or his counsel to establish why his name should not be included on the List of Excluded Persons. In the absence of such a request, the commission proceeds on its own time to meet and act on the board's recommendation. The commission meeting, too, is held publicly, again with the state deputy attorney general for gaming presenting the board's case, followed by the attorney for the nominee presenting the case against inclusion. Witnesses may be called. Evidence is presented. Summations follow. A vote is taken.

As a regulatory procedure, the rules of evidence in establishing the conditions for entry into the Black Book need not meet the standards required of criminal proceedings. This principle has been given a very liberal interpretation by the regulators. Thus, evidence to establish a person's threat to the gaming industry might include testimony of confidential informants, national and international arrest and conviction records, or merely mention of one's associations and activities in media accounts, crime commission reports, and in scholarly and not-so-scholarly publications (including even fiction).

As a rule, those who have been nominated by the Gaming Control Board for inclusion in the Black Book have been entered by vote of the commission, and only one such entry has been made without a unanimous vote. Following the entry of 11 men in 1960, 21 of the 27 remaining entries have been placed in the book since 1986, with the latest having been entered in July 1994. Only six individuals were entered in the 26-year interim, three for a period of only a few weeks in 1965, two in 1975, and one in 1978.

Seven additional persons have been nominated to the Black Book but not entered. Two of these were removed from nomination because of imprisonment, another died in prison while appealing his nomination, and one recent nominee is awaiting action by the commission. Numerous others have been investigated,[6] and some have been recommended publicly to the regulators for inclusion but not entered.[7] A list of those nominated and entered into the Black Book is shown in table 1.1.

TOWARD A THEORY OF THE BLACK BOOK

The maintenance of social institutions depends on the designation of certain behaviors as deviant,[8] which implies that even the essentially immoral institution of gambling must effect control in this manner. Such designations not only control activities that might disrupt routine operations in the area, but also symbolically affirm the norms, standards, and beliefs required for institutional persistence.[9]

Profound reactions to deviance are especially likely to occur during periods of perceived threat to established institutional arrangements,[10] suggesting that the development and implementation of the Black Book are responses to threats to the integrity of gaming or its regulatory body. Indeed, gaming is a tenuous institution, faced with both internal threats of corruption and external threats of a lack of public confidence, which might result in declining patronage. It is thus perceived as essential that both the industry and the public believe that legalized gambling can be and is being controlled. Within this context, regulatory bodies must dramatize their effectiveness by employing mechanisms that go beyond affecting their more mundane activities to publicly affirming their capabilities of controlling the industry. Emphasizing the wrongs of and designating as deviant those who stand in contrast to the social norms are critical to the legitimation of the established order and to the assurance of its viability over time. Such denunciation promotes not only a public perception of the legitimacy of institutional arrangements, but also an illusion of the ability of control organizations to police problematic situations effectively within these institutions. The ritualized transformation of designated individuals into persons of a lower kind—that is, those who stand outside legitimate society and are opposed to its values[11]—is central to this process, because it publicly communicates the power of the state to rid the industry of even its most sinister elements.

The perceived importance and dramaturgical quality of the Black Book in maintaining control over the gaming industry are reflected in the statements of the state's deputy attorney general, Jeffrey Clontz, in the first formal hearing involving placement of an individual in the book:

> Now how is the Nevada Gaming Commission to implement this State policy? How are you to maintain the public confidence and trust and insure that criminal or other corruptive elements do not gain a toehold into this most sensitive of our State's industries? . . .

10

Now, in the ordinary course of events the licensing or suitability process provides you with an extremely efficient method by which you can weed undesirable elements out of Nevada's gaming industry. However, on rare occasions you are confronted with a situation which does not lend itself to resolution through the normal channels of the licensing process, a situation that does not involve a person who can be scrutinized through the normal licensing or suitability process—a person who may not have any direct or visible ties to a licensed gaming establishment . . .

We all know that the Nevada Legislature has provided you with a unique and extraordinary tool to utilize in those situations where the normal licensing and suitability processes are simply not enough. This unique tool is known as the list of excluded persons.

Although it is not often used, the list of excluded persons is the single most powerful weapon in the arsenal of gaming control. It is the ultimate civil sanction at your disposal to use against those persons allegedly belonging to criminal or otherwise corruptive elements who elude the grasp of your licensing statutes because on the surface they do not appear to be directly connected with a licensed gaming establishment . . .

Considering the awesome sanctions that befall an individual who is included in the list and the numerical paucity of individuals who have actually undergone inclusion, I think it is more than fair to conclude that it takes a very special type of person to be considered for candidacy.

We might even consider the individuals whose names are currently in the list to be members of a very exclusive, if infamous, club.[12]

Within the context of an economy built on vice, the choice of how to maintain boundaries is a major task for those who would proclaim and enforce morality during times of crisis. To the extent that some groups control the law and its application, such designations of deviance reflect and legitimate relations of dominance and subordination.[13] Distinctions among groups, as well as the power of the state to effect the law, are thus affirmed through the deviance defining process. Those who speak on behalf of the legitimacy of the industry—its moral entrepreneurs—are, like dominant groups elsewhere, white Anglo-Saxon Protestants. In Nevada, a number are also Mormon. Those chosen for inclusion in the Black Book tend to be distinctively different from the domi-

11

nant group. By contrast, they are alien, weak, and exemplify behavior publicly denounced as disreputable. As a result, they are easily discredited.

Although blatant in some respects, discrimination in this area is not entirely an overt process. Rather, it operates through an institutionalized stereotype, that of the American mafia, which presumes that organized crime is the domain of Italians, is divided into specific families, is engaged in a conspiratorial fashion, is enforced by violence, and is structured in a hierarchical fashion.[14] Although largely a mythical definition,[15] it is clearly this imagery that has served as the basis for the selection of those to be included in the Black Book.

American social values mitigate against more overt forms of discrimination, even in this setting where negative assessments of out-groups seem predominant. Because the mafia stereotype reflects more general beliefs and is validated by its official application, it has evolved into taken-for-granted assumptions that are blind to their underlying biases.[16] Its use accordingly obscures prejudice and discrimination and lends legitimacy to the decision making. By rationalizing discriminatory actions, the stereotype also functions to avert any cognitive dilemmas on the part of decision makers.[17]

However, we shall see that not all these cases fit neatly into the mafia stereotype. It is in these atypical cases that cognitive dilemmas and deviations in the process of routine decision making are likely to occur. The appearance that such cases are given more time and effort on the part of the decision makers suggests that they are cognitively more problematic. Once the stereotype has been applied, however, the tendency is to search for evidence that corroborates the definition.[18] Persons thus tend to avoid conflicting information[19] and to hold to stereotypical beliefs even when information to the contrary is presented.[20]

CONCEPTUAL FRAMEWORK

Grounded in the preceding theoretical arguments, the conceptual framework for our analysis of the Black Book may be summarized as follows: First, we argue that the origin and use of the Black Book as a means of social control are responses to perceived threats to the gaming industry or to its regulatory body. Emanating from both inside and outside the industry, such events are gauged by the regulators as threats to the extent that they have generated negative publicity. The issue of threats is explored through an analysis of the events that both preceded the development of the Black Book and coincided with subsequent periods in which the regulatory procedure has been aggressively activated. These events include: (1) promised federal intervention in the late 1950s following underworld conflict in Las Vegas; (2) the extortion conviction of a major industry figure in the mid-1960s; (3) the indictments of several industry figures for skimming and hidden interests in the late 1970s; (4) the federal convictions of these same figures in the early 1980s; and (5) questions of institutional corruption, including gaming regulation itself, in the early 1990s. Appendix A provides a chronology of these and other important events and the regulatory and legislative acts in Nevada gaming that followed them.

The regulators act to prove their power to handle threats to the industry by proclaiming certain individuals as persons of ill repute who are conspiring in activities that undermine the interests of gaming and the welfare of the state. As we have noted, not only has local law enforcement been instrumental in this process, but so have the city's newspapers. Contributing to the public perception of threat, Las Vegas newspaper editorialists have commented regularly on the reputations and activities of those who are nominated, those who might be nominated, and those who they feel should be nominated. Nominees are accordingly described as felonious criminals with notorious and unsavory reputations, and are generally said to have ties to organized crime as stereotypically conceived. Even the few small-time gambling cheats recently entered into the Black Book are portrayed as serious criminals engaged in conspiracies that threaten the state's economy.

In this dramatization of evil, regulators also tend to ignore or seek to discredit any ties that the individual might have to conventional society. Although some of these individuals have families and are employed, even in relatively high-ranking occupations, such information is seldom mentioned in the hearings and is objected to when introduced, which suggests that there is a concerted effort to portray the nominees as persons without legitimate positions in society.

13

Further affirming the disreputability of the nominee is the regulatory attention to the issue of aliases (see appendix B). The introduction of aliases has the effect of amplifying the criminal character and threat of the individual. The nominee appears to be one with deceptive intent and to have possibly committed numerous other crimes under other names.

Further, the threats to the industry are most often seen as emanating from forces alien to established groups and those who represent them. Thus, the selection of individuals for the Black Book reflects cultural conflicts and the differential ability of groups to institutionalize their interests with the result that persons of subordinate groups are more often selected for denunciation. As we have noted, dominant groups in Nevada are typical of those elsewhere in the United States in that they tend to be Anglo-Saxon. In addition, the state has a historical tradition of political and civic involvement on the part of its northern and Mormon population. These population and social trends are reflected in the composition of the Gaming Control Board and Nevada Gaming Commission during the years in which the Black Book has been in existence. The regulatory procedure's differential application to out-group members is evident in its exclusive application to those who have migrated to Las Vegas (largely Italian) from the ethnic urban areas of the Midwest and Northeast.

ORGANIZATION OF THE BOOK

The story is told in a chronological fashion, noting the specific crises that occurred in the history of legalized gambling and discussing the particular persons who were entered into the Black Book following or concurrent with each crisis. It is divided into four parts. Part 1 deals with the early period of Nevada gambling and includes chapters 2, 3, and 4: "Babylon in the Desert," "Genesis of the Black Book," and "A Savior Comes to Babylon." It covers gambling from the saloon bordellos of the silver mining towns to statewide legality and the entry and conflict of underworld entrepreneurs. The conflict and notoriety of syndicate figures vying for increased power within the industry in the 1950s brought the threat of federal intervention. Rather dramatically and without apparent legislative or gubernatorial approval and due process considerations of hearing and notice, the state gaming regulators banned 11 men from its casinos. They were the first of those to be denounced as notorious and unsavory and placed in the Black Book. Then, in 1965, when a major casino owner and his associates were convicted in federal court of attempted extortion, they were added to the book, but only for a short period of time, largely because of their positions within the industry. The section ends with the relative peace of the Howard Hughes's era and how his purchase of major casinos was thought to have removed mob interests from Las Vegas.

Part 2 deals with the period of internal crises in the industry, and includes chapters 5 through 7: "Enemies from Within," "Control Comes to Babylon," and "Tamer 'the Atypical.'" It covers the industry crises that began in the mid-1970s. There was the death of Howard Hughes, who owned six major casinos at the time. There was the disclosure of Teamsters' loans to casinos, loans which were tainted because of their links to organized crime. And there were federal indictments of industry figures for hidden ownership and skimming in several Las Vegas casinos. While for 10 years the regulators battled with these figures, they entered a few men into the Black Book, some of whom were not connected to these crises.

In Part 3 we address the revitalization period of Nevada gaming. It includes chapters 8, 9, 10, and 11: "Renewed Zeal," "Cusumano 'the Typical,'" "Contemporary Moral Crises," and "Return to Morality." The focus is on how the regulators were compelled to demonstrate their ability to police and maintain a viable industry in light of its changes, expansion to other states, federal convictions for the industry figures in the 1980s, and allegations of institutional corruption at the outset of the 1990s, including the regulation of gaming itself. The result was the Black Book entry of some of the major industry figures, as well as a number of others— relatively small-time bookies and hoods who were caricatures of the mafia stereotype and several individuals with histories of cheating at gambling. The decade of the 1990s brought an unprecedented number of inconsequential persons to the Black Book.

Part 4 on denunciation and inequality contains chapter 12, "Righteous Indignation and the Mark of Cain." The chapter deals with the dynamics of the denunciation itself and the differential application of the regulatory mechanism to members of alien groups and Italians in particular. It suggests that, by setting apart and emphasizing the evilness of those who are said to present threats to gaming, the regulators cleanse gaming of its corruptive elements and assert their ability to effect the controls necessary to achieve those ends. The sharp contrast between the ethnic backgrounds and orientations of the regulators and those of the excluded persons is said to explain how regulators bought into the mafia myth and were manipulated by more conventional industry entrepreneurs.

Finally, we close with a brief epilogue which describes where the members of the Black Book are now, and comments on the efficacy of denunciation and exclusion in this context.

PART 1

The Early Period of Nevada Gambling

2

Babylon in the Desert

THE CULTURAL CONTEXT AND EARLY PERIOD

In the minds of many, gambling is synonymous with Nevada. Indeed, it has always been an integral part of the state. Because of Nevada's long-standing reputation as the nation's gambling capital, it may come as a surprise that the state has historically had a strong Mormon influence. It was originally part of the Mormon state of Deseret that was established in 1849.[1] These followers of Joseph Smith, or saints as they are referred to in the Mormon church, settled in Washoe County in the north, around Reno and the capital of Carson City. When the Comstock lode of gold and silver was discovered in 1860, the county was said to be ruled out of Salt Lake City, the capital of the Mormon church.[2]

Of predominately English and Scandinavian ancestry, Mormons are one of the millennial groups that migrated from New York and, in 1849, established the large part of their state of Deseret in what is now Utah and Nevada. Unlike the general pattern of millennial groups, they chose the Judaic, rather than the Christian, world view.[3] They believe that their origins are with a sixth-century B.C. Near East voyager to Central America, a man of Jewish descent. One of the voyager's sons, Laman, who was cursed with a skin of blackness for his continual evilness, was the father of the Lamanites, a "dark and loathsome" people. The other son, Nephi, father of the Nephites, who symbolize good, was "white and delightsome."[4] Mormons believe that they are the spiritual descendants of the fair-skinned people.[5] These be-

19

liefs have contributed to a strong in-group–out-group orientation among Mormons.[6]

Given this orientation, the early Mormon influence in northern Nevada may have contributed to the historical antagonism that developed between this region and the less conservative Las Vegas in the south. Las Vegas has always been largely populated by non-Nevadans, which seems to have contributed to its being viewed by the north as "vulgarish [and] criminalish."[7] These demographic and social patterns, and the north's position at the center of economic activity in the state until the 1950s—whether it was mining, railroads, livestock, or gambling—have also meant that Las Vegas has not, until recently, been admitted to full participation in Nevada politics.[8]

Contributing to the early northern and Mormon influence in Nevada was the temporary intrusion of non-Nevadans into state government at the time of statehood. In 1865, Nevada came under the influence of major eastern and California investors, first in mining, then in railroads, and finally in livestock. These industries were located in the north and had primarily absentee owners who were heavily involved in national and, to a lesser extent, state politics.[9] Then, by the turn of the century, Nevada began to take control of its government, demanding that its officials be long-time natives. They were, therefore, of necessity from the north. This practice has continued until very recently, regardless of changes in the location of the state's economic base, with Las Vegas now being its major contributor. Many of these officials have also been Mormon. Although not as often from the north in more recent years, Mormons have, for example, traditionally occupied major roles in the state's most important Senate committees: finance, government affairs, and the judiciary.[10]

To this day, Mormons continue to play major roles in Nevada state government, including the regulation of gambling.[11] Their morality and somewhat distinctive cultural experience are reflected in the ambivalence that surrounds law in this most important of the state's industries. Especially evident are the conflicts produced by the Mormon taboo system with its strict proscriptions against a plethora of hedonistic pleasures, proscriptions clearly at odds with the life-styles and activities that accompany gambling.[12] There is also the strong in-group–out-group orientation[13] that seems to create difficulties in understanding and accepting the plurality of ethnic groups that have been attracted to Nevada gambling as both patrons and industry entrepreneurs and personnel. At the same time, their cultural commitment to capitalist principles and the reality of the state's economic dependence on gambling have inclined Mormons to tolerate gambling and "try to make the best of the situation" for both the state and themselves.[14]

Although the Mormon church has only recently (1987) allowed its more devout members to be employed in gaming activities, such as dealing, church members have had long-standing involvement at the managerial level.[15] They have also been major financial backers of the industry. The largely Mormon (and Jewish)-owned Bank of Las Vegas (later merged to become Valley Bank of Nevada and recently purchased by Bank of America) was the first Nevada financial institution to provide loans to casinos. The bank's long-time head and principal owner, Parry Thomas, is said to be a Jack Mormon (a less-than-active church member who might drink or smoke) who used his Mormonism to establish himself in Las Vegas. He is purported to have remarked that he worked for "the Mormons until noon, and from noon on for my Jewish friends," the latter presumably being those who ran the casinos. The Bank of Las Vegas is said to have provided financing for the development or expansion of the Sahara, the Fremont, the Sands, the Desert Inn, the Dunes, the Hacienda, the Stardust, the Riviera, and the Thunderbird.[16]

Even in the territorial years during which Mormons settled Nevada, the silver mining towns were dominated by saloon-bordellos where gambling was common. In spite of the first governor's efforts to quell the activity by making it a felony, gambling continued to flourish into the period of early statehood.[17] Then, in 1869, the Nevada legislature approved a bill to legalize gambling. Although the bill was at first vetoed by Governor Henry Blaisdel, who saw gambling as a "vicious vice," it was ultimately put into law by a legislative override.[18] Gambling continued as a legal activity until 1910, during which time license fees were charged, with half the monies going to the county and half to the state.

In the two decades that followed, gambling was only sporadically legal, and then for only certain types of card games. Enforcement is said to have been lax, with illegal operations being widespread and the state losing considerable revenues.[19] Then, in 1931, in efforts to revive a depressed economy and to regain state revenues, the Nevada legislature passed its "wide open gambling" bill.[20] Reflecting the sentiments underlying the long-standing love-hate relationship between Nevadans and gambling, Assemblyman Phil Tobin introduced the bill, stating that "as long as we don't seem to get rid of [it], we might as well derive a tax from it."[21]

WIDE-OPEN GAMBLING AND UNDERWORLD INVOLVEMENT

Immediately following the passage of the new gambling bill, the state's first real night club, the Meadows, was opened in Las Vegas. The club was built and owned by "Admiral" Tony Cornero (born Stralla), a reputed criminal who was well known for running gambling ships off the coast of Los Angeles.[22] Soon, a number of other individuals who had been operating illegal gambling clubs in Los Angeles would flee municipal reforms there to establish casinos in downtown Las Vegas. Gambling's legal status in Nevada gave this formerly underworld group a new legitimacy, as well as new opportunities. They, in turn, provided the funds and skills required for the more sophisticated industry that was to develop there.[23]

By the mid-1940s, postwar Las Vegas was a boomtown, and gambling was a major part of the state's economy. During this period, a number of other investors with illegal backgrounds bought into the industry. They came from poor ethnic neighborhoods in New York, New Jersey, Cleveland, Boston, and Chicago, where they had originally been bootleggers. About half were eastern European Jews, a quarter Italian, and the remainder Irish and Polish.[24] They included Frank Costello, Frank Erickson, Meyer Lansky, Benjamin "Bugsy" Siegel, and Abner "Longie" Zwillman from New York and New Jersey, Morris "Moe" Dalitz and partners from Cleveland, and Jack Guzik and Tony Accardo from Chicago (p. 150). Following the repeal of Prohibition, they developed, often as partners, regional illegal gambling operations and invested in horse racing and nightlife entertainment in New Orleans; Hot Springs, Arkansas; Covington and Newport,

Kentucky; Cicero and East St. Louis, Illinois; and Havana, Cuba (p. 150). They eventually extended their operations to become Las Vegas' casino and entertainment entrepreneurs.

Wanting to protect its burgeoning economy, officials were at first reluctant to interfere with the industry.[25] Thus, by 1950, licenses to own and operate casinos had been granted to several persons alleged to be members of organized crime. These included Bugsy Siegel, Moe Dalitz and his associates, and former Michigan gambling syndicate member Lincoln Fitzgerald. Some of these individuals would come to obtain respectability in the state, and Dalitz would even receive the city of Las Vegas' Humanitarian of the Year Award in 1976.

Until 1945, Nevada gambling was overseen by local city and county officials. At that time, the state legislature shifted authority to the Nevada Tax Commission,[26] and by 1949 required that the commission investigate the backgrounds of applicants for licensing. Even after official control shifted to the state, however, local law enforcement continued to be involved in efforts to keep criminal elements out of gambling. Thus, in October 1946, a Las Vegas newspaper reported that, after receiving a confidential tip, local police became concerned that a large segment of the Los Angeles underworld was infiltrating Las Vegas. "Word received here indicated that the southern metropolis was becoming 'too hot' for the lads with shady backgrounds as a result of the gangland wipe-out and recent cafe slugging of James Utley, associate of 'Admiral' Tony Cornero in the current gambling ship controversy."[27] Emphasizing that the police had to protect established business and property interests, Sheriff Glen Jones said he would crack down on such persons by requiring them to comply with a city and county ordinance that mandated that felons register at police headquarters upon arrival in Las Vegas.

THE THREAT OF FEDERAL INTERVENTION

During this time, most of the gaming industry was centered around Reno in the northern part of the state. Then, in the 1950s, Las Vegas in the south began to overtake the former leader in total state revenues from gaming.[28] It was also during the early 1950s that a national crisislike preoccupation with organized crime developed. The crisis began with a series of congressional investigations into the issue—the Kefauver committee hearings, which included attention to Las Vegas.

The Kefauver committee hearings had tremendous national public impact in the early 1950s. The hearings were held in 14 cities across the nation, one of which was Las Vegas. Senator Estes Kefauver of Tennessee chaired the five-member investigatory committee, which for the years 1950 and 1951 turned the heads of the nation to the phenomenon of organized crime. Television was becoming a focal aspect of social life, and the medium provided a stage for the spectacle of notorious and unsavory types testifying about their activities or knowledge of activities relative to organized crime in the nation. Notables such as Mickey Cohen, Moe Dalitz, Bugsy Siegel's former girlfriend, Virginia Hill, and Frank Costello testified before the committee while the people of the nation watched, glued to their television sets.

The popular sentiments of the day were mirrored in the hearings' conclusions that there was an American mafia, "a sinister criminal organization" operating throughout the country, dealing in gambling, narcotics, and prostitution. The very use of the word *mafia* to describe the organization of these activities reflected the belief that the problem was a predominately Italian one, a belief that would soon diffuse from these Senate investigations to the public at large. The committee further concluded that there were two major syndicates in the nation and that both were operating in Nevada.[29]

The federal investigations into Las Vegas focused on the alleged involvement of organized crime figures with major casinos and were fueled by violent attacks on industry figures. The most noteworthy was the 1947 gangland murder of Bugsy Siegel. Siegel was a former bootlegger and reputed New York organized crime figure who, only several months prior to his murder, had opened the first major hotel and casino on the Las Vegas Strip— the Flamingo. Newspapers following his murder said that he "had committed twenty to thirty murders, was a director of Murder, Inc., and had an arrest record like a village phone book."[30] Although Gus Greenbaum took over the management of the Flamingo following Siegel's murder, the hotel was thought to have remained under the control of the New York mob through its ties to the notorious Meyer Lansky, Siegel's friend and partner, who was later found to have maintained behind-the-scenes interests in the business.[31] Then, in 1949, there was the near-fatal, alleged gangland shooting of Lincoln Fitzgerald, co-owner of the Nevada Club in Reno and reputed member of a Michigan gambling syndicate also with ties to Meyer Lansky.[32] It is said that officials in Michigan wanted Fitzgerald returned to the state in the late 1940s, but a Nevada judge, Harry Watson, released him from extradition.[33]

These violent events and the suspicions about underworld involvement in the industry that followed raised questions about the ability of the Nevada Tax Commission to "eliminate the undesirable element in Nevada gaming."[34] It was among the conclusions of the Kefauver committee that

> too many of the men running gambling operations in Nevada are either members of existing out-of-state gambling syndicates or have had histories of close association with the underworld characters who operate those syndicates. The licensing system which is in effect in the State has not resulted in excluding the undesirables from the State but has merely served to give their activities a seeming cloak of respectability.[35]

Several casino owners were called before the Kefauver committee. Of note among them was Moe Dalitz, head of the so-called Desert Inn Group, which also included Morris Kleinman, Thomas McGinty, and Samuel Tucker. The group had purchased 59 percent of the Desert Inn stock in 1947 when Wilbur Clark was unable to finance completion of the building project (pp. 67–69). The U.S. senators raised questions about Dalitz and his partners' illegal gambling activities in Ohio and northern Kentucky, and indicated that sources had linked him to New York organized crime figures Lucky Luciano, Benjamin Siegel, and Meyer Lansky.[36] When the senators called Wilbur Clark to give an account of his alliances with these individuals, he is said to have appeared to be "a confused little fish who had been bodily swallowed by the sharks from the underwater catacombs of Cleveland."[37]

This portrayal of Dalitz and his partners is greatly at variance with the perceptions of Nevada regulators at the time. This is especially evident in the recent reflections of the state's first regulator of the gaming industry, former head of the Nevada Tax

Morris "Moe" Dalitz, *center,* at ceremony honoring him. Dalitz was alleged to have been a former bootlegger and operator of unlicensed gambling houses, and believed to have been an associate of Meyer Lansky. He would, nevertheless, gain respectability in Las Vegas and become one of the most powerful figures in the history of the city. His success has been attributed to his charitable activity, and to his political savvy. Courtesy *Las Vegas Review Journal.*

Commission's Gaming Division Robbins Cahill. Cahill is said to have "greatly admired" Dalitz and to have viewed him as markedly different from many of the others who had sought to enter the industry during its early years. For Cahill, former bootleggers and illegal gamblers like Dalitz were not "gangster[s] in the true sense," but merely men who wanted to "come to Nevada and do legally what . . . [they] had been doing illegally in other states. . . . The guys from Cleveland were silk glove men," he said, and Moe Dalitz in particular, he felt, had "done more good for the city of Las Vegas and done more to build Las Vegas than any single man connected with the industry."[38]

26

The Kefauver hearings promised the threat of federal intervention in Nevada gambling, either by shutting it down or by regulating it and imposing substantial taxation. Adding to this threat were the highly publicized 1955 recession in the industry and disclosure that the Thunderbird hotel and casino had been secretly financed with loans from Jake Lansky, Meyer Lansky's brother. In the same year, there was the suspicious death of Tony Cornero, who expired while shooting craps at the Desert Inn.[39] At the time, Cornero was about to open the Stardust, a hotel that was instead opened by Moe Dalitz, then owner of the Desert Inn, where Cornero met his untimely death.* It was against this backdrop, in 1955, that Governor Charles H. Russell closed the Thunderbird, imposed a 90-day moratorium on new gambling licenses, and organized the three-member Gaming Control Board within the Nevada Tax Commission. The responsibilities of the new board would be to conduct investigations into applicants and to oversee the enforcement of gaming regulations throughout the state.[40]

Suspected underworld involvement in the industry nevertheless continued. Of particular concern was that underworld conflict would continue to accompany such involvement in the lucrative industry. This concern was fueled by the McClellan Senate investigations into organized crime, which began in 1957, and by several additional incidents of suspected gangland violence. There was the 1957 near-fatal shooting of reputed Chicago underworld figure Frank Costello. At the time of the shooting, it was disclosed that he had ties to Louis J. Lederer and Charles "Babe" Baron, two investors in the Tropicana hotel and casino, which had just opened on the Strip. Confirming one of these ties was Costello's possession of a slip of paper in Lederer's handwriting with figures that matched the casino's first three weeks' winnings.[41] In 1958, Gus Greenbaum, the former manager of the Flamingo, and his wife were found with their throats slashed at their home in Phoenix.

*In his recent study of Italian Americans in Las Vegas, Alan Balboni (1994: 29–30, 52–55) points out that Tony Cornero was the only Italian to have been involved in the construction of a major Las Vegas hotel and casino. Most of the early builders were Jewish. The association of organized crime with Italians seems to have caused them greater scrutiny than was given Jewish investors who, in addition, actively sought legitimacy through civic activities.

Adding to the suspicion that organized crime was becoming entrenched in Las Vegas was the disclosure of Teamsters' pension fund loans to several of the city's largest casinos. Identified among them were the Fremont, the Dunes, and the Stardust. The monies did not stop at the doors of the casinos; they extended throughout the city. A total of $12 million was invested not only in casinos but also in golf courses and real estate at the time.[42] Even one of the city's hospitals was financed in this manner. A $1 million loan from the pension fund of the Central States Southeast and Southwest Conference of Teamsters was made to the Desert Inn Group in 1959 to build Sunrise Hospital. Not surprisingly, the project was a profit-making venture, one so cost-effective that fire safety codes were said to have been violated in order to cut construction costs. The issue created considerable controversy, with Hank Greenspun, owner and editor of the *Las Vegas Sun*, charging that Dalitz and his partners had used their political influence "to override the objections of a building inspector."[43]

CONTROL COMES TO BABYLON

The concern with keeping criminal elements out of Las Vegas escalated during the late 1950s. Attention was directed especially to the more notorious individuals who were coming to the city for the gambling and entertainment that it offered. As the chairman of the Nevada Tax Commission commented, "There was always the innuendo that they were [in town] to . . . collect their money in their secret interests."[44] Although the regulators themselves seemed to have been ambivalent about any real underworld threat, they responded to public pressure by obtaining industry support to keep notorious persons out of the casinos. Casino owners expressed difficulty of excluding their often long-time acquaintances, but agreed to try and encouraged the regulators to provide them with a legal mechanism (pp. 943–944). Relating his conversations with casino owners, executive secretary of the Nevada Tax Commission Robbins Cahill explained:

> We'd go to 'em, and tell them of our problems, and say, "Look, can't you keep these people out?" They told us that it was a difficult thing, but they said, "Look, all you've got to do is to tell us to keep these people out of here, and give us the direction. [If]

28

we've got something that we can show to them—and say, 'Look, I'm sorry, but you're not wanted here. We were told to keep you out.'—we'll do it. But we want one understanding with it—we don't want 'em going out of this place and going across the street to somebody else. If we keep 'em out, everybody's got to keep 'em out." . . .

This was . . . before the Black Book was thought of . . . (p. 944)

The Gaming Control Act

Continued public concern about mob involvement in Nevada gambling, along with the fear of federal intervention and taxation, prompted executive and legislative efforts to draft regulations that would better control organized crime.[45] These efforts resulted in the 1959 Gaming Control Act. The act provided for the separation of the Gaming Control Board from the Tax Commission and for the creation of a five-member Nevada Gaming Commission with powers to grant licenses, enact regulations, collect taxes, and oversee the board as its enforcement and investigative arm.[46] The act also authorized the board to require gaming establishments to be "operated in a manner suitable to protect the public health, safety, morals, good order and general welfare of the State of Nevada." The new regulations were drafted and moved through the legislature under the leadership of Mormon politician James Gibson.[47]

In 1959 and 1960, many applicants for licensing continued to have criminal records, most of which were related to illegal gambling, and some had even testified before the Kefauver committee. Thus, they were not substantially different from many of those who had been licensed before them. Given the pressures to clean up the industry, the newly appointed regulators thus struggled with criteria that would allow them to make fine distinctions among the generally problematic applicants. Although verbatim transcripts were not kept at that time, the available records reveal the frustrations of the regulators in dealing with this problem. So basic was the problem that they even struggled with what terms to use as an official basis for the denial of a license. Decisions of whether the term should be *unsatisfactory antecedents* or *unsuitable background* or *unsatisfactory past experience* or *questionable associations* consumed inordinate amounts of time and discussion.[48]

Within a year of passing the Gaming Control Act, the newly

29

The first Nevada Gaming Commission in session. *From left*: James W. Hotchkiss, Chairman Milton W. Keefer, Pete Petersen, Norman D. Brown, and F. E. Walters. At the table below are two Gaming Control Board division chiefs and administrative assistant, Michelle Cardinal. Beginning in 1959, the commission was charged with the administration and supervision of gaming in Nevada. Its members were well-respected men with backgrounds in ranching, federal law enforcement, public service, and business. Courtesy Nevada State Library and Archives.

established commission had before it the application of a man who had been trying to obtain licensing for nine years. The man was a brother of an alleged "strong arm lieutenant to Abner 'Longie' Zwillman," a former New Jersey bootlegger who had specialized in the transportation of illegal liquor. At this time, the board nevertheless decided to grant the license in a vote of two to one. However, the commission overruled the board's decision, stating that the applicant was of unsuitable background.[49] Then, within a month, another man applied for a license who had been an associate of the unsuitable applicant. The board again approved the application and forwarded it to the commission. After struggling with the issue, Commissioner Bert Goldwater suggested that the commission could "best control the suspicious circumstances if a physical exclusion for all purposes . . . [was] made." In accordance with this suggestion, the commission voted to grant the license with "limitations" that the formerly denied applicant "not be [permitted] on the premises."[50] Only a few months later, the board entered 11 men into the first Black Book.

The Black Book

The first 11 men were placed in the Black Book without any formal notification or hearing. All were reputed to be notorious associates of organized crime, said to be linked primarily to the Chicago, Kansas City, and Los Angeles crime families. Several had previously been subpoenaed to testify in the Kefauver hearings and the McClellan investigations. Without apparent formal sanction of the commission, the board and its chairman, former FBI agent R. J. Abbaticchio, Jr., decided that these individuals presented a threat to the industry, and instructed the enforcement agents to distribute the List of Excluded Persons to all state-licensed gaming establishments.[51] The list was accompanied with the following statement:

> The notoriety resulting from known hoodlums visiting Nevada gaming establishments tends to discredit not only the gaming industry but our entire state as well . . . In order to avoid the possibility of license revocation . . . your immediate cooperation is requested in preventing the presence in any licensed establishment of all [such] "persons of notorious or unsavory reputation" including the above individuals as well as those who subsequently may be added to this list.[52]

Each of the book's entries included mug shots, various aliases, often a local arrest number for some American city, a Federal Bureau of Investigation file number, a physical description, and the last known residence. Reflecting the preoccupation with organized crime in Las Vegas, each entry also included a statement regarding the extent of the individual's presence in the city, with the majority described as frequent visitors. Interestingly, none of the entries in this state regulatory mechanism was described as presenting a threat outside Las Vegas.

THE PRIVILEGED IN THE INDUSTRY

Not all who might have presented a serious threat to gaming at the time were placed in the Black Book. This would have been impossible in light of the historical development of the industry. As we have noted, many of those who were major investors during the early years had backgrounds that included bootlegging and illegal gambling, and some reputedly had ties to organized crime. It would seem to have seriously injured the economic base of the state to clean house completely. So, when the regulators were under pressure to get the "notorious and unsavory" elements out of gaming, apparently only some were chosen. Others were in essence "grandfathered in."[53] Not only were they not placed in the Black Book, but they also sustained and were granted new licenses. A considerable number of these individuals were identified in the Kefauver hearings as being linked to Meyer Lansky.

Only a few months before the board moved to institute the Black Book, it considered the application of Frank Soskin for a 1 percent interest in the Desert Inn partnership of Samuel Tucker, Ruby Kolod, Thomas McGinty, and Moe Dalitz. Although the board chairman noted that the applicant had at one time been involved in illegal gambling, the chief of investigations implied that such histories were so commonplace in the industry that it really didn't matter.[54] Not surprisingly, Soskin's application was approved.

Then two months later, in May of 1960, the Gaming Control Board considered the application of Lincoln Fitzgerald for 100 percent ownership of Nevada Club, Inc., in Reno.[55] At the time, Fitzgerald was also licensed as an owner of two other casinos in the northern part of the state. The regulators discussed his criminal record, including income tax evasion, gambling, bribery, and conspiracy to run a gambling operation, as well as his association with Daniel Sullivan and Mert Wertheimer, reputed members of a gambling syndicate in Michigan. Interestingly, Wertheimer had been licensed as an owner of the Riverside Casino in Reno.[56] The chief auditor of the board also questioned Fitzgerald's ability to provide the required finances. In his defense, local police praised the applicant for his cooperation and for having provided part-time employment for law enforcement personnel, and references

described him as a successful and respected businessman with no "connection with Eastern elements."[57] Board chairman R. J. Abbaticchio, Jr., added that Fitzgerald's "reputation in this state is good as a square gambler and businessman . . . [and that] there is no question about . . . [his] complete solvency" (pp. 15–18). Fitzgerald's application was approved, in spite of his criminal record and associations, albeit on the condition that he submit "an acceptable personal financial statement to the Board" (p. 19).*
This decision surely must have been made with the knowledge of the Kefauver committee's observation nine years earlier that "operating in Reno are Mert Wertheimer, a big-time Michigan gambler who has been in partnership in Florida with such notorious gangsters as Joe Adonis, the Lanskys, and Frank Erickson, and with Lincoln Fitzgerald and Daniel Sullivan, members of the Michigan gambling syndicate."[58]

Also before the board in May of 1960 was Sanford Waterman's application for 13.33 percent of Cal-Neva Lodge in Lake Tahoe. The regulators discussed at length Waterman's history of illegal bookmaking and noted that the Kefauver committee showed him to be a dealer at Club Bohème in Florida, owned by Jake and Meyer Lansky, Vincent Alo, and Frank Erickson.[59] They noted further that he had been licensed in Nevada on a seasonal basis since 1956, and approved his application on this occasion as well.

Eleven days later, Samuel Cohen, Daniel D. Lifter, and Morris Saks Lansburgh, who had previously joined forces in obtaining ownership of five other hotels, applied for 87.75 percent of the Flamingo.[60] From the time that the first public notice of the applications appeared, the board received allegations that Cohen and/or Lansburgh might be fronting for "notorious hoodlums" seeking a foothold in Nevada gaming (p. 14). The investigation by the board indeed revealed that reliable sources linked the men to Meyer Lansky when they both owned hotels in Havana. Lansky had tried both to borrow money from the group and to sell them the Havana Riviera with the plan of leasing it back. The applicants said that they had declined both propositions.

---

*And Fitzgerald would continue to receive favorable decisions by the regulators, being approved for 99.98 percent of the Nevada Club in Reno in May 1965 and for 99 percent of the Silver Dollar Club in Reno in February 1967 (NGCB and NGC microfiche summaries for May 1965 and Feb. 16, 1967).

Despite the seeming contradiction, summary reports of the investigators described the men as "most cooperative" and as having forcefully and sincerely "denied hoodlum or undesirable associates and any negotiation and/or business dealing with the mob element" (p. 26). References from bankers, brokers, accountants, and attorneys provided testimony of the applicants' solvency, business acumen, character, and civic contributions. An account of their having ejected an "important figure in an Italian syndicate"—Charlie "the Blade" Tourine—from their Casablanca Hotel in Miami just days after they had acquired the property seemed to be additional evidence of their clean business practices (p. 14). Tourine was reputed to have been sponsoring a handbook and floating games that operated openly there before the group took over the hotel. The regulators must have been impressed; the board approved the application and the commission concurred, with Commissioner Bert Goldwater abstaining because his brother represented the three as their attorney.[61] Later it was learned that Lansky had been paid a large finder's fee for turning up these buyers and some of the partners, and Lansky was indicted for skimming from the casino. Then, in 1973, Lansburgh and others pleaded guilty to conspiring to hide Lansky's continued interest in the Flamingo and for skimming $36 million from it over a period of eight years. Lansky himself never stood trial on the matter, at first because he was out of the country in Israel, then later because of questionable claims of ill health.[62]

Just five days before the Black Book was instituted, the board considered the application of another man with a prior record of bookmaking for another 13.33 percent of Cal-Neva Lodge. Although the record of the man, Ike "Cheesecake" Berger, was "not clean," he too had been licensed since 1956 and was approved again.[63]

Also appearing before the board in June 1960 was Charles "Babe" Baron, a Chicago man and former investor and employee at the Tropicana, and general manager of the Havana Riviera.[64] Baron left Cuba in the early months of the Cuban revolution in 1960 and took employment as a host at the Sands hotel and casino. He appeared before the Gaming Control Board to apply for 1 percent ownership of the Sands. The board's investigation into his Chicago background revealed a police record for carrying a concealed weapon; additionally, confidential sources said that he had also been twice arrested for murder, first in 1929 and again in 1933. With the exception of a record of the grand jury having returned a no-bill on the 1929 charge, most of the information on the arrests "had been removed from the files by persons unknown" (p. 54). However, a December 3, 1929, *Chicago Herald Examiner* article told of the applicant shooting a man in "a gangsters' duel" over a prize fight bet and of his alleged admission to the killing. And an October 28, 1933, *Chicago Tribune* article told of the "alleged West Side hoodlum" being freed on charges of carrying a concealed weapon after being arrested in connection with questioning in regard to the murder of Gus Winkler, a "notorious Chicago mobster" (pp. 55–56).

Baron admitted that he was a former bookmaker and that he had opened a legitimate business in association with other former bookmakers. One of these business associates, Louis J. Lederer, had formerly divested his investments in the Sands, the Fremont, and the Tropicana hotels and casinos when revocation proceedings approached following the 1957 disclosure of his connection to Frank Costello (pp. 58–59). The regulators also noted that Baron was a frequent associate of John Rosselli, a man reputed to have obtained control of Los Angeles organized crime following the 1957 death of its former head, Jack Dragna.[65] In spite of Baron's criminal record and unsavory associations, the board not only did not nominate him to the Black Book, it also approved his application for the 1 percent ownership in the Sands.

However, in all fairness to the regulators, some applications of individuals of questionable background were denied at the time, even though they were applying for minor changes in their existing licenses. An example may be seen in the case of Leo Roy Frey, who applied for approval of additional slot machines at his Moulin Rouge Hotel in Las Vegas.[66] Born in Germany, Frey had immigrated to the United States and become a citizen in 1951. Following a short stay in New York City, he moved to Los Angeles, where he resided at the Ashbury Hotel, which his corporation eventually acquired. When the hotel was sold and Frey moved to Las Vegas in 1959, the new owners "discovered that it had been running as a regular house of prostitution and it was necessary to evict nineteen girls from the hotel" (p. 64). People who knew Frey in Los Angeles "said he was a 'nice fellow' but 'a con man from way back'" (p. 64).

In addition to a 1950 arrest in Paris for forgery and using forged documents (a passport), Frey's Interpol record showed a 1957 conviction in Attari, India, for attempting to export currency illicitly. "During a customs search before entering Pakistan, 8,500,000 Indian rupees and . . . 10,000.00 [U.S. dollars] were found hidden in a special compartment in the gasoline tank" of Frey and his companion's car (p. 52). Frey also had illegal possession of a .22 caliber pistol and ammunition. He was convicted and sentenced to three years in an Indian prison. The following excerpt from an article in the *Los Angeles Examiner* entitled "King of the Smugglers" describes the incident:

> Two American con-men, Thomas Dana and Leo Roy Frey, with records as long as adding machine rolls, got a bright idea. They bought an American diplomat's car in Paris and bribed the garagemen to leave the *Corps Diplomatique* plates on.
> They shipped the car to Pakistan, loaded it with 100 pounds of gold hidden behind the front seat . . . But the third time the Indian customs agents went over the car, [they] spotted $90,000 worth of gold and nabbed the pair.[67]

Although Frey was denied his application for the additional slot machines, there is no indication that his original license was revoked. Further, he was initially licensed in Nevada following his release from the Indian prison, and was again renewed only a month before the *Los Angeles Examiner* article appeared.[68]

Finally, the denial of licensing for the new machines may have had more to do with the problems of the Moulin Rouge than with those of Frey himself. The casino had been licensed for only a few months in 1955 and then went bankrupt. Thereafter it operated off and on, primarily as a hotel and nightspot, with several changes in ownership. It is said that some Las Vegas casino owners welcomed, if not contributed to, its failure. Unlike other casinos of its day, the Moulin Rouge had no racial restrictions and was located in one of the city's black neighborhoods. When it became a favorite after-hours place for black entertainers, such as Sammy Davis, Jr., who could perform at the major casinos but not stay there, it attracted substantial crowds. Thus, at a time when the city was experiencing an economic recession, the Moulin Rouge's efforts to remain solvent did not receive support and may have even been undermined by those threatened by its popularity.[69]

A CRITERION OF THREAT

It is clear that a number of applicants of questionable background were licensed during the late 1950s and early 1960s. This raises the question of what criteria formed the basis for the selection of those thought to present so great a threat to the industry that they should be placed in the Black Book. This is a question that has been raised since the time that the book was instituted. Considering the numerous other potential candidates at the time, some have suggested that board chairman Abbaticchio had simply chosen the men randomly.[70] The backgrounds of these individuals would suggest otherwise.

The conclusions of the 1950s U.S. congressional investigations into organized crime seem to have played an important part in the regulators' thinking and decisions in this regard. The Kefauver hearings (1951) and the McClellan investigations (1957) concluded that there was a "mafia" operating in the United States of largely Italian and Italian-American origins. It was believed that this mafia was organized into regional "families" that were structured bureaucratically, and that these families conspired to monopolize gambling, prostitution, and various rackets.[71] These conclusions formed the basis for an "alien conspiracy theory" of organized crime.[72] Thus, not surprisingly, when the first 11 men were entered into the Black Book in June of 1960, the overwhelming majority were of Italian ancestry.

This is especially interesting in light of the generally problematic backgrounds of those who entered the industry in its infancy. Virtually all these men had previously been bootleggers and were engaged in illegal gambling. The large majority were Jews, outnumbering Italians two to one. Yet, the threat of organized crime to the industry is seen as emanating from Italians. So pervasive is this belief that, when Jews are identified with organized crime, they are seen as "fronting" for Italians. Even when circumstances suggest that Jews control casinos and some Italians may be working for them, the evidence is sometimes twisted to fit with the more popular belief. This may be seen in the anonymous statement of a high government official quoted by Wallace Turner in *Gamblers' Money* (1965).

> ... where the Italians get hold of a good gambling joint, they have somebody run it for them and that somebody is usually Jewish.
>
> I don't know why this is, but you can see examples of it all along the line. Meyer Lansky is a Jew, and he has very, very close ties with the top hoods in the Cosa Nostra outfit. Bugsy Siegel was a Jew and he was hooked up real close with the Italian mob.
>
> Some of the places in Las Vegas today are really controlled by the Mafia and we know this because we see some of their muscle men around. But the front men are almost always Jews.[73]

This is an incredible statement when one stops to consider that the front man in the case of Siegel was said to have been responsible for some 20–50 murders, depending on whose account you accept. More recently it has been suggested by a former FBI agent that Moe Dalitz was fronting for both New York and Chicago mob interests in Las Vegas.[74] Nevertheless, Dalitz was, as late as 1978, named in a California Organized Crime Control Commission list (along with several Black Book figures) as one of 92 persons whose associations with organized crime activity have been substantiated.[75] One cannot help but wonder what kind of disorganized "mafiosa" might try to hide behind the skirts of individuals such as Siegel and Dalitz.

3

Genesis of the Black Book

THE FIRST ELEVEN

The Black Book began with the entry of 11 men who were known nationally and internationally as organized crime figures. They were identified as members of mafia families in Chicago, Kansas City, and Los Angeles, with the families from the last two cities viewed in law enforcement circles as under the control of the family in Chicago. Most interestingly, none of the first 11 was associated with the New York and Cleveland syndicates that had gained a stronghold in Nevada gambling, that is, the Lansky and the Dalitz groups. Among the notable entries were Murray "the Camel" Humphreys, Joseph "Wild Cowboy" Sica, Marshal Caifano (alias John Marshall), the brothers Carl and Nicholas Civella, Louis Tom Dragna, and Sam Giancana (see table 1.1).

Humphreys, an alleged lieutenant of Al Capone, was said to have been involved in labor racketeering in the mid-1940s and to have been a "Washington lobbyist" for Sam Giancana in the 1950s and 1960s.[1] Sica was reputedly a strong-arm thug of Mickey Cohen, a notorious Los Angeles bookmaker in the 1940s and 1950s, and was said to have subsequently taken control of the racing news-wire service there. He is also said to have been the lieutenant in charge of narcotics for Los Angeles crime boss Jack Dragna in the 1950s.[2] Caifano, a dapper and frequent visitor to the casinos of Las Vegas, was said to have been a high-ranking member of the Chicago mob. Newspaper accounts suggest that he was entered into the Black Book because of problems that had arisen between

39

him and the management of the Desert Inn and Tropicana hotels.[3] The Civella brothers were reputed bosses of the Kansas City organized crime syndicate. Sometime after the death of his uncle, Jack Dragna, in 1957, Louis Tom Dragna was reported to have become acting boss of the Los Angeles mob. He, too, was said to have had problems with the Desert Inn prior to his entry into the Black Book. He was arrested and searched there in February 1960 and ordered to leave Las Vegas.[4]

Finally, Sam Giancana was reputed to have been the Chicago syndicate boss and "one of the twelve overlords . . . [of the American] 'Mafia.' "[5] Giancana was subsequently linked to John F. Kennedy's 1960 presidential election and to a 1963 CIA plot to assassinate Fidel Castro.[6] He also cost Frank Sinatra his gaming license at the Cal-Neva Lodge in Lake Tahoe when it was learned that he and singer Phyllis McGuire were staying at the lodge following his entry into the Black Book. Giancana and his close associate, John Rosselli, were murdered gangland style shortly after being subpoenaed to testify before a congressional committee regarding Kennedy's assassination.

EARLY CHALLENGES TO THE BLACK BOOK

Challenges to the Black Book began almost immediately following the closed-door, initial, unannounced listing. Within a month of his entry, Louis Tom Dragna checked into the Dunes hotel and casino armed with two prominent civil rights attorneys, William B. Beirne and A. L. Wirin.[7] Wirin had gained notoriety for his energetic, though futile, efforts to save Carl Chessman from the California gas chamber only a year earlier. The hotel management quickly became aware of Dragna's presence and inquired of the Gaming Control Board about how they should proceed. They were referred to the letter that accompanied the Black Book and the regulation which stated that it was an "unsuitable manner of operation" for a licensee to cater to persons of notorious or unsavory reputation.[8] Dragna was then asked to leave, but refused and proceeded to a night on the town. He had a complimentary dinner and saw an early show at the Sands, then proceeded to a midnight show at the Tropicana and an early-morning lounge show at the Stardust. Throughout the evening, he was followed by three gaming agents, who informed the hotel executives of his presence. Other than the brief problem with the management at the Dunes, Dragna did not encounter any other difficulties in obtaining services. Casino officials were probably uncertain about the constitutionality of the Black Book, and it was implied that lawsuits would follow if they were to interfere with his freedom. Following his stay in Las Vegas, Dragna did indeed file a suit asking the federal court to find the Black Book illegal and void.[9]

Only a few months later, in October of 1960, Marshal Caifano (aka John Marshall) came to Las Vegas and proceeded to taunt the regulators openly. He was suspected of having committed several gangland executions, which may also have made his presence generally intimidating. Edward Olsen said of one occasion that "all he would do is stare at me, and I've never seen colder eyes in my life."[10]

Caifano stayed at the Tropicana his first day in town (Thursday). When the management there discovered who he was, he was told that rooms would not be available for the remainder of the weekend. He then moved to a motel without gaming facilities for the next two nights and then back to the Tropicana on Sunday, when the hotel could no longer contend a lack of rooms at the close of the weekend. During his stay, he visited numerous casinos on the Strip, often accompanied by singer Roberta Lin. He went to the Stardust, the Sands, the Desert Inn, the Flamingo, the Riviera, the Sahara, the Silver Slipper, the New Frontier, and the Last Frontier. During his rounds, he was frequently joined and warmly greeted by owners and ranking executives of the hotels, such as Wilbur Clark, owner of the Stardust, where Roberta Lin performed.

When Gaming Control Board chairman, R. J. Abbaticchio, Jr., learned of Caifano's activities, he flew from Reno to Las Vegas, taking with him almost his entire Carson City staff. In an effort to convince the casinos not to cater to the Black Book figure, he led an all-out effort to curtail their business.[11] His strategy was to embarrass publicly the casinos that Caifano visited by openly confiscating their cards and dice for inspection. An account of the incident is given by Edward Olsen, former Associated Press bureau chief for Nevada, and Abbaticchio's 1961 replacement as chairman of the Nevada Gaming Control Board.

They hit the Tropicana first, then the Desert Inn, the Stardust, Flamingo, Sands, and Riviera. At each hotel what seemed like a small army, with Abbaticchio in the forefront, moved into the casino pit, demanding cards and dice from selected tables. These were elaborately placed in brown envelopes, which were then sealed and ceremoniously signed by the dealers and the shift boss as well as by agents.

The practice of picking up cards and dice for inspection is an ongoing one in Nevada, but usually requires no more than two agents and is carried out so discreetly that the players are unaware of the operation. On this Monday night, however, the puzzled players in the luxury hotels were well aware of the activity, and by the time Abbaticchio's raiders reached the third hotel, even the press had reporters on the scene, resulting in gaudy headlines in the morning editions. (p. 7)

During these episodes, several of the casinos tried to eject Caifano, but eventually caved in to his threats of lawsuits. It was at Moe Dalitz's Desert Inn that he was finally escorted out of a casino, whereupon he got into an altercation with a news photographer who was popping flash pictures of him. He nevertheless stopped his rounds of the casinos at this point and left for Los Angeles the next morning, where he met with his lawyers, who also were Wirin and Beirne. He soon brought civil suits against Governor Grant Sawyer, gaming regulators, and the Desert Inn,[12] and, like Dragna, appealed the regulators' actions in federal court.

This episode produced unfavorable press regarding the Black Book and Abbaticchio's approach to enforcement.[13] Much of the criticism was directed toward Governor Grant Sawyer for allowing it to happen. Public reaction and concern over the effects of the publicity on Nevada's already tarnished image prompted the governor in 1961 to replace former FBI agent Abbaticchio with Edward Olsen, the Associated Press bureau chief in Reno.

Dragna and Marshall* launched a major attack against the regulators by immediately taking their cases to the federal courts.[14] They argued that being declared undesirable without notice constituted a violation of their Fourteenth Amendment right to due process. Attorneys for the state argued, on the other hand, that

---

*We have drawn upon regulatory transcripts (NGC transcripts, June 20, 1961; Mar. 20, 1962; July 17, 1962) and the published works of Edward Olsen (1972) and Bowers and Titus (1987) in our interpretations and discussion of the appeals of Louis Dragna and Marshal Caifano. In the discussion, we will refer to Caifano as John Marshall or simply Marshall, for this is the name form used in these sources as well as in the legal cases.

entry into a casino was not a basic human right, but rather a local right (if not a privilege) and, therefore, challenges to the Black Book should be dealt with in the Nevada courts. Deferring to the state, a federal trial court dismissed the Dragna and Marshall cases on the basis of the rule of abstention. The men then appealed to the U.S. Court of Appeals for the Ninth Circuit, which reversed the lower court dismissal and agreed to hear their cases.[15] In 1962, however, the federal appeals court ruled in *Marshall v. Sawyer* that the state's classification of those who were or were not "notorious" was reasonable and not a violation of Fourteenth Amendment rights.[16] This decision reinforced the state's position that to enter casinos is a local right or privilege, not a basic human right.

The decision in *Marshall v. Sawyer* held that the due process rights of the Fourteenth Amendment are relative to their context, in this case the special economy and needs of the state of Nevada. Because the state itself is engaged in the gambling business and its people depend so heavily on it, it must, of necessity, go to great lengths to protect its welfare by keeping the wrong kind of people out of gambling. The justice stated in his decision:

> The opportunities for rich pickings in this sanctuary for gambling would assuredly be tempting to hoodlums and gangsters. At all hazards these enterprises must be preserved for indigenous Nevadans whose law-abiding propensities could be relied upon. Let the gangsters move in from the underworld where they were forced to operate elsewhere, and the resultant crooked games, cheats, frauds, swindles leading inevitably to gangland style kidnappings and killings would mean the end of Nevada's rich gambling take. The good people of the State would not tolerate it, and even if they failed to move, the federal government would be pressured to move in and licensed gambling in Nevada would come to an end with even greater celerity than that which saw the end of polygamy in Utah . . .
>
> It follows from these considerations that where the anticipated evils, sought to be prevented or restricted, are particularly serious, or where extreme harm may be anticipated, the remedies to be applied may be more drastic if the State authorities reasonably regard such drastic remedies as necessary to protect the State against the anticipated harm. The more serious the threat to the State's welfare, the more drastic the remedy which may be applied.[17]

The federal appeals court decision in *Marshall v. Sawyer*, however, did not keep the most notorious of all the members of the Black Book from entering a casino. From July 17 to July 28, 1963, Sam Giancana literally lived at Frank Sinatra's Cal-Neva Lodge in Lake Tahoe.[18] Sinatra had reportedly associated with Giancana at various other places around the country, and there had previously been rumors of "undesirable people" around north Lake Tahoe. This along with a federal investigation into alleged interstate transportation of prostitutes to the lodge and incidents of suspected violence involving lodge employees are said to have raised concerns that the regulators had earlier communicated to Sinatra.[19] These circumstances also suggest that the lodge had been the object of considerable law enforcement inquiry prior to Giancana's visit.

Giancana had just won a federal court harassment charge against the FBI and went to Cal-Neva Lodge to stay with his girlfriend, singer Phyllis McGuire, who was performing there. Sinatra is said to have made no effort to have Giancana leave and to have talked with him during his stay. The Black Book figure is said to have been graciously entertained at the lodge and to have had use of one of the lodge's cars.[20] Allegedly he also got into a fight at the lodge, and Sinatra and his valet are said to have broken it up, although the entertainer denied any knowledge of the incident. During the board's investigation, Sinatra was also said to have stated that he would continue to associate with Giancana outside Nevada "whenever he felt like it."[21] Within two days of the board having informed the FBI of the findings of its investigation, a detailed story of Giancana's visit appeared in the August 2 issue of the *Chicago Sun-Times* under the headline "Moe's Visit Perils Sinatra License" (pp. 378–379). It was not until the board had issued subpoenas to executive staff members at the lodge a month later, however, that a Las Vegas newspaper got hold of the story and, to quote then control board chairman Edward Olsen, "all hell broke loose in the press and all over the country" (pp. 384–385).

When Sinatra heard the early reports of the story he is said to have become infuriated with the publicity (which he felt was a result of the subpoenas) and requested through his accountant to meet with the control board chairman at the Cal-Neva Lodge. When Olsen refused, Sinatra is said to have phoned him and, according to Olsen, "maligned and vilified" the regulators and tried to "intimidate and coerce" him into dropping the investigation (pp. 398–399). Olsen then issued a formal complaint. The complaint informed Sinatra of the violation (including what he had allegedly said in the phone conversation), the board's recommendation that his license be revoked, and the requirement that he defend his actions before the Nevada Gaming Commission. Promising at first to fight the matter, Sinatra had the considerable support of his friends, and it appeared to some that the Black Book was in for a setback. Then, following two days of sessions between his attorneys and the board, and on the night before he was required to respond to the complaint, Sinatra surprisingly issued a statement that he was divesting his interests in Nevada gambling. He gave as his explanation an earlier decision to devote his full time and efforts to an entertainment company with which he had recently become associated.

As one of the best-known Italians in America, Sinatra was the perfect target of symbolic law enforcement at a time of considerable federal interest in organized crime. By then the government had identified individuals whom they considered to be leaders of the mafia, and Sinatra was said to have openly associated with one of them. For some he may have accordingly come to symbolize this "Italian problem," especially to those resentful of his success. They therefore gave support, if not impetus, to the regulatory action. Olsen states that, when the board was pursuing the matter,

> there were literally hundreds of letters that came from every part of the nation. And . . . so many people had a—apparently an ingrained resentment of Sinatra because he had been successful, or he came from a poor background and made money, or something like that. And so many of these things were racial overtones. People were just "bitter" about the man. So they were very complimentary to the state for trying to do something with him. (pp. 400–401)*

*It was not until 1974 that the state would again be faced with the need to enforce the sanctions of the Black Book. At that time, Nicholas Civella visited Las Vegas. He stayed at the Dunes, where he was accorded VIP treatment (NGC transcripts, Mar. 23, 1978: 14–16). He was given a special double-room suite, his favorite liquor, flowers, and free license to withdraw cash from the casino cage at any time. He registered at the hotel under a pseudonym, and it was believed that the management sought to conceal his presence. However, the incident became known, and the regulators proceeded to take action against the Dunes.

We return now to the appeal of Black Book member John Marshall. Marshall attacked the regulators on several legal fronts. Even before a decision was rendered in the case against Governor Sawyer in the U.S. Court of Appeals for the Ninth Circuit, Marshall also brought a civil suit against the governor and the regulators in the U.S. District Court for Nevada. He asked for monetary damages for being restricted from his liberty to register and eat at certain hotels and, as in his federal case, for being declared undesirable without notice of hearing. He was again unsuccessful, however, because the district court upheld Nevada's use of the Black Book as part of the police power of the state as contained in the Tenth Amendment.[22] News accounts also indicate that he filed a civil suit against the Desert Inn and the Gaming Control Board for $151,000 in the U.S. District Court.

While his civil case was pending before the district court, Marshall also appealed to the U.S. Court of Appeals for the Ninth Circuit on the basis of failure to be notified prior to his inclusion in the Black Book. Again, the circuit court ruled in favor of the state, and held in 1966 that his inclusion was legitimate because of his criminal record. The court recommended, however, that future Black Book nominees be given a hearing,[23] a recommendation that would not be implemented until many years later and after several others had been entered into the book. Still not deterred, Marshall finally took his case to the U.S. Supreme Court, which in 1967 denied him a hearing.[24]

OTHER REGULATORY DECISIONS OF THE 1960s

Joseph D. Pignatello is an Italian cuisine chef from Chicago. He came to Las Vegas in the 1960s without a criminal record or history of gambling, and applied for licensing as a 50 percent stockholder in a restaurant with four slot machines.[25] Described as having worked in a "major hoodlum hangout" of Marshal Caifano, Felix Alderisio, and Sam Giancana in Chicago and in another "hoodlum owned" restaurant in Florida, and as having

---

The hotel's defense was that the state had not clearly specified the procedures that licensees were to follow in dealing with those listed in the Black Book. The Dunes was nevertheless found to be in violation of gaming regulations, and was required to pay a fine of $10,000.

been a personal chef to Frank Sinatra, Pignatello was denied licensing "on the grounds of questionable antecedents." There were also the dubious bits of evidence of a car registered to Pignatello allegedly having been observed at the funeral of Marshal Caifano's father, and the belief of "reliable" informants that he was acting on behalf of Sam Giancana in his application; these too apparently played a part in the regulators' decision. It seems to us absurd, however, even to suggest that Pignatello might have been fronting for one of the reputed 12 overlords of the mafia (Giancana) in trying to obtain a license for a restaurant with only four slot machines. It is more likely that he was denied his license because he cooked for the mob.

Yet, while some were denied licensing because of their associations, others, even those with criminal histories, were licensed. At the same board meeting in which Pignatello was denied his license, two of six applicants for operation of the Thunderbird hotel and casino were discussed—Charles J. Rich and Sidney Wyman (pp. 40–46). Though both men were prior licensees, they were, according to national identification records, said to have extensive bookmaking records, and to have appeared before the Kefauver committee, where they invoked the Fifth Amendment right on several occasions. Yet, the board concluded that these records were "so limited in factual detail that it . . . [was] impossible to obtain a true picture of their entanglements with law enforcement agencies" (p. 40). Further, it was suggested that "because of their thorough knowledge of all phases of gambling and their colorful personalities, [they] have a flare that attracts people and thus business to any establishment with which they are associated" (p. 46). While Rich and Wyman soon withdrew their application for the operation of the Thunderbird, only a few months thereafter they applied for 30 percent ownership of the Dunes and were approved.[26] Although it was said that there had been an updating of their backgrounds in the interim, the information was not entered into the record.

MORE PROBLEMS AND MORE MEN

The entry of the three men in 1965 is one of the most interesting events in the colorful history of the Black Book. It is the only instance in which individuals have been removed from the book

Ruby Kolod. Kolod was a member of Dalitz' Desert Inn
Group that owned several hotels in Las Vegas in the 1950s
and 1960s. Receiving national notoriety for his involvement
in what was referred to at the time as a "shady oil deal,"
Kolod was put in the Black Book in 1965. His power and
influence, however, resulted in his immediate removal, the
only such instance in the history of the Black Book. Courtesy *Las Vegas Review Journal.*

48

for reasons other than death. The event illustrates how regulation is influenced by negative publicity in one instance and by powerful interests within the industry in another. It also raises questions about the influence of powerful industry interests on the origins and use of the Black Book more generally.[27]

In what would become a familiar pattern, the men were entered into the Black Book because of negative publicity and governmental efforts to convey an image of a legitimate industry. Most notable among the three men placed in the book in 1965 was Ruby Kolod, a member of the Dalitz Desert Inn Group, which controlled a large portion of Las Vegas gambling at the time. From New York City, Kolod had moved to Cleveland in 1930. He and his partners had formerly run illegal gambling operations in Ohio and Kentucky, and had since gained respectability in Las Vegas. In addition to the Desert Inn, the group had acquired ownership of several other major Las Vegas hotels and casinos, including the Stardust and the Royal Nevada.[28]

However, apparently Kolod's share of the profits from his lucrative casino investments was not enough. To supplement his income, he is said to have joined forces with "Icepick Willie" Alderman in investing $68,000 in a "shady oil deal" with a Denver attorney, Robert Sunshine, who was eventually convicted of embezzling monies from the investment. Alderman is said to have held stock in the El Cortez from 1945 to 1948, in the Flamingo from 1948 to 1954, and in the Riviera from 1954 to 1959.[29] When the oil deal went sour, Sunshine told authorities that Kolod had gotten the money from the Desert Inn cage and that he and Alderman had sent "two hoods," Felix "Milwaukee Phil" Alderisio and Americo DePietto, to Denver to convince him "to return the money or be liquidated."[30] Alderisio was alleged to be a top lieutenant of Sam Giancana.[31] Along with Kolod, Alderisio and Alderman would be added to the Black Book.

Apparently desperate to stay out of prison, Kolod fashioned an incredible defense that involved taking on the FBI.[32] Contending that it would prove his innocence, he challenged J. Edgar Hoover to produce the tapes of phone conversations in which he had allegedly threatened Sunshine. Since phone taps were a violation of both federal and Nevada state law at the time, and admission of such activity on the part of the FBI would have resulted in incrimination of one of their own officials, the tapes were never produced. Kolod and his two assistants were nevertheless convicted of conspiring to use interstate communications to threaten the Denver attorney.[33]

From the day that the oil deal became public, it produced newspaper accounts that have been described as resembling "a Damon Runyon sequel."[34] At the time, Kolod faced a loss of his interests in Las Vegas casinos, which amounted to $1 million— 13.1 percent in the Desert Inn as the single largest stockholder, and 8 percent interest in the Stardust.[35] Within a week of his conviction in Denver of conspiracy to extort money by threatening violence, the newspapers carried the story of the Gaming Control Board notifying casino operators that the presence of the three men would be considered "dangerous to the best interests of the state." On April 15, board chairman Olsen was quoted as saying that "casinos catering to these men will be placing their licenses in jeopardy."[36] Then, within a week, on April 22, the commission issued an emergency order to suspend the licenses of Kolod.

While there was indeed a great deal of unfavorable publicity surrounding the crime given the position of Kolod in the industry, there was an even more pressing threat to the state. Within the several months previous to the press coverage of the attempted extortion, the Nevada legislature was attempting to find additional revenue to support various state institutions, including its schools, cities, and counties. The state was apparently gripped by a major economic crisis. A proposal had been made in February of that year (1965) that the needed monies could be obtained from gaming, by increasing the gross tax on the industry from the existing 5.5 percent to 15 percent. The governor and the gaming regulators responded in horror to the proposal, maintaining that it would seriously damage the industry. The threat to the economy of the state was very real, and Kolod and his associates were caught in the middle of the crisis.

Because of Kolod's position in the industry and the national publicity given to his crime, his entry into the Black Book is said to have been used by Governor Grant Sawyer to demonstrate just how determined Nevada was to keep unsavory elements out of gambling. A Las Vegas editorial explicitly suggested that the action toward Kolod served to communicate the degree of determination on the part of Nevada's regulators, even to the federal government.

Most Nevadans expected it, but the state's action to boot Ruby Kolod and his pals from the gambling industry should come as a surprise to a number of our uninformed critics.

Conviction of the trio in a Colorado extortion case was all the State Gaming Control Board needed to move to strip Kolod of his casino interests and to declare all three persona non grata in gambling places. The action gives testimony to Nevada's determination to police its major industry and demand that all licensees conform to the standards of this privileged business. This won't silence our detractors but it should have an effect on many who haven't the faintest idea about the self-imposed controls on gambling and gamblers in Nevada.

We have no illusion about the Kolod removal reversing the tide of unfair criticism which has been running against Nevada gambling—some of it within the state itself. After all, the Sinatra divestiture case worked no miracles on public opinion either. But, it will, we believe, take the sting out of the argument that holds that gamblers write their own rules in Nevada. This may come as a surprise in some quarters—even in the Justice Department.

. . . The multitude of favorable publicity stories emanating daily from Las Vegas is both good and necessary. However, for impact where it counts, nothing can benefit Nevada more than accounts of the State exercising its proper authority over businesses operating as a privilege of the people of Nevada. These stories discount with fact what has been given currency through fiction.[37]

Thus, for a few weeks, when the state drove out those convicted of extortion, it appeared that the industry was indeed clean, and this condition may have even implied that the present economic crisis would pass. The message had been communicated to the public and even to the federal government that Nevada was tough. It was two weeks later, on May 6, however, that the board lifted its ban. Kolod and Alderman could once again enter casinos. Of the three, only Alderisio remained banned, for how long a time is unclear.[38]

The governor's earlier actions toward Kolod apparently backfired, however, and ultimately cost Sawyer his reelection. In placing Kolod in the Black Book, he had taken on too respected and powerful a group, especially in the person of Dalitz.

Dalitz . . . , through one of those strange and inexplicable sociological developments, . . . [had] come to have in Las Vegas

51

the reputation of standing as a force for righteousness between the Strip gambling houses and the Mob. Various elements of officialdom look[ed] on Dalitz as a known quality, a gambler they . . . [could] figure . . . [was] less likely to be a part of some terrible criminal conspiracy. Dalitz . . . [was] widely respected among observers of the gambling scene. The Desert Inn management . . . [was] a sort of aristocracy among the gamblers who control the casinos in Las Vegas.[39]

Dalitz and his associates were not only influential enough to have Kolod and his alleged accomplice removed from the Black Book; they also had the respect and power to mobilize public opinion against the governor so as to cost him his reelection. Their friends in the industry were said to have been especially outraged by Sawyer's actions. The Desert Inn also became the largest hotel contributor to the campaign of Sawyer's opponent, Paul Laxalt, and Kolod was the single largest individual contributor. Terminally ill at the time, Kolod is said to have so wanted to destroy Sawyer before he died that he personally contributed $200,000 to Laxalt's campaign.[40] During Laxalt's term as governor no new entries were made to the Black Book.

Even at this early period it is clear that the regulators directed their efforts principally toward Italians. Not only were almost all those entered Italian, but also the regulatory mechanism seems to have been selectively enforced against Italians, with preferential treatment given to Jews. The most extreme example we have seen is the case of the removal of Kolod and one of his Jewish associates from the book and the retention for a time of his Italian associate.

4

A Savior Comes to Babylon

The mid-1960s brought the eccentric Howard Hughes to Las Vegas. His presence was like a miracle. He immediately bought several casinos that were thought to have been controlled by organized crime. Some of these had been owned by Moe Dalitz and his partners, though Hughes is said to have thereafter enlisted Dalitz's advice on Desert Inn operations and to have wanted his involvement in decisions regarding "other deals" that he had been considering.[1] And there were indeed other deals. By April of 1968, Hughes had acquired six major casinos on the Strip—the Desert Inn, the Sands, the Castaways, the Frontier, the Landmark, and the Silver Slipper. He had become the state's largest employer, owning a quarter of the business done in Las Vegas and contributing a seventh of the state revenues.[2]

Because Hughes was believed to have obtained his fortune honestly, he was trusted by the regulators and increased public confidence in the legitimacy of gaming. Several transcripts of regulatory meetings pertaining to his properties reflect the esteem in which he was held and the deference shown him by the regulators. "Desperately anxious to keep him in Nevada, the state waived most of the mandated investigative procedures necessary for licensure." [3] Also, because Hughes bought hotels and casinos that were thought to have been under mob influence, there was the perception that the underworld no longer posed a serious threat to the industry. Indeed, it has been suggested that the eastern mobs sold their Las Vegas interests to Howard Hughes.[4] With Hughes now in town, presumably regulators felt little need to activate the Black Book. But just what do we know about this man who went to such great lengths to avoid social contact and to keep his life secret?

Billionaire Howard Hughes died in 1976 at the age of 70 on a plane from Acapulco to Houston, Texas—a victim of malnutrition, gross neglect, and drug abuse.[5] For the last 15 years of his life, he lived in blackened rooms and complete secrecy. The regulators of the Nevada gaming industry, as well as the general public, were unaware of the many bizarre aspects of Hughes's life because of the elaborate "secrecy machine" that he had constructed to guard his privacy. James Phelan, who chronicled how Hughes maintained his invisibility and fostered a myth of his sanity and control over his business empire, wrote:

> In the everyday world, a recluse who cowers naked amid self-neglect in his bedroom is called insane. A billionaire who thus flees the world is termed eccentric.
>
> The charade was played out by . . . [Hughes's] aides for fifteen years. It succeeded because the truth about Hughes was confined to a tight, taciturn little group and because Hughes had stretches of lucidity when his mask of sanity stayed in place. (p. 43)

Born in 1905, Hughes inherited the Hughes Tool Company from his father, which proved to be the basis of his wealth. He used these monies to make movies and to build a major international air transportation company, Trans World Airlines. These business machinations were the large part of his public image. But Hughes also was the beneficiary of government contracts and favors amounting to $6 billion, sometimes secured by cash, and he escaped any accounting of his transactions in court or by governmental or regulatory agencies (pp. xii, 75, 187–189). His personal life was equally unknown (pp. 24–43). Though a legendary womanizer in the 1940s and 1950s, he maintained residences for women he never visited, and was completely without female companionship for the last 10 years of his life. During this time, he lived a Spartan-like existence as a hypochondriac and drug addict, prone to compulsive meticulousness and obsessive cleanliness.

On Thanksgiving Day in 1966, Hughes moved unseen to the penthouse of the Desert Inn, where he lived for the next four years. At the time, he was embroiled in a complicated and expensive legal battle over alleged mismanagement of TWA that had forced the sale of his $546 million interest in the airlines and resulted in a $145 million default judgment against him by the court (pp. 49, 56). To organize the "counterintelligence" necessary to keep him out of court, Hughes hired Bob Maheu, who as a CIA operative had earlier recruited Johnny Rosselli and Sam Giancana in the failed attempt to assassinate Fidel Castro in the early 1960s (p. 51). Maheu kept Hughes out of court and, without ever seeing him, became his second-in-command in Las Vegas (pp. 60–81).

On his arrival in Las Vegas, Hughes was to use the funds from the sale of his TWA stock to buy into the Nevada gaming industry, where he eventually owned seven casinos, in apparent violation of antitrust laws but with the approval of Attorney General John Mitchell (p. 75). By 1970, in addition to the casinos, Hughes had acquired additional land on the Las Vegas Strip, an airport, a huge ranch and a large tract of undeveloped land outside town, and a television station, and is said to have had "the state administration in his pocket" (pp. 101–102).

Summa Corporation, of which Hughes was the sole stockholder, was the parent company of his Nevada holdings. By 1971, Bob Maheu was deposed as Hughes second-in-command, and Frank William Gay, a powerful Mormon who had risen from a potato chip salesman and chauffeur, had gained control of Summa (p. 10). Maheu's firing followed closely upon Hughes's furtive exit from the Desert Inn penthouse on Thanksgiving eve in 1970; never to return to Las Vegas, he left a bedroom with a four-year supply of empty bottles of pain-killing drugs and filled jars of urine (pp. 112–113). Then Gay and Chester Davis, Hughes's chief attorney, were put forward for licensing with Summa (pp. 117–119), and, following Hughes's death, Gay was elected president of the corporation (p. 200).

During the final 10 years of his life, Hughes was personally attended by an elite entourage of six bodyguards, referred to by the press as the Mormon Mafia and Palace Guard. They were in place to do Hughes's bidding without question and to protect him from the world, and, at times, even from others in his own employ. While this group was at Hughes's command, whisking him about from place to place and catering to his eccentricities, they also exercised a degree of power over his empire, in that they had control of information going to and from him (p. 99). This situation becomes all the more intriguing when one considers that five of the six guards, two of the four doctors, and his barber (who was occasionally called in to cut his foot-and-a-half length hair) were Mormon, and that, in addition, Gay had appointed Mormons to various positions in the top echelons of Hughes's empire. It suggests that the special treatment that Hughes received in Nevada was in many respects quite fitting, given the state's long-standing tradition of Mormon influence in government and regulation of gaming.

Hughes was licensed in Nevada gaming with almost a complete absence of official protocol. Nevada governor Paul Laxalt, Maheu's regular tennis partner, was said to be extremely receptive to allowing Hughes to have privacy, and the regulators followed suit:

> Hughes was not required to furnish a contemporary photograph, to appear before the gaming board in person, to be fingerprinted, or to provide a detailed financial statement. Once when he wanted a license in a hurry for a newly purchased casino, the control agency members, scattered around the state, gave their approval in a few hours by "meeting" via a conference telephone call. (p. 78)

After Hughes's 1970 abrupt exit from Las Vegas and bad publicity surrounding his said-to-be authorized biography by Clifford Irving, the regulators grew suspicious and less malleable. Although Hughes denied the Irving book as a hoax in a telephone interview with several newsmen, the denial itself fostered more doubts and disbelief on the part of the public (pp. 125–127). As usual, the regulators responded to the adverse publicity. Thus, Nevada's new governor, Mike O'Callaghan, and Gaming Control Board chairman Phil Hannifin insisted on seeing Hughes personally to confirm the reorganization of his casinos. With Gay and Davis in attendance, O'Callaghan and Hannifin met briefly with Hughes, who was attired in a bathrobe and slippers, wearing an old-fashioned hearing aid, which he pointed in their direction. Though agreeing to keep the details of Hughes's appearance secret, the Gaming Control Board chairman later reported that "he seemed ... eccentric but articulate."[6]

BEGINNINGS OF THE CORPORATE ERA

While the advent of Howard Hughes might have seemed like a panacea to the regulators and a break from the problems associated with the licensing of those of questionable background, the Hughes era was to bring another problem—that of the corporate structure. Beginning in the late 1960s and early 1970s, it was large corporations that began to dominate the gaming industry. The change came about when the Nevada legislature gave in to the lobbying pressures of Las Vegas casino owners and in 1969 passed a corporate licensing act.[7] The act provided for the purchase of Nevada hotels by public corporations "without requiring each shareholder to submit to individual licensing."[8]

The bureaucratic structure of the corporation soon provided in the gaming industry what it had provided in society generally—an ostensibly legitimate structure, where individual action and responsibility were nearly impossible to locate and ascertain. Within this complex structure, the specifics of financial matters and relationships thus became increasingly difficult to discern. Tracing the origins and hence the appropriateness of loans to casinos through the corporate structure, for example, became increasingly difficult for the board's Audit Division.

Adding to this problem for the board was the increase in the number of loans that its Audit Division was responsible for monitoring.[9] By 1975, there were at least 30–40 declared loans each month. By 1976, there were nearly 150 per month. By 1978, there was an average of more than 200 per month. The Audit Division was obligated to review each and every loan, and refer suspicious ones to the board's Special Investigations and Intelligence Division. By 1979, the Hilton, the Thunderbird, Caesars Palace, the Sands, the Frontier, and the Riviera had cases in state court dealing with audit assessments.[10]

The magnitude of this problem is evident in the case of Argent Corporation. Headed by Allen R. Glick as sole stockholder and president, Argent was seeking registration as the sole stockholder of Recrion and Karat, the corporations that operated the Fremont and the Stardust hotels and casinos, respectively. Glick financed the buyout with a $62,750,000 loan from the pension fund of the Central States Southeast and Southwest Conference of Teamsters. This was the single largest Teamsters loan ever

Allen R. Glick being sworn before the Nevada Gaming Control Board. A man with a sterling background, Glick rose rapidly from a job as a real estate salesman in San Diego to become, within five years, the president and sole stockholder of Argent Corporation, the parent company of the Stardust and Fremont casinos in Las Vegas. The backing for his ventures was obtained from loans received from the Teamsters Pension Fund in amounts totaling $160 million. The regulators were plagued with suspicions of hidden ownership and skimming from his casinos for a decade following the formation of Argent. Although Glick was believed by law enforcement to be fronting for mob interests, he was never convicted of such acts. Courtesy *Las Vegas Review Journal.*

made for the purchase of a casino, and was approved in only nine days without a personal financial statement from Glick.[11] The loan is said to have been obtained through a connection with an influential pension fund trustee when the fund was controlled by Alan Dorfman, a Teamsters' official who was thought to have friends in organized crime. Glick eventually obtained a total of $160 million through additional Teamsters loans for these and other ventures. After approving Glick's application for Argent, the regulators were plagued with problems from the corporation for the next decade. The problems centered around questions of hidden ownership and skimming from the casinos, problems that eventually resulted in a major national scandal within the industry and in convictions of several Argent figures. Although Glick himself was not convicted, the Nevada Gaming Commission revoked his license and fined him $125,000 in August of 1979.

Steven Brill researched Glick's background for his book *The Teamsters* and provides a detailed account of events that preceded and were coincidental with the formation of Argent.[12] Born and raised in Pittsburgh, Glick had a very conventional middle-class background. The son of a local scrap iron dealer, he attended college at Ohio State University and went on to complete a law degree at Case Western Reserve. He served as a helicopter pilot in the military and received a Bronze Star for his duty in Vietnam. Upon discharge as a captain in 1969, he and his family moved to their frequent vacation spot of San Diego, where he took a $200-a-week job as a real estate salesman. A year later, he moved up to a $500-a-week position with Saratoga, a multi-million-dollar real estate firm with whom his previous employer had been involved in several ventures. In just one more year, he parlayed this new job into a 50 percent ownership of the company, acquired by a $2,500 note from his partner. It was this business from which he was able to borrow $2.3 million to enter into partnerships in the gaming industry. First, he jointly purchased the Hacienda on the Las Vegas Strip in 1972, and then later, in 1973, he jointly purchased King's Castle near Lake Tahoe.

True to his form, he wasted neither time nor his own money in borrowing from the Teamsters' fund to purchase the Stardust and the Fremont hotels and to form Argent Corporation. When Teamsters' official Alan Dorfman was asked why he had given Glick so much money for the venture, he responded, "Alan was a nice kid. This is America. You see a smart young honest kid who has an

idea and you give him a chance" (p. 246). But others had surmised that there was more to it than a mere liking for the intense
and bright-appearing young executive. Rather, it has been suggested that Glick's clean, if not sterling, background made him an
excellent front for mob interests in the casinos. He more than
qualified for licensing, given his background relative to the backgrounds of most of those who had come into the industry before
him. Indeed, some of the regulators who were worried about the
decline of the Hughes's dynasty must have felt that the appearance of Glick in Las Vegas—a man no one had ever heard of—was
a "second coming"; he was another savior, another Hughes. But,
the second coming soon became hell for the regulators.

When Glick formed Argent Corporation, he made a Stardust
21 pit boss chairman of its executive committee. The pit boss's
name was Frank "Lefty" Rosenthal, a reputed former bookie
with a record of gambling violations and alleged ties to organized
crime. The new chairman's problems didn't stop there. He also
had the dubious distinction of being an old friend of Anthony
Spilotro, alleged loan shark and enforcer for Chicago mob interests in Las Vegas. Spilotro had and continues to have a local
reputation as the most notorious and ruthless of any organized
crime figure who has allegedly operated in the city. Soon all the
pieces were in place for what became one of the industry's major
skimming operations. As one FBI agent put it:

> Think of it as a corporation . . . Dorfman arranges the loans.
> Then, there's Spilotro, who's the company's corporate vice-
> president from Chicago. Rosenthal is his manager of skim. And,
> Glick—well, they let him run the hotels and be the front, but he
> stays away from the casinos. (p. 238)

It did not take long for law enforcement to get the picture. As
early as 1975, a California police agency memorandum on Glick
stated the belief that

> . . . the plan was for Rosenthal and the others to "skim the 'gub'
> out of the two casinos, driving them into bankruptcy, and [then]
> be unable to make his payments to the Teamsters [pension fund].
> The Teamsters [pension fund] would then be forced to fore-
> close . . . leaving the Teamsters the owners of Recrion [actually
> renamed Argent]." (p. 238)

Argent is not the only corporation to have received financing from the Teamsters' fund. The Dunes, under M and R Investment as the parent company when Morris Shenker was a corporate officer, was the recipient of $40 million, a loan that caused the regulators considerable concern. It has in fact been suggested that much of Las Vegas was built with Teamsters' money.[13] Near the end of the Hughes's dynasty, it was believed that loans to several major casinos from the Chicago Teamsters' pension fund were being used by the Chicago underworld to regain their influence in Las Vegas.[14] With the fear and publicity of Teamsters' money flowing into the city, and their "savior" no longer holed-up in the penthouse of the Desert Inn surrounded by Mormon bodyguards, the regulators started to get nervous. Hughes was out of the country, and Chicago was back in town. The regulators again circled their wagons by nominating five new men to the Black Book. The new nominees were Wilford Kalaauala Pulawa, Alvin George Kaohu, Anthony Giordano, Michael Santo Polizzi, and Anthony Joseph Zerilli.

NOW, TWO HAWAIIANS AND MORE ITALIANS

The first 11 men were put in the Black Book without notice or hearing. The board decided that they presented a threat and, without formal approval of the commission, sent their photos and descriptive information to all licensed gaming establishments in the state of Nevada. When the three men were put in the book in 1965, they were entered for only a short time and then removed. By 1975, when two more men were entered, several regulatory and legislative changes had taken place. The decision of the U.S. Court of Appeals for the Ninth Circuit in the Marshall case recommended that nominees subsequently be awarded a hearing.[15] The Gaming Control Act, as revised in 1967, provided for an administrative hearing as well as for notice and judicial review of such hearing.[16] In 1972, the commission put into effect Regulation 28, delineating the specific criteria that were to be used in determining whether an individual is an appropriate candidate for the Black Book.

Yet, when Wilford Pulawa and Alvin Kaohu were blacklisted in 1975, they received no prior notice and had no hearing. Although the commission did issue a single Final Order of Exclusion for both men, it was little more than a one-page document acknowledging that it had "received the [board's] Petition for Final Order of Exclusion . . . and . . . found that the procedural requirements of Regulation 28 . . . [had] been satisfied in full."[17] The reasons given for inclusion of the men were less than specific. It was stated that they had notorious reputations and that Kaohu (only) had been convicted of a crime which would be a felony under the laws of Nevada and the United States. Thus, on January 23, 1975, when Pulawa and Kaohu were excluded from Nevada gaming, the regulators seem to have acted both in violation of their own regulations and in opposition to a federal court recommendation.

In our review of the agenda for all board and commission meetings in 1974 and 1975, any mention of Pulawa, Kaohu, or the List of Excluded Persons failed to surface. Thus, we have had to rely on general transcripts of the time in reconstructing the circumstances surrounding the entry of the two men. The transcript for the Nevada Gaming Commission meeting in July 1974 reveals two concerns: the pension fund loans of the Central States Southeast and Southwest Conference of Teamsters to Las Vegas casinos; and the granting of junket representative licenses to several individuals operating out of Hawaii.*

In considering the suitability of the several applicants for junket licenses, the board submitted evidence that the men had associations with Wilford Pulawa, the alleged head of organized crime in Hawaii. Two of the men had "paid tribute" to Pulawa, and when one of them stopped, his life was threatened.[18] Of additional concern was that the man had agreed to testify against Pulawa and that there might be repercussions. The board recommended denial of the junket representative licenses, stating that "the influence which dominates these particular individuals is an illegal, improper influence that we can't tolerate" (p. 5). While the regulators were not unsympathetic with the man who had had his life threatened, their concern was with the effects of possible

---

*Often owners of travel agencies, junket representatives are retained by a hotel and casino to identify and coordinate the regular visits of patrons known to be gamblers in the cities in which the junkets originate. Such patrons are usually provided with free air transportation, rooms, meals, and entertainment in return for a deposit of specified sums of money with the casino, for which they use "markers" when gambling.

ensuing events on the reputation of Nevada gaming. This concern is expressed in the following statement of commission chairman Peter Echeverria regarding the man in question:

> His associations, the fact he is under threat of death, the fact he is associated with the syndicate, all that situation is just rampant with danger; that is certainly not consistent with the best interest of the State of Nevada. It is a volatile situation.
> What if that guy got knocked off right in front of Caesars Palace? (p. 56)

The commission decided that three of the four applicants were unsuitable for licenses as junket representatives, and Chairman Echeverria suggested that the board "proceed to place . . . [Wilford Pulawa and his 'right-hand man,' Alvin Kaohu] among the list of those individuals who cannot come into the casinos of . . . [the] State" (p. 219). Within five months and without a formal hearing, Pulawa and Kaohu were nominated and entered into the Black Book. It is noteworthy that there is no indication in the available records that either Pulawa or Kaohu had ever even been in the state of Nevada, which raises questions about the perceived threat that the men posed to gaming. Their absence did, however, make them easy targets.

Again, in 1975, the regulators nominated three other men to the Black Book—Anthony Giordano, Michael Santo Polizzi, and Anthony Joseph Zerilli. And, again, an official record of neither a board meeting nor a commission meeting on these men could be located. Yet the commission's computerized "Events Index System" (a computer data base initiated in 1989 by the board's executive secretary) and newspaper accounts[19] provide some, however scanty, information on the men. According to newspaper accounts, Giordano, from St. Louis, Zerilli, from Detroit, and Polizzi had been convicted of having hidden interests in the Frontier. They appealed their Black Book nominations, but the commission postponed the hearings because they were serving prison sentences and could not enter Nevada casinos. By April of 1976, their cases were vacated.

Finally, the nominations of Giordano, Polizzi, and Zerilli bear directly on our argument that the decline of the Hughes's dynasty was a major factor in reactivating the Black Book. The Frontier, in which the three men were alleged to have held hidden interests, was one of Hughes's holdings, which must have confirmed the regulators' worst fear that Hughes was no longer in control of his empire. With Hughes's death in 1976, that fear became a reality.

PART 2

Internal Crises in the Industry

5

Enemies from Within

The relative peace of the Hughes's era seemed to end abruptly when regulators faced major problems that erupted from within the industry itself. In the late 1970s, the Nevada Gaming Control Board was involved in ongoing investigations of several Las Vegas casinos. The inquiries involved the Aladdin Hotel Corporation, the Hotel Conquistador, Inc., doing business as the Tropicana hotel and casino, the Argent Corporation, the corporation operating the Stardust and the Fremont hotels and casinos. An hotel executive and others in the entertainment sector of the industry were thought to be involved in skimming and behind-the-scenes influence on the operations of these establishments. The men were Frank Larry Rosenthal, entertainment director at the Stardust, James Tamer, executive show director at the Aladdin, Joseph Agosto, show producer at the Tropicana, and Carl Wesley Thomas, casino executive at Circus Circus and owner of Bingo Palace and Slots-A-Fun. All but Rosenthal were convicted of felonies in federal court, and all were eventually nominated to the Black Book.

The industry was in disarray following the death of Hughes. The industry was also tainted by the revelation that several of the largest casinos were recipients of Teamsters loans. There was clearly a need to restore confidence in the integrity of gaming. But with federal indictments pending against the several individuals who were presenting problems, the regulators did not move against these enemies from within. Instead, they moved against one so notorious, so unsavory, and so linked to Chicago that

Nevada Gaming Commission Chairman Harry Reid, May 1977. Now a U.S. Senator, Reid had high political aspirations even before his appointment to the commission. He had run for the posts of Nevada governor, U.S. senator, and mayor of Las Vegas all within little more than a year. A convert to Mormonism, the young commissioner set a strong moral tone in Nevada regulation. During his tenure public attention was brought to the alleged underworld connections of several major industry figures, a number of whom were later entered into the Black Book. Courtesy *Las Vegas Review Journal*.

they appeared strong. They moved against Anthony Spilotro, or Tough Tony as he was called. Indeed, it was a dramatic event. As the first public hearing involving the placement of an individual in the Black Book, it provided an opportunity for the regulators to demonstrate the power of the state to rid Nevada gambling of organized crime. Interestingly, the majority of the Nevada Gaming Commission members on this auspicious occasion were Mormon. Chairman Peter Echeverria introduced the incoming chairman, Harry Reid. Referring to Reid as a former distinguished lieutenant governor and legislator and an outstanding lawyer from Clark County, and in anticipation of the press response to Reid's appointment, Echeverria said:

> Before the press can make much jargon of this, I want to steal the appellation that so naturally fits into the new Chairman of the Commission . . . we will have three Mormons on the Commission . . . [George] Swarts, . . . [Clarence] Haycock . . . a Jack Mormon, . . . [and Reid]. When Harry Reid takes this chair, I know the press is going to . . . [say that] the Mormon Mafia will control gambling in the State of Nevada.[1]

Reid (now a U.S. senator) and George Swarts would experience failed car bombing attempts on their lives shortly after leaving their posts on the commission.[2]

Before his appointment to the commission, the politically aspiring Reid had run for the posts of Nevada governor, U.S. senator, and mayor of Las Vegas, all within little more than a year. Though himself a prior object of public accusations of questionable ethics,[3] the young Mormon set a strong moral tone for commission meetings under his chairmanship. He required that all applicants for nonrestricted licenses personally appear before the regulatory body, and he even introduced the pledge of allegiance into commission meetings.[4]

THE ENTRY OF SPILOTRO

Spilotro was a person of considerable notoriety and on the streets was thought of as an enforcer for Chicago organized crime interests in Las Vegas. He was attributed extensive and wide-ranging underworld involvement in southern Nevada. As an editorialist put it: "If you have lived in Southern Nevada a few years, it is a devil you know: Tough Tony. The Ant. The Chicago mob's Las Vegas overseer. Former ruthless ruler of the street rackets. Suspected of killing several dozen people."[5] Indeed, a recent defense of a woman charged with the death of her husband in 1986 is based on the allegation that Spilotro ordered the hit. A *Las Vegas Review Journal* editorial dealing with the issue reflects the legacy of his reputation: ". . . the Blame Tony Syndrome . . . [is] a virus that impaired the judgment of some detectives and reporters during the hood's heyday. If a bookmaker turned up in a ditch, Tony did it. If a salad fork came up missing at a Strip buffet, Tony did it . . ."[6] Reflecting the extent to which Las Vegas' crime problem was attributed to Spilotro was the seemingly incongruous belief that this major underworld figure was also the head of a local burglary ring known as the Hole in the Wall Gang.[7]

It is said that in the months before Spilotro moved to Las Vegas in 1971, several newspapers reported speculation that he was among those likely to become Chicago's next mafia boss. It naturally made sense to some, then, that he must have been sent to Las Vegas to oversee Chicago mob interests in the casinos. He already had a reputation as an enforcer, and by the time of his arrival, had been suspected of having carried out numerous executions, though he had never been convicted. He is said to have learned his trade from Felix Alderisio, also a reputed executioner for the Chicago mob and one of the men added to the Black Book in 1965 along with Ruby Kolod.[8]

Soon after his arrival in Las Vegas, Spilotro leased the jewelry-gift concession at Circus Circus as a suspected front for his illegal activities. He is said to have then recruited a gang of burglars and assorted heavies, and to have quietly gained control of bookmaking, loan-sharking, narcotics, and prostitution along the Strip. He was soon seen as the city's chief loan shark, overtaking Gaspare Speciale, a man who himself would be placed in the Black Book almost two decades later. Speciale was reputed to be a New York mafia associate who for 15 years had operated a loan-sharking and bookmaking business out of his Tower of Pizza restaurant. But unlike Speciale, a soft, dapper fellow, jokingly said to have on occasion dispatched his pizza waitresses to collect his loans, Spilotro was said to be tough on "deadbeats" and "welchers," using threats and unnecessary force.[9]

A short, stocky man of about 5 feet 4 inches, Spilotro was said to have used intimidation as the chief means of getting his way. Newspapers and magazines are replete with statements of law enforcement officials about him that are remarkably similar to former Gaming Control Board chairman Edward Olsen's depiction of John Marshall decades earlier. "He had those icy eyes, [a former law enforcement official said] . . . I could see he had the potential to become violent if he had to be."[10] And there is the account of his having once been introduced to a federal agent in the Las Vegas airport, whereupon he just "looked him coldly in the eye, stuck out his finger and moved his thumb up and down like a hammer." The power that Spilotro gained in Las Vegas was said to be second only to that of Moe Dalitz.[11]

Whatever obscurity Spilotro might have had when he first arrived in Las Vegas came to an abrupt end on August 30, 1972. On that date, the Chicago Police Department issued a warrant for his arrest in connection with a murder of another alleged loan shark nine years earlier. He was implicated in the crime along with his reputed former loan shark boss, Sam DeStefano, and Sam's brother, Mario, when one of Sam's enforcers turned witness for the government and testified that he had helped Spilotro and the DeStefanos with the murder. Having to stand trial with Sam DeStefano was said to have caused Spilotro great consternation. Newspapers reported speculation that Sam might provide testimony against his brother and Spilotro in return for a reduced sentence, because he was critically ill and fearful that he might die in prison. When Sam was murdered shortly before the trial, Spilotro and Mario were naturally the prime suspects. But they were only suspects in Sam's murder and, although forensic evidence corroborated the eyewitness testimony alleging Mario's role in the original murder, Spilotro produced witnesses to testify in regard to his whereabouts at the time of the offense and was acquitted.[12]

However, this was to become the beginning of Spilotro's problems in Las Vegas. The arrest and circumstances surrounding the trial led local and federal authorities, in retrospect, to suspect him of what they perceived to be an increased number of gangland murders since his arrival in the city. "Every time there was a 'hit,' we'd rush out to Spilotro's house," recalled a former Las Vegas officer. Because authorities were unable to substantiate an arrest (and Spilotro was said to have boasted about this), their public image was threatened and they grew increasingly frustrated. The result was for Sheriff Ralph Lamb to order Spilotro's arrest on suspicion of murder and, according to one newspaper account, pledge that Spilotro would "rot in jail." Spilotro protested and, when a judge opened the courtroom the following Sunday morning to hear the case, he told the judge that when the arresting officers were trying to book him, they were unable even to tell him whom he had allegedly murdered. The judge ordered his release, which went unchallenged, and Spilotro received the apology of an assistant district attorney.[13]

Beginning in 1975, Spilotro is said to have held court at the poker area of the Dunes, which, like Circus Circus, was heavily indebted to the Teamsters' pension fund at the time. He spent most of his days there for about a year, until he was forced out by

Anthony Spilotro surrounded in a Las Vegas courtroom. Spilotro was an object of extensive law enforcement activity during his years in Las Vegas, much of which is said to have been unwarranted. These entanglements would ultimately be used to substantiate the necessity of his entry into the Black Book. Even nine years after his murder, he continues to be blamed for crime and corruption in Las Vegas. Courtesy *Las Vegas Review Journal.*

Anthony Spilotro being defended by his attorney, Oscar Goodman. Goodman represented Spilotro in many of his entanglements with the law. And Spilotro appears to have kept his lawyers very busy as a result of his notorious reputation. Indeed, the mere allegation of association with Spilotro was sufficient for the regulators to deny an applicant a gaming license. Courtesy *Las Vegas Review Journal.*

regulatory pressure on owners Morris Shenker and Major Riddle. He then moved shop to the gated Las Vegas Country Club and Estates, where he is said to have had more privacy to conduct his affairs, although his presence there too seems to have met with some resistance from Moe Dalitz and other club members. He soon moved again, this time to his own jewelry store, the Gold Rush.[14]

The perception of more murders and disappearances between 1975 and 1978 brought additional media attention to Las Vegas. National newspapers and magazines picked up on the incidents and most often mentioned Spilotro's name in connection with them. A result was that the government closed in from several fronts, with the FBI, IRS, local police, and state gaming authorities accelerating their efforts to obtain information on him. A dozen or more FBI agents are said to have maintained around-the-clock surveillance over Spilotro and his associates, and at least one undercover agent sought to infiltrate the group. The surveillance was so great that at one point there were even plans to place a video camera on a phone pole near Spilotro's home, a plan that is said to have been aborted only because of a lack of funds.[15] Spilotro responded in kind, turning his jewelry store into a veritable fortress against government surveillance. With look-outs stationed upstairs, in adjoining buildings, and in automobiles, the store is said to have had an elaborate alarm system complete with buzzer-operated doors, to have been equipped with radio scanners to monitor FBI and police frequencies and radio transmitters and receivers, and to have been swept routinely for "bugs" by a private security firm.[16]

Spilotro's picture was constantly in the newspapers and on television, so virtually everyone knew his face. Like a celebrity, he therefore attracted crowds wherever he went. Not only did reporters and surveillance teams from various agencies constantly follow him, but also there were crowds of curiosity seekers that frequented his local haunts to sneak a glimpse of him.[17]

By June 1978, enough information was gathered to convince a U.S. magistrate to approve FBI warrants to search the homes, businesses, automobiles, and person of Spilotro, his brother, and his associates.[18] After all the surveillance, however, the seizures are said to have produced evidence of only questionable significance, almost all of which was eventually ruled inadmissible because of the government having gone beyond the scope of the warrants.[19] But the damage had already been done: at least in the minds of the people, Spilotro was everything the media and law enforcement had suggested that he was. It is no surprise then that, just a week after the search warrants had been executed, newspapers reported that Spilotro might become a candidate for the Black Book. In connection with the report, former Nevada Gaming Commission chairman Peter Echeverria was quoted as saying that Spilotro "is a very dangerous individual and [from] the reports I hear . . . is supposed to be in Las Vegas watching after the mob's interests and his brother . . . is going to take over after he goes back to Chicago and joins the 'Big Three' and runs the Chicago mafia there."[20]

The perceived importance and dramaturgical quality of the Black Book in maintaining control over the industry are especially relevant in what was this first formal hearing involving placement of an individual in the Black Book. A reflection of the state's concerns with Spilotro and with preserving the reputation of the industry at this time may be seen in excerpts from Jeffrey Clontz's opening statement in the state's case to enter Spilotro into the Black Book.[21] Responding to allegations of counsel that moving the hearings from the offices of the Gaming Control Board to the Las Vegas Convention Center and holding them on a Saturday to accommodate a larger public was to have created a "three-ring circus . . . [and put his] client's reputation . . . at stake" (p. 8), Clontz stated:

> . . . the reputation of Anthony Spilotro is not the only reputation that is at issue at today's hearing. For over half a century the Nevada Gaming Authority, including this present Commission, [has] worked towards building a reputation as the strongest gaming regulators in the world, and I submit that that reputation is also at issue in today's hearing. When I began my opening remarks today I mentioned that the list of excluded persons had not been overly utilized in prior years and when we consider the awesome sanctions that befall an individual as a result of inclusion I think that it's a healthy sign that the list has not been over utilized. There are, however, certain—for want of a better term—select individuals whose reputations are so notorious or so unsavory or whose mere physical presence on the premises of a licensed gaming establishment is so highly inimical to the continued well-being of this State and its people and its well-deserved reputation for tough gaming control that the continued efficacy of that reputation can be satisfied by nothing less than the inclusion of that individual's name on the list of excluded persons. (pp. 23–24)

In presenting the state's case for the entry of Spilotro into the Black Book, the deputy attorney general stated:

> As . . . evidence of Anthony Spilotro's history of involvement with criminal activities the Board will . . . offer into evidence a very recent copy of his criminal arrest record—more commonly known as his rap sheet. When you examine this record you will see that Anthony Spilotro has enjoyed a long and colorful history of encounters with various law enforcement agencies . . . (p. 19)

It is questionable, however, whether Spilotro's reputation is as well-deserved as is popularly believed. Although Spilotro had, in fact, been arrested 19 times for offenses ranging from traffic violations to murder (p. 19), the only crime of which he had been convicted in the United States was "making false statements of material fact on mortgage loan applications to a federally insured lending institution . . . the sentence received . . . was a $1 fine on each of two counts" (p. 21). In addition, he had been charged with the crime of jewel robbery in Monaco in 1964 and two years later was convicted in absentia (p. 20), having been previously excluded from the country. Other than the one-dollar fines, Spilotro had never been sanctioned for any of the alleged offenses.

The magnitude of Spilotro's criminal record is also drawn into question by circumstances surrounding his March 1974 Las Vegas arrest for murder. An account of this incident is given by Robert Legakes, justice of the peace in Clark County, Nevada, in response to questions from Spilotro's counsel, Oscar Goodman. The following is a portion of the direct examination record, with Goodman posing the questions:

Q. Please state your name.
A. Robert Gus Legakes.
Q. And will you spell your last name for the record?
A. L-e-g-a-k-e-s.
Q. Where are you employed?
A. Clark County, Nevada, Justice of the Peace.
Q. And were you so employed on March the 3rd of 1974?
A. Yes, I was.
Q. Did you have an occasion to be sitting as Justice of the Peace at that time?
A. Yes, I did.
Q. Was there a matter which came before you on that date concerning one Anthony Spilotro?
A. Yes, there was.
Q. And what day was March the 3rd of 1974?
A. Sunday.
Q. Would you please tell the honorable Commission what took place in your courtroom?
A. There was a hearing concerning the release of the defendant Anthony Spilotro from custody as a result of his being arrested the previous date.

Q. Was he incarcerated in the Clark County Jail to your knowledge overnight?

A. I have no personal knowledge. He was in custody at the time
he was brought before me.

Q. Do you know when he was arrested?

A. I have no personal knowledge of that.

Q. Was there a law enforcement Metropolitan Police officer in
the court at the time that the hearing took place?

A. There was a jail employee, who brought Mr. Spilotro into the
courtroom.

Q. What was the nature of the matter which brought Mr. Spilotro into custody?

A. He was arrested for homicide.

Q. Was there ever a complaint filed?

A. No criminal complaint was ever filed against Mr. Spilotro.

Q. And at the time that the arrest took place did the District
Attorney's Office even appear at the bail hearing?

A. The District Attorney's Office did not appear. They advised
the Court personally that they felt that the Defendant was
entitled to a bail, whether or not he was entitled to his own
recognizance would be discretionary with myself.

Q. And did you in fact place Mr. Spilotro in his own recognizance on March the 3rd, 1974 after he had been arrested for
murder?

A. Yes, I released him on his O.R. without bail.

Q. And did there come a time when there was another court appearance scheduled for Mr. Spilotro on or about March 19th,
1974?

A. Yes, there was.

Q. And did Mr. Spilotro in fact appear in court at that time?

A. I do not recall.

Q. Could you tell us what you do recall about the hearing of
March 19th, 1974?

A. The Court was advised by the Clark County District Attorney's Office that no criminal complaint had been filed, charging the—charging Spilotro with a crime; that no request had
been received from the Metropolitan Police Department considering—or concerning the arrest, and no Metropolitan Police documents had been turned over to the District Attorney's Office concerning the arrest.

Q. Did you then exonerate the own recognizance and let Mr.
Spilotro go?

A. Yes, I did.

Q. Do you know of anything else that happened as far as that arrest is concerned which resulted in the filing of a complaint at any time?

A. No, I do not. (pp. 98–101)

Again, the target of the regulators appears to have been an easy one. Spilotro was highly visible and believed locally to be a major organized crime figure. His having been arrested for felonious offenses on numerous occasions but never convicted was seen as additional evidence of his nefariousness. Many believe that he was so feared and influential as to be immune to the criminal process. Social scientists familiar with gambling and organized crime seem to have come to share in this belief. A classic example may be seen in the comment of a prominent scholar in this field. In response to our observation that Spilotro's official record did not measure up to his criminal reputation, he wrote, "Spilotro was a particularly vicious thug and hitman . . . [who] was tough to convict since he had no scruples about killing witnesses." In light of Spilotro's never having been convicted of such crimes, one cannot help but ask how this individual can say with certainty that Spilotro killed his witnesses. Nevertheless, even eight years after his badly beaten body was found buried in an Indiana cornfield, a deceased Spilotro continues to be blamed for crime and corruption in Las Vegas.

THE STARDUST AND FRANK LARRY ROSENTHAL

Frank Rosenthal was the first of the industry figures to come under the suspicion of the board. Although he had earlier been approved for 2.84 percent of Circus Circus in 1969, he was called forward for key-employee licensing in 1976 in connection with his managerial duties at the Stardust as director of Nevada operations.[22] In accordance with gaming regulations, the board can discretionarily call forward for investigation anyone who applies for key licensing for casino duties that appear to constitute a certain degree of influence and carry a salary of more than $40,000 annually; this process allows the board considerable latitude to inquire into the background of suspected associates of organized crime. Rosenthal had a record of illegal bookmaking and bribery, and had been investigated by the McClellan committee in 1968. A

Frank Larry Rosenthal appearing before the Nevada Gaming Control Board for key employee licensing with Argent Corporation, January 14, 1976. *Left to right*: attorney Harry Claiborne, attorney Oscar Goodman, Frank Rosenthal, and Allen R. Glick speaking on behalf of Rosenthal. The applicant encountered great difficulty with the Board because of his earlier alleged bookmaking activity, and his long-time friendship with Anthony Spilotro, and was ultimately denied licensing. Courtesy *Las Vegas Review Journal*.

1969 report of the Chicago Crime Commission also named him as an affiliate of organized crime. The expressed concern in calling Rosenthal forward was that he might have a role in the operation of the race and sports book at the Stardust. A large part of the board's inquiry also focused on his long-standing friendship with Anthony Spilotro. Having grown up in the same neighborhood in Chicago, Rosenthal had known Spilotro since birth. The offenses which concerned the regulators most were a 1959 Miami arrest for bookmaking and a 1963 conviction for conspiracy to bribe a New York University basketball player in a 1960 national tournament game with West Virginia University. The Miami arrest had been a major subject of inquiry in Rosenthal's investigation by the McClellan committee. In his closing statements, Senator McClellan said, ". . . the testimony regarding accused fixer, gambler and handicapper, Frank Lefty Rosenthal, provides us a sordid example of the crooked and contemptible operations in which some of these characters engage."[23]

The licensing hearing, like that on the excluded persons issue, is a show cause process. The burden of proof in establishing suitability rests with the applicant. This was obviously clear to Rosenthal, inasmuch as he took an unusually active and aggressive stance in arguing his case before the regulators.[24] He denied any regular association with Spilotro or any other wrongdoing since his arrival in Las Vegas in 1970. He attributed a large part of his criminal record to police harassment, citing one instance in which he had been arrested three times within 24 hours for failing to register as a felon with the Las Vegas Metropolitan Police Department. He told of how his unwillingness to pay protection money and to serve as an informant for law enforcement resulted in the 1959 raid on his apartment and subsequent arrest for bookmaking. There were beatings by the FBI and threats on his mother's life; she was told, " . . . if you don't smarten your son up you'll find your head in Chicago and your body in Chicago Heights" (p. 119).

Rosenthal said that he had been framed by his codefendant in the bribery charge. He said two New York detectives had told him that the North Carolina county solicitor had informed his codefendant that if he could "deliver Frank Rosenthal, [he would] have a chance to walk away free." He characterized his codefendant as one who "would have given his mother up to stay away from what he had to face, [given] what had been substantiated, all the admissions of attempted fixing, and all the positive identifications" (pp. 188–189). He maintained that out of ignorance of the law and because he was a Jew in "Baptist Country," he entered a plea of nolo contendere rather than risk the possibility of going to prison (p. 192).

At times the regulators seemed to believe Rosenthal's story, but at other times they shook their heads in dismay at what must have seemed to them to be outlandish fabrication. His account of the 1959 raid on his apartment and arrest for bookmaking exemplifies the kinds of issues and arguments that the regulators faced in assessing the applicant's suitability. These kinds of stories, together with Rosenthal's vociferous and self-confident style, appear to have tried the patience of, if not offended, some of the regulators.

After I had decided to leave Chicago, . . . to go down to Miami, . . . I took an apartment there . . . In a . . . very short period of time I was contacted by a gentleman who had the name of Eli the Juice Man . . .

. . . he advised me that he was well aware of my reputation as a "big time national gambler out of Chicago." We tossed around some small talk, and then he came to his point. He suggested to me—I use the word loosely—that it would be in my best interest to make available to him—I believe at the time it was $500 a month. He never stated why, and naturally I was curious and only curious, and he explained to me that my reputation, one who had—I was considered to be one of the biggest gamblers in the United States known from coast to coast. I believe he even mentioned the possibility that I might be a bookmaker.

I assured him that I had no intentions of being a bookmaker . . .

I reminded Eli the Juice Man that I was actively engaged on a venture with my father . . . with thoroughbred racing, and I could not resolve the issue of the fact that I would have to pay him or anybody else $500 a month, . . . to operate those racehorses.

He didn't quarrel with me, but he didn't agree with me. He left . . . I believe he indicated he'd be back to see me. He even suggested someone else might be seeing me. I wasn't quite sure what he meant by "someone else."

Subsequently, as I left my apartment . . . I was met by an agent of the FBI . . . He offered me identification, customary procedure. He asked me if I would allow him a few minutes of my time. I said, "Yes."

He informed me that he was on a special mission specifically with the interest of the Director, referring to J. Edgar Hoover, and that Mr. Hoover had a personal interest in Frank Rosenthal, and that his interest would be, would I be willing to provide and supply information to this agent, or a designee, with respect to gaming around the United States, with respect to associations, bookmakers, et cetera. That was his request.

In turn, he promised me if I would look upon this favorably that he would guarantee and provide me with near total immunity, with the exception of murder. He promised me immunity from state, from local, from federal, from every agency in this country.

In addition to that he said, "Lefty, you can write your own check. You name the amount."

Obviously I didn't accept his offer.

He also told me he'd be back to see me. He did come back to see me.

The next time that I met this agent his conversation was, I guess you might say, it was somewhat similar, but certainly his tone was not. He was no longer asking me, he was telling me what I was going to do and what I wasn't going to do, and he reminded me that without his protection, without that of the Bureau, without that of the Director, that my life could become very, very miserable, and he was very, very accurate in his statement.

He asked me if I would consider, and I told him I wouldn't. He reminded me that that wouldn't be the last I'd hear about it, and that he had brought my message to the Director, and the Director told him, "You better smarten this guy up," meaning me.

Shortly thereafter Eli the Juice Man came over to see me and asked me if I had changed my mind, and I told Eli the Juice Man—I wasn't so cordial to him, and I made the mistake by telling him to take his best shot . . . that I would not concede to any payments, and that I would continue to do what I was doing, and he took his best shot.

The next I knew about it . . . [was] when an arrest was made in North Bay Village . . . and that was my answer for refusing to pay the money to Eli the Juice Man and refusing to work as an informant for the FBI; but that was not the end. (pp. 92–95)

The 1959 arrest for bookmaking occurred on New Year's Eve. A raid was conducted on Rosenthal's apartment by the chief of police and deputy sheriff of North Bay Village, Dade County, Florida, and members of the state attorney general's office. When the police entered the apartment, they found Rosenthal seated on his bed in his pajamas with a phone in one hand and a small black book in the other. The chief described the incident to the McClellan committee:

The search warrant was read to him by a deputy sheriff from the Metropolitan County Sheriff's Department, at which time I took the telephone from him and I asked the person on the other end who was talking. I said I was Lefty [Rosenthal]. He said, "This is Cincinnati." He said, "You have 10 and 10 on Windy Fleet, and I will take 4 and 4 of it." We later learned that Windy Fleet was a horse running at Tropical Park that afternoon. He came in second. (pp. 100–101)

The chief went on to explain that he took other calls:

I answered several phone calls dealing with, as I recall, the Florida–Baylor game, the East–West game, one call in particular from an Amos in Indiana. I answered the telephone, and he asked if this was Lefty, and I replied, "Yes." I asked him, "Who is this?" And he said, "This is Amos from Indiana." He wanted to know what we were doing with the East–West game. I asked Mr. Rosenthal what he was doing, and he gave me a point spread. I think it was five and a half points for the East. I gave it to Amos as the West; anyway, I gave him the opposite team. I asked Mr. Rosenthal if he wanted to talk to this particular man in Indiana, and Mr. Rosenthal took the phone, and he said, "Do you know who you are talking to? You are talking to a cop, you stupid s.o.b.; keep on talking." With that, Amos hung up the telephone. (pp. 101–102)

The police said that they found several phones and an elaborate intercom system in the apartment, along with the usual items found in a lay-off betting operation: rundown sheets, baseball cards, and the like. They also indicated that there were two loaded 0.38 revolvers in the nightstand near Rosenthal's phone. Rosenthal denied that the apartment was set up for bookmaking operations and that any bookmaking was taking place at the time of the raid. He said that he was simply watching one of the games on television at the time and felt that the entire episode was a result of his having not cooperated with Eli the Juice Man and the FBI.

Although Rosenthal said that he had not maintained regular association with Anthony Spilotro in recent years, he did not deny their long-standing friendship. He acknowledged that he had testified on Spilotro's behalf at a bail hearing following Spilotro's 1972 Chicago indictment for homicide. He also told a story of his long-time friend saving him from a beating by the FBI.

I was at a red light in Miami, in the left lane, trying to make a left turn, waiting for the green arrow to go on, and I turned on the green arrow, and as I turned I noticed two cars behind me. One was obviously a local police; the other was easy to identify as the FBI. They put their red light on the first car, and the second car didn't do anything, just trailed. They cited me with a ticket for failing to put my turn signals on . . .

I accepted the violation, and the local police pulled away, and the remaining car which I described to you as [a] Bureau car, they didn't, and they were making gestures, laughing, and had a few words to say.

This was at nighttime, and it was on—it was not on a—it wasn't heavily trafficked, kind of quiet.

And as Frank Rosenthal, that's the way I am, I walked back to
that car. They didn't come to me, I walked back to them, and we
had a few words. I reminded them about some of the members of
their family, kind of a nasty thing, back and forth. With that they
got out of the car. One was out and one was in. The one was in,
got out, and they pushed me off, physically pushed me off to the
side, and the one agent said, "We finally got you. We are going to
give you the beating of your life, you son of a bitch."

And I was already pushed off. They tried to get me a little
further into the bushes. There was no contest. They were two big
agents, they were armed, and I wasn't that big.

With that, another car pulled up very quickly, and two fel-
lows jumped out of the car, and one of them was Anthony Spilotro, and he wasn't armed, and there were just a couple of words
went back and forth, just a couple, very, very few. He is about
five foot two or five foot three, and they got back in their car, and
as they went back in their car we kind of changed the momentum
a little bit. (pp. 255–256)

However, the regulators did not believe Rosenthal. His stories
and explanations were just too far afield from law enforcement
accounts. The regulators were also concerned with the national
notoriety given to the incidents and issues in question. Thus,
after all the inquiry and probing, it was unanimously concluded
that the applicant should not be licensed as a key employee at the
Stardust.

Rosenthal appealed the commission's decision to the Nevada
Supreme Court and lost, but was able to continue to work at the
Stardust in a non-key-employee position. He returned to Argent
as a senior member of its executive committee. After a brief period, he was made director of food and beverage at the Stardust
and later entertainment director of the hotel's Lido Show.

As entertainment director at the Stardust, Rosenthal was again
called forward on June 22, 1978, for licensing as a key employee
of Argent. He requested that the commission reconsider its decision, and there was a hearing on October 6, 1978. A major witness
at the hearing was Allen Glick, executive and owner of Argent
Corporation.[25]

The first of the state's questions of Glick had to do with Rosenthal's role in the operations of the Stardust race and sports book,
a book run by Martin "Marty" Kane and Joey Boston (born Jo-

seph I. Gurwitz), well-known reputed Las Vegas bookmakers and friends of Rosenthal. There was the implication that Rosenthal might be influencing the book through Kane and Boston (p. 118). Having been employed in various capacities at the book since 1975, the two men came under investigation for key-employee licensing at about the same time as Rosenthal. Although they withdrew their applications and terminated employment with the Stardust, the board entered their criminal activities and associations into the record, including FBI wiretaps of conversations with Spilotro regarding line information on wagering.[26] Later, candidates to the Black Book were discredited for associating with Kane, although neither he nor Boston was ever nominated to the book. Instead they have been eulogized in recent years—Kane as "a gentle old-schooler who paid his debts," and Boston as being no "tough guy . . . [though he] always wanted to be a gangster."[27] In addition to the problems posed by his association with Kane and Boston, Rosenthal had a television show that was broadcast from the Stardust, advertising him as "one of America's foremost sports handicappers."[28] The "Frank Rosenthal Show" also raised considerable suspicion among board members regarding his influence on decisions at the race and sports book. But Glick contended that the applicant did not influence the policies of the book and that he did not confer with Rosenthal on such matters. He said that he talked with Rosenthal only on a personal basis about specific games or to obtain his opinion about a particular team. He added that, although he might occasionally ask Rosenthal for his ideas regarding the race and sports book, there were never any inquiries of a specific nature.

Another major issue was Rosenthal's employment contract with Argent. In 1975, Argent had contracted to employ him for 10 years at a salary of $250,000 per year. It stipulated that the sum was to be paid whether he was licensed or not. The state's deputy attorney general, Jeffrey Clontz, construed the agreement to mean that Rosenthal was a creditor of Argent Corporation. The total debt would have been in excess of $2 million at the time Rosenthal was denied licensing. Clontz further implied that the contract was used by Rosenthal to return to the Stardust after he was turned down.

Rosenthal's attorney, Oscar Goodman, argued the merits of Rosenthal's new role as entertainment director of the Lido

Show.[29] He explained that the show brought considerable pride to Las Vegas and had gained in popularity since Rosenthal had taken over as director. He also inferred that the matter would likely go into litigation and that he was prepared to enter into the record whatever information was necessary to substantiate his client's case. These actions were viewed by some members of the commission as threats and a waste of their time. The body responded by denying the petition and sustaining their earlier motion to call Rosenthal forward for licensing. They held that his contract made him a creditor of Argent and constituted significant involvement with the corporation's activities. It was further believed that his influence extended to administration and supervision at the Stardust, and that his salary and ability to offer complimentary services there made him a key employee. The vote was unanimous. Immediately following the vote, Rosenthal got into a televised heated dispute with the commission chairman, Harry Reid.

By the time that Rosenthal was called forward again, his old friend, Anthony Spilotro, had been entered into the Black Book. If the saying "With friends like these, who needs enemies?" has any validity, it certainly did in this instance. Also adding to Rosenthal's problems at the time were the Florida Racing Commission's recent action to exclude him from racetracks in that state and considerable publicity regarding his alleged organized crime activities and associations.[30] The Florida exclusion was based on many of the same concerns that had come up in Nevada, and was construed by counsel for the Nevada Gaming Control Board and Gaming Commission as the equivalent of having been placed in the Black Book. Several news articles chronicling Rosenthal's background had also appeared in the *Miami Herald* (Oct. 29, 1978), the *Nevada State Journal* (Dec. 5, 1978), and the *Reno Evening Gazette* (Dec. 5, 1978). The *Miami Herald* article appeared as front-page news. There was a picture of Rosenthal and his television show with headlines that read, "Vegas Can't Shut Out Organized Crime."[31] It was said of the articles that they would "shock the faith of anyone in the regulatory structure."[32] There were also recently published books that addressed issues of the state's difficulty in controlling Rosenthal: Steven Brill's *The Teamsters* (1978) and Jerome Skolnick's *House of Cards* (1978). Brill's book told of an interview that Rosenthal had had with *Business Week* in which he had informed the reporter that he was the casino boss and that, while Glick handled financial matters, he made the policies. The author also gave a gruesome account of a murder of a San Diego woman who had made several investments in Glick's real estate ventures and threatened to report him to the SEC when the deals went sour. He told of how law enforcement surmised that Glick may have mentioned the problem to Rosenthal or someone else behind the Argent front and, to prevent her from making trouble for Glick, "Rosenthal or Spilotro or someone else . . . had . . . [her] killed."[33] All these events were viewed as bringing disreputability to gaming in the state of Nevada and became additional reasons for the denial of Rosenthal's application.

Then, just two days before the unprecedented joint meeting of the board and commission to determine his suitability, Rosenthal seems to have sealed his fate when he allegedly used his television show to malign the regulators. Rosenthal also appeared on a local news commentary show in which he expressed similar views. His comments caused considerable stir among the regulators, which spilled over into the licensing hearing. An exchange between Rosenthal and board member Jeffrey Silver, the applicant's major antagonist, reveals the issues and resentments on both sides. Silver posed the questions in the following portion of the record:

Q. Do you think that the members of the Control Board and Commission's respect for jurisprudence in general is disgraceful?
A. . . . I think that at times in my experience, Frank Rosenthal, that in my personal experience there's no question that what you've just said is true. Without question I think your actions are disgraceful.
   Would you like some examples?
Q. Let me ask the next question.
A. In case you might, I'm prepared.
Q. Did you feel in your own mind then that the members of this agency, the Control Board and the Commission, are men without conscience?
A. I think that based upon my experience with those two agencies over eight years that you have displayed manners, methods, lack of consideration for people in general, completely unconscious of constitutional rights, being overzealous, wild pursuit in order to gain your objective . . .

... there isn't one man up here that hasn't determined my suitability prior to me walking in this room. And then you ask me do I consider the Board to be disgraceful—at times—or men without conscience. That one example, if I am correct, would give me reason to believe that. I have more.

Q. Well, let me interrupt again.

A. I have heard—

Q. Do you feel that the Commission lacks human dignity?

A. I think the Commission at times, once again, has displayed a manner and methods that are irresponsible of human dignity. When a man like Commissioner Haycock can sit in a private institution—

Q. Without getting personal now.

A. I'm not getting personal. You asked me to give you a justification—and gloat over the fact what he will do to me, I consider that could be unconscionable.

Q. Those things that you've said here tonight, did you, in fact, vocalize those responses on your television program that's seen by over a million—

A. What responses? If I haven't, I probably will. Will that help you?

Q. Did you, in fact, make these statements on the air?

A. What statements?

Q. The fact that you felt that the control authorities lacked jurisprudence, that in general we were disgraceful, that we lacked human dignity and were men without conscience. Did you vocalize that on the air?

A. I'm not exactly sure when I have done it, but one thing for sure, you just heard it now, haven't you?[34]

Rosenthal argued that he had complied with the laws governing his employment with Argent following the original denial of his application and the Nevada Supreme Court decision. He said that when he returned to work, he had an agreement with Glick that he would set aside their contract as long as he was working with the corporation or if he were to be licensed. He also contended that he had conferred with the board regarding the specific terms of his employment, his salary, responsibilities, changes from his position as director of food and beverage to entertainment director, and the like. According to Rosenthal, the demand that he come forward for licensing as a key employee was without grounds. He was adamant in his views when he expressed his intent to pursue the matter to its finality:

> . . . there is no system in this country that allows for a man to become labeled or excluded from an industry he has given his entire adulthood to because of a whim of a writer of a magazine or a book. It does not work that way, and I doubt very seriously that anybody up here really thinks it does.
>
> It's beyond being inconceivable that men with good conscience can sit there in judgment and try to exclude a person without giving him the benefit of a proper and fair hearing before a legally constituted board that will, in fact, consider the evidence rather than the individual . . .
>
> We all realize here today that your decision to me as an applicant for a key employee license is not reviewable, but please keep in mind that it will not end here and it is my sincere intention and my dedication to pursue this matter with every ounce of strength of energy that I know.
>
> Someone asked me, Mr. Chairman, just recently, . . . why would I as one man allow myself to accept the intimidation and humiliation that I found here today and in many months past and every day[?] And I will give you one phase of my philosophy of why I will stand here and come back again and again and again. Because, number one, I cannot be intimidated, at least by nonprofessionals as far as intimidators, and I'm sure you'll agree with me there's nobody I'm looking at who would consider themselves as professional intimidators . . .
>
> I know you do not consider my rights to be that of yours. That's a difference of opinion we have. There is the process that we are all governed under, and once you lose your real value for that process you are no better than the man that you seek out. (pp. 143–145)

Responding to Rosenthal's statement about the question of why he would accept this intimidation, counsel for the board and commission said, "very simple, . . . $250,000 a year" (p. 159). The counsel explained further that Rosenthal's right to work was not being denied. Granted, a denied applicant could not return to work with the same employer, but he could go to work as a non–key employee in any other casino in the state, including at the executive level. Finally, he argued that the constitutional issue of due process did not apply to determinations of suitability. He said that the state relied on the decision of the U.S. Court of Appeals for the Ninth Circuit in *Marshall v. Sawyer* in determining suitability for licensed participation in, as well as exclusion from, gaming. The decision held that due process rights are not absolute but relative rights. They are relative to their context, in this instance the problems of corruption thought to be endemic to the unique economy of the state and their impact on the welfare of the state's inhabitants. This context, the court held, sometimes requires measures beyond those normally employed to protect state interests. According to this rationale, Rosenthal's rights to due process in assessments of his suitability to work did not extend to the privileged area of the Nevada gaming industry. Like going into a casino, participation as a licensed member of the industry is said to be a privilege. In the end, Rosenthal was unable to establish his suitability for licensing.

A decade later, Frank Larry Rosenthal was entered into the Black Book. During his hearing before the commission, he was asked to recall why he had been denied key-employee licensing. Responding that he felt the denial was political and that there were people in the industry who made him "look like a choir boy,"[35] he blamed then commission chairman Pete Echeverria in particular, stating:

> ... there were several personnel changes at the Hacienda Hotel at the request of Mr. Glick. One of those ... changes was a gentleman by the name of Glenn Neely, who was a good old boy of Pete Echeverria's ...
>
> Pete sequestered half of ... the executive corporation down to this particular room because the Argent Corporation felt personnel changes were justified and needed in order to help the corporation. Glenn Neely made no bones about it, we will get even. And he kept his word, he did. That was the first hearing.
>
> The second hearing was a situation ... [in which] the appointed officials ... just ... wanted it their way.
>
> And I was one of the few people that took them on, ... and was successful.
>
> ... And they just kept gunning me and gunning me and gunning me. And it's just almost impossible to continue your fight.
>
> ... I have no influence. Pete Echeverria was a very influential,

very persuasive, very intimidating type of person. And I think he had members on that Commission that were in a sense intimidated by him. (pp. 279–280)

Rosenthal was a problem for the regulators in part because of his manner. In addition to being self-assured and well-spoken, he was defiant, accusatory, and challenged the very credibility of the regulators. No other individual who has gone before them has appeared to have presented them so many problems, including John Marshall and Frank Sinatra.

THE ALADDIN AND JAMES TAMER

In 1976, the Aladdin hotel and casino came under investigation when Mae Ellen George applied for licensing as a part-owner. Investigations linked her to James Tamer, the Aladdin's executive show director, who was thought to be associated with organized crime in Detroit. As a result of these ties, Mrs. George was denied her license and Tamer came under the further scrutiny of the board. Within a year, in 1977 and in the midst of a Detroit federal grand jury inquiry into Tamer's alleged involvement in hidden ownership of the Aladdin, the board called him forward for key-employee licensing. Following his indictment on that 1977 charge, he was denied his license. In 1979, he was convicted of conspiracy to assist three other men in maintaining illegal ownership of the Aladdin. Immediately after the federal conviction, the board issued an order excluding the men and four officers and directors of the Aladdin Hotel Corporation, Mae Ellen George among them, from the premises of the hotel—a ruling reminiscent of the Black Book. Tamer's actual entry into the Black Book followed almost 10 years later.

THE TROPICANA CASE

Carl Wesley Thomas

At about the same time in 1979, a federal indictment was entered in Kansas City charging 11 defendants with various offenses in connection with the hidden control and skimming of money from the Tropicana. The publicity accompanying the indictment proved to be a severe embarrassment to the industry and particularly humiliating to one of the defendants, Carl Wesley Thomas, a casino owner and well-respected member of the Las Vegas community. Thomas was the owner and manager of Bingo Palace and Slots-A-Fun, and a shareholder and manager of Circus Circus; also, during his 23 years in gaming, he had been a casino executive at the Riviera, the Stardust, and the Tropicana.[36] The national publicity accompanying the indictment's mention of a taped meeting in 1978 in Kansas City between Thomas and several individuals was said to have become a "source of great anguish to him, . . . [and] the state of Nevada."[37] Thomas immediately and voluntarily left the management of Bingo Palace and Slots-A-Fun, and proceeded to sell his interests in Circus Circus.

The regulators were apparently not sufficiently appeased by his action, however. While Thomas was a respected family man, a college graduate, and without a criminal history, he was seen as having betrayed their trust in him as an owner and licensee. So it was in June of 1979 that the board sent an order to the commission to place the name of Carl Wesley Thomas on the List of Excluded Persons.[38] Although a commission hearing was set for September, the board's order was withdrawn because the transcripts of the federal wiretaps implicating Thomas in skimming activities—transcripts that formed the basis of their case for inclusion—had been suppressed in Kansas City (p. 5).

Though frustrated in these initial attempts to exclude Thomas from licensed gaming establishments, the regulators proceeded to revoke his licenses.[39] They expressed some ambivalence in the process, however. Commissioner Swarts expressed disappointment and shock because he had held respect for Thomas in the past, and then complimented him on his acceptance of his punishment (p. 11). Thomas appeared briefly and offered this apology:

> Mr. Chairman, fellow members of the Commission, I'd like to say that I'm sincerely sorry for the embarrassment I've caused the State of Nevada, my partners, my employees, and most of all my family.
>
> I would further like to say that from this day on with this revocation that I'm out of the gambling business after twenty-three years. (p. 9)

Any ambivalence the regulators had may have been heightened because Thomas differed from the popular image of organized crime: he was Anglo-Saxon and without criminal background and involvement in the mafia. But even this atypicality may have disadvantaged him, as his counsel, Frank Schreck, suggested: "... [Thomas is] a man contrary to almost everybody else that's been before the Commission and may be before the Commission—and in certain respects that makes his actions or alleged actions maybe even more unpalatable and indefensible" (pp. 7–8).

Not his atypicality, his apology, or any ambivalence could ultimately dissuade the regulators from acting against Thomas. The commission revoked his licenses, fined him $50,000, and ordered that he pay board costs up to $10,000 (pp. 14–15). Their formal action was viewed as adding further to Thomas' already public disgrace. As commission chairman Harry Reid stated:

> I'm sure if Mr. Thomas or some of the other people who have been before us, if they could take a good beating they would certainly take that and walk away from it happier than the public ridicule and humiliation that they're held up to because of the events that have transpired.
>
> So that's part of the punishment that this Commission metes out, whether it wants to or not. It is the public ridicule and castigation that just comes as a result of the type of hearings that we have. (p. 13)

The commission's resolution of any ambivalence and its willingness to punish Thomas suggested that it had rejected some common explanations of his behavior, including being corrupted and greedy. Even the sentencing judge in the Tropicana case saw Thomas as a victim—of his own greed, the general corrupting influences of Las Vegas, and the seductions of organized crime figures.[40] On the other hand, the regulators' view of Thomas was quite different and appeared to have developed in large part from the highly publicized telephone call he had had with Nicholas Civella, reputed Kansas City syndicate boss and among the first Black Book members. News accounts of that call credit Thomas as the one who gave instructions to Civella.[41] Furthermore, the indictment quotes Thomas as the one making decisions regarding how the money was to be taken from the casinos

rather than following the orders of syndicate members. Here are
Thomas' responses to questions:

> Q. Did you have any discussions with Nick Civella concerning
> how you wanted to take money out of the casino?
> A. Yes.
> Q. What discussion was that?
> A. I wanted to take the money out of the boxes, the cash money.
> No fill slips out of the money boxes, just cash, all cash.
> Q. What did Nick Civella respond to that idea?
> A. He thought it was a good idea. He said, "Everything takes
> time."[42]

The specifics of the Tropicana case, including how monies
were skimmed and who, in addition to Thomas, was involved in
the skimming, were enumerated in the 1979 Kansas City indictment.[43] The indictment refers to the skimmed monies as "stolen,
converted and taken by fraud" (p. 33) and names, notably, Carl
Wesley Thomas, Joseph Vincent Agosto, Carl Angelo DeLuna,
and Carl and Nicholas Civella. At the time of the indictment,
some might have questioned the effectiveness of Black Book exclusion, at least as far as the Civella brothers were concerned, because they were alleged to present a contemporary threat, though
they had been banned more than a decade earlier. As specified
in the indictment, Agosto made management-type decisions at
the Tropicana and coordinated the conspirators' activities there.
Under the direction of Thomas, Donald Shepard, casino manager, and Billy Caldwell, assistant casino manager, removed the
money from the casino floor and gave it to Agosto. Agosto gave
the monies to Carl Caruso. Caruso transported them to Kansas
City on an irregular basis for about nine months during 1978 and
1979, usually in "sandwiches" of $40,000, for which he was paid
$1,000 per trip. He delivered the sandwiches to DeLuna, reputed
Kansas City underboss, and Charles David Moretina. And the Civella brothers and DeLuna distributed the monies among themselves and among persons in Chicago.

In addition, the indictment lists the code names said to be
used by the defendants to disguise their true identities and avoid
detection in their activities at the Tropicana. The use of such code
names in the indictment indicates how such cases are built by law

enforcement. Further, while none of the names has an extremely negative connotation, their introduction into Thomas' hearing reveals the mindset of regulators who lent importance to such appellations.

> . . . "Caesar," represent[s] . . . Joseph Vincent Agosto; "Mr. Zoppo" and "C. Dogman" . . . Carl Angelo DeLuna; "Zio" and the letters "ON" . . . Nick Civella; "the brother," and the letters "MN" . . . Carl James Civella; "cump" and the letters "CP" . . . Charles David Moretina; "legs" and the letters "LGS" . . . Peter Joseph Tamburello; "Opera Singer," "Mr. Singer" and "Enrico" . . . Carl Caruso; "Mr. C," and the letters "C.T." . . . Carl Wesley Thomas; "Baa-Baa" and "Pecoradu" . . . Donald Joe Shepherd [sic]; "Stompy" and the letters "stm" . . . Anthony Chiavola, Sr.; "Two-Two" and the numerals "22" . . . one resident of Chicago . . . ; and "the one underneath" and the numerals "21" . . . another resident of Chicago . . . (pp. 26–27)

While the indictment appears to be very specific regarding the conspiracy and the acts, there are disparities with regard to the total amount of monies skimmed. The total losses from the Tropicana were variously estimated at $280,000 and at $380,000 (p. 127). Even if one accepts the higher figure, which is the figure referred to by the sentencing judge,[44] one has to question whether over a two-year period the removal of that sum would constitute the kind of threat to the industry that one could expect from the efforts of several major organized crime families.

Although regulatory efforts to place Thomas in the Black Book were not ultimately achieved until 1990, he was, in the interim, convicted in the Tropicana case and served prison time.

Carl Angelo DeLuna

Another man named in the 1979 Kansas City indictment for skimming from the Tropicana was also nominated to the Black Book— Carl Angelo DeLuna. DeLuna, said to be second-in-command to the Civella brothers in Kansas City, was nominated that very year. His Black Book nomination remained in pending status, however. The commission waited to proceed on the board's recommendation because Anthony Spilotro had appealed his 1978 nomination to the Nevada Supreme Court, challenging the constitutionality of the Black Book (p. 102). In 1983, the state supreme court ruled in the Spilotro case that the Black Book was not a violation of the Constitution. In the interim, DeLuna was convicted of the Tropicana skimming charges and then later convicted of additional skimming charges and sentenced to 16 years in prison.[45] Finally in 1989, his nomination was dismissed because of his age and the lengthy prison term he was serving.

Joseph Vincent Agosto

Joseph Agosto was also nominated to the Black Book the same year he was named in the Kansas City indictment. Agosto was an immigrant from Sicily who was having difficulty obtaining U.S. citizenship because of alleged criminal activity in his homeland. He admitted the crime to the commission and explained that it was a wartime violation of Russian law, and one that was committed "because . . . [he] was hungry . . . [and] had to resort to all expedients to survive the war."[46] As the owner of Joseph V. Agosto Productions and Leasing, Limited, he was under contract to Hotel Conquistador, Inc., doing business as the Tropicana hotel and casino, to produce the Folies Bergère, a major Las Vegas show at the Tropicana.

Agosto had come to the attention of the board in 1977 when it was believed that, as part of a property settlement in his divorce, he had agreed to award his former wife an option of $500,000 worth of stock in the Tropicana (p. 106). Because he was doing business on the premises of the hotel, and under the presumption that he was a stockholder in the corporation, the board exercised its discretion of calling him forward to determine his suitability for licensing. Although his counsel established that he was not a stockholder in the Tropicana, Agosto himself admitted that he had received a note in the amount of $560,000 from the corporation (p. 149). In return for the commission's temporary stay of action on suitability for licensing, Agosto and the Hotel Conquistador agreed to terminate their debtor-creditor relationship and to establish in the courts that he had a "bona fide entertainment contract" with the corporation.[47]

Nevertheless, concurrent with his 1979 indictment in Kansas City on skimming charges, Agosto appeared on the agenda of the Gaming Control Board in June of that year for consideration of

Joseph Vincent Agosto. A Sicilian immigrant who had never obtained U.S. citizenship because of alleged criminal activity in his homeland, Agosto produced the Folies Bergère for the Tropicana. The regulators, however, made known their belief that he had a behind-the-scenes interest in the casino and following his indictment for skimming from it, nominated him to the Black Book in 1979. Said to be a man with great staying power, Agosto was still appealing his nomination when he died in federal prison four years later. Courtesy *Las Vegas Sun*.

his nomination to the List of Excluded Persons. Again, his case and the presentation of evidence was continued, until finally in August of 1979 the commission ruled that the nomination be "continued indefinitely," although it acknowledged that there would be a "continuing investigation going on."[48] It was obviously an understatement when Commissioner Haycock said: ". . . [Agosto's] got tremendous staying power. He's proved it with the immigration authorities. I don't know how many courts have ordered him deported, and he's still here. He seems to have that same staying power with this Commission for some time."[49]

It was also in the summer of 1979 that federal wiretaps revealed statements by Agosto that persons connected with the Tropicana and Argent Corporation had paid large sums of money to a member of the Nevada Gaming Commission in return for favorable treatment in regulatory matters.[50] Referred to by Agosto as Mr. Clean or Clean Face, the individual was identified by federal authorities as commission chairman Harry Reid. Comments in the transcripts of the wiretaps suggested that Reid had ignored the ownership problems at the Tropicana and assisted in saving sports book licenses at two of the Argent casinos. Investigations into the matter failed to confirm Agosto's comments, however, and Reid was cleared. The comments were ultimately attributed to mere boasting about control over the regulators, to Agosto's "trying to be a big shot," as Reid put it.[51] They nonetheless created considerable public stir and questions about the efficacy of Nevada regulation.

Finally, affirming his "staying power," Agosto appealed his nomination to the Black Book to the U.S. District Court for Nevada in 1979. When the district court dismissed the case on grounds that the state should rule on the case first, Agosto again appealed to the U.S. Court of Appeals for the Ninth Circuit in 1981. It was not until his death in prison in 1983 that the federal circuit court dismissed his case, and the board removed him from nomination to the List of Excluded Persons, a list that numbered only nine individuals at the end of the 1970s.

6

Control Comes to Babylon

Although knowledge of the enemies within major casinos was disclosed in the 1970s, those involved were not entered into the Black Book until the 1980s. Control came to Babylon only after Spilotro's appeal of his entry was denied by the Nevada Supreme Court. At that time, the Black Book was reactivated with the board's actions against Carl Wesley Thomas, Frank Larry Rosenthal, and James Tamer, the major industry figures in the Argent, Tropicana, and Aladdin cases. At the same time and with the assistance of the Las Vegas Metropolitan Police Department, the board took action against a number of other individuals. The decade of the 1980s was marked by tremendous expansion of the Black Book.

RESOLUTION OF THE SPILOTRO APPEAL

When the regulators entered the decade of the 1980s, the crises they had previously faced from within the industry had not abated. In many respects, their problems had worsened. The Aladdin, the Stardust, and the Tropicana were not under control, and skimming was found to be occurring at several additional casinos. Contributing to the difficulty of addressing the problems was Anthony Spilotro's state-level appeal of his entry into the Black Book. Questioning the constitutionality of the regulatory procedure, the appeal, for the time, tied the hands of the regulators while they waited for state validation of their ultimate weapon.

99

Attorney Oscar Goodman walks with his client Anthony Spilotro before a court session. Although Spilotro was nominated to the Black Book in 1978, the two men held the regulators at bay for five years. Not until 1983, when the Nevada Supreme Court upheld the constitutionality of the Black Book, was Spilotro finally entered. Courtesy *Las Vegas Review Journal.*

Spilotro first appealed his Black Book entry to a Nevada district court on the grounds that punishment based on status—his alleged notorious and unsavory reputation—is unconstitutional. When the lower court affirmed the commission's action, he then

appealed to the Nevada Supreme Court. In 1983, the Nevada
Supreme Court also affirmed the commission's action, ruling that
statutes that permit punishments on the basis of reputation are
not unconstitutional if they protect the interests of the state. The
court further stated that punishment in this instance is possible
only if a person acts in opposition to the statute,[1] that is, if he
enters a casino and is convicted of a gross misdemeanor. It did
not accept the notion that entry into the Black Book is, in itself, a
punishment. The court did, however, remand the case to the commission, ordering that it specify the basis for Spilotro's entry. The
Nevada Supreme Court decision in the case of Spilotro has become popularly regarded as the decision that established the constitutionality of the Black Book.[2]

Two months before the state supreme court decision, Richard
Bryan took office as the new governor of Nevada. With the recent
support of the higher court, he made the new appointments to
the Nevada Gaming Control Board and Gaming Commission
with the mandate that the newly composed bodies "revitalize the
Excluded Persons List."[3] To aid in the mandate, the board directed its Special Investigations and Intelligence Division to devote much of its efforts to preparing reports on potential candidates for periodic nomination to the Black Book.[4] The Las Vegas
Metropolitan Police Department was also adamant in its "desire
to have persons entered into the Book," and, within the next few
years, prepared packages on 55 persons—all alleged organized
crime associates—and submitted them to the board for consideration.[5] The gubernatorial mandate and active law enforcement
effort jointly contributed to the adamant pursuit of those who
were seen as presenting threats to gaming. They also led to more
routinized procedures for nominating and entering individuals
into the Black Book.

Three years after the Nevada Supreme Court ruled that Anthony Spilotro's entry into the Black Book was constitutional, he
ceased to pose either a personal or a legal threat to gaming. In
1986, he disappeared. His disappearance was linked to conflict
between rival mob interests in Las Vegas. These suspicions were
confirmed in the minds of law enforcement and regulatory officials when the badly beaten bodies of Spilotro and his brother
were found in an Indiana cornfield early that same year. Again

Spilotro brothers. Anthony Spilotro, *left,* and his brother, Michael, *right,* are shown here leaving the federal building in Chicago after a 1983 bond hearing. On the far left is Spilotro's attorney, Oscar Goodman. The photo appeared again in the papers in June 1986, when Michael's wife filed a missing persons report. The badly beaten bodies of the brothers were later found in an Indiana cornfield. Photograph from AP / Wide World Photos.

national attention became focused on the problems of crime and corruption in Las Vegas.*

*The murders of Spilotro and his brother remain unsolved, and some in law enforcement believe that they were killed by the Chicago mob itself because of Spilotro's failure to maintain the mob's position in Las Vegas (German 1994).

THE BANNING OF CARL WESLEY THOMAS

In October of 1983, the 1979 federal indictments for skimming and maintaining hidden interests in the Tropicana resulted in convictions for Carl Wesley Thomas, Joseph Vincent Agosto, Carl Anthony DeLuna, and Carl and Nicholas Civella, among others. Then in December of the same year, additional federal indictments were filed in Kansas City on 15 defendants for crimes against Argent Corporation casinos: the Fremont, the Hacienda, the Stardust, and the Marina.[6] Again, the charges were for various offenses related to skimming and hidden control of the casinos, and again those named in the indictment included Agosto, DeLuna, Thomas, the Civella brothers, and reputed organized crime interests in Chicago, Kansas City, and Milwaukee. The case became known as the Argent case, and Carl Wesley Thomas played a key role.* His testimony in the case eventually resulted in the conviction of several other men and disclosed his own involvement in skimming from other casinos as well.

In June of 1985, the federal court affirmed Thomas' earlier conviction in the Tropicana case, and he began serving a 15-year prison sentence at Leavenworth.[7] Within a month of his incarceration, a Las Vegas newspaper reported, "Now, informed sources confirm, some law enforcement authorities want to add . . . [Thomas'] name to the Nevada Black Book."[8] Then, at the end of November, the U.S. District Court for Kansas in Kansas City dismissed the charges against Thomas in the Argent case, and, within a week, he testified against others named in the indictment.

The circumstances surrounding Thomas' testimony in the Argent case are not clear. Some have suggested that the charges against him were dismissed in exchange for his testimony.[9] His lawyer, Richard Wright, however, contended that the case was dismissed and the testimony compelled simultaneously:

*Newspapers reported that the Argent skim took in between $7.2 million and $20 million from November 1974 to May 1976, costing the state as much as $1.1 million in revenues. The operation was said to have involved a wiring of the electronic coin scales at the casinos so that they would show 30 percent less weight. The additional unweighed coins were then distributed to change booths, where they were converted into cash that was put into marked envelopes in the auxiliary banks of the booths, and then later removed. It was felt

103

... [His] testimony ... was not the result of any plea bargain or agreement between ... [him] and the government. [He] ... was immunized upon application of the United States and by order of Judge Stevens and compelled to testify against his will in a case in which he was a defendant. (p. 53)

True to the rumors that were then circulating in Las Vegas, Thomas was again being considered for inclusion in the Black Book. Recall that he was first nominated in 1979 concurrent with his federal indictment in the Tropicana case. The chronology of the next series of events is revealing of the regulators' renewed efforts to enter him into the book. Two days after Thomas' Kansas City testimony in the Argent case, his attorney petitioned the court for a reduction in his sentence (p. 130). At the same time and on two occasions, one as late as January 9, 1986, the board members approached him regarding the possibility of his providing them with information about ongoing skimming operations in the Nevada industry. But Thomas, through his counsel, declined to talk with them. Ron Hollis, chief of the board's Special Investigations and Intelligence Division, nevertheless continued to pursue Thomas' cooperation, approaching board member Michael Rumbolz about a possible incentive. Although Rumbolz told Hollis that he had nothing to offer, Hollis "went further and specifically asked ... [him] if he could offer the Black Book, ... [about which Rumbolz] told him specifically, no, he could not" (p. 44). Such contemplated action appears to have had the intent to pressure Thomas to cooperate.

It was also in January of 1986 that the board learned that Thomas had entered a motion for a reduction in sentence for the Tropicana conviction. In the process of reviewing files in Kansas City, a board agent came across the motion for reduction and apparently relayed that information to board chairman Barton Jacka (p. 129). Jacka then wrote to the sentencing judge that very month. In the letter, Jacka informed the court of Thomas' refusal to cooperate with the board and, in light of this, raised the question of whether he was "rehabilitated."

---

that the success of the operation required the knowledge of many people connected with the corporation's hotels (Dahlberg 1979a, 1979b).

> This agency has always supported and cooperated with the federal government and the federal courts . . . However, noting that . . . [Thomas'] attorney . . . has indicated to your court . . . that Mr. Thomas "has been sufficiently rehabilitated," this agency believes that the . . . refusals on his part should be brought to the court's attention for whatever consideration deemed warranted in this matter. (p. 131)

The letter was obviously intended to dissuade the judge of any reduction in sentence.

On March 1, 1986, before a decision had been rendered regarding any sentence reduction, the board took the initial step toward placing Thomas in the Black Book by issuing a formal order of exclusion (p. 136). Then, within two weeks, and over the written objections of Jacka, the judge ruled:

> In assessing the appropriateness of a sentence . . . the court considers it important to note . . . [that Thomas] is bright, ambitious, personable, and greedy and he made a life-changing mistake in succumbing to the blandishments of Nick Civella and his ilk . . . Irrespective of his recently expressed reluctance to talk with the Nevada authorities, the court finds . . . that the sentence originally imposed was clearly too harsh and that it should be substantially reduced. (pp. 134–135)

Indeed Thomas' sentence was reduced, from 15 to 2 years, of which he ultimately served 17 months.

By the end of March, the board held Thomas' nomination hearing. In August, when he was transferred from prison to a halfway house, a board employee informed authorities there of his lack of cooperation (p. 154). A hearing before the commission was scheduled for December, a month after the nominee's release into the community. This chronology of events raises the obvious question of whether the regulators ultimately acted to enter Thomas into the Black Book because of his refusal to cooperate.

The state's case to exclude Carl Wesley Thomas from licensed gaming establishments was argued on several grounds: his 1983 conviction for skimming and hidden control of the Tropicana; the infamous episode in which he gave Kansas City syndicate boss

Nicholas Civella instructions on how to skim; his Argent testimony, wherein he admitted to participating in skimming at Circus Circus, the Stardust, the Hacienda, and the Fremont casinos during the 1970s, and to giving $80,000 to Frank Rosenthal on orders from Alan Dorfman; and, finally, his association with various organized crime figures (pp. 38–41). The sentencing judge in the Tropicana case captured the part played by Thomas and how his actions were seen as damaging to the image of Nevada gaming:

> . . . certain residents of Kansas City, specifically Carl Angelo DeLuna, Nick Civella, and Carl James Civella, secured and maintained a hidden interest in the Tropicana . . . [and] enlisted the support and assistance and expertise of certain veterans of the Las Vegas scene, specifically Joe Agosto and this defendant, Carl Thomas.
>
> . . . Mr. Shepard and Mr. Caldwell . . . had experience working with . . . Carl Thomas, and they took their orders from . . . [him] . . .
>
> Carl Thomas' services were, however, essential to the success of the operation . . . and the court finds . . . a substantial damage to the image of the confidence and theoretically or allegedly regulated gaming community in Nevada by reason of this intrusion into the fabric of the regulatory process. (pp. 60–61)

Contributing to the offensiveness of Thomas' actions was his position of trust in the industry, as Commissioner Hillyer commented:

> Carl Thomas was a respected member of this gaming community. He was trusted by business associates, his friends. He was given a privileged license based upon the state's belief and confidence in his integrity, honesty, and good character. It is my belief that Mr. Thomas is a traitor. He betrayed the trust placed in him by many innocent business associates, employees, friends, and respected members of the community, but most of all, he betrayed the State of Nevada. (p. 42)

Commissioner Gragson followed in kind that Thomas was "like a policeman that takes a bribe or a public figure that is on the take" (p. 95).

Nicholas Civella, *center,* answers questions. Nick Civella was the younger of the two Civella brothers. Reputed to be a boss of the Kansas City syndicate, Civella was among the first eleven men to be entered into the Black Book. But even after his entry, he was said to have been on one occasion given VIP treatment at the Dunes. And, he was thought to have had a behind-the-scenes influence on Nevada gaming more than twenty years after his exclusion. The man in glasses behind Civella was not involved in the issue in question. Photograph from *The Kansas City Star.*

But, Thomas' attorney, Richard Wright, argued that neither the activities that Thomas had engaged in nor his violation of the industry's trust was sufficient reason for his inclusion in the Black Book. He held that such inclusion constituted a violation of Thomas' right to equal protection, that he was being arbitrarily singled out from among others who were similarly situated but were not being considered for the Black Book. The board acted in

Carl Civella, at age 74, entering the U. S. Courthouse in Kansas City to post bond in 1983. The older of the two Civella brothers and also among the first eleven to be entered into the Black Book, Carl is reputed to have become head of the Kansas City syndicate when his brother Nick died in prison. He, too, was implicated in certain behind-the-scenes influence on Las Vegas casinos in the 1970s and 1980s, and only recently died in prison while serving time for gaming-related offenses. Photograph from *The Kansas City Star*.

retaliation, argued Wright, when his client failed to cooperate and invoked his Fifth Amendment rights.[10]

In support of his arguments, Wright presented records of over 150 persons with felony convictions or gaming violations who had received approval to work in the industry within the four-year period prior to the hearing (p. 79). Their offenses included murder, child molestation, burglary, bookmaking, racketeering, and the like (p. 94). He questioned how the board could allow these people to work in the industry and at the same time exclude Thomas? Counsel also petitioned for additional records, including those for all licensees with felony convictions, along with the positions that they held. He maintained that the board, as the official regulatory body, was statutorily responsible for having such information. After much discussion, the board proclaimed that the information was unavailable except through an extensive manual search of the records (pp. 207–211).

Wright continued to press the "selectivity" issue by pointing to Thomas' codefendants in the Tropicana case, some of whom were equally situated in the industry, had been convicted, and were identified as members of organized crime, but were not proposed for the Black Book. He also compared Thomas' treatment with that of seven other individuals with highly problematic backgrounds who were similarly situated in the industry (pp. 163–184). Like Thomas, four of these individuals either had been convicted of or admitted to gaming violations involving skimming or hidden ownership, and six had not cooperated with the regulators. The consideration of only one of the seven for inclusion in the Black Book was said by counsel to constitute further evidence of Thomas' differential treatment.

Counsel's argument that Thomas was the object of board retaliation found some support in the regulators' expectations of his cooperation and in the sequence of their actions, including those following their initial investigation. When the board's chief of Special Investigations and Intelligence, Ron Hollis, assigned an agent to investigate Thomas, the agent was also assigned to gain Thomas' cooperation. The extent to which this is a common practice in investigations of candidates for the Black Book remains an unanswered question. Although an investigative file on Thomas was developed as early as January of 1985, and a preliminary report was prepared in April of that year, the final report was not submitted to the board until February 24, 1986—after

Thomas had refused to cooperate (pp. 142–143, 147). Under questioning by Wright, Hollis revealed that he felt Thomas would not cooperate and that this might have affected his thinking about proposing Thomas for the Black Book.

> I was personally never convinced that Mr. Thomas would cooperate with us, and that in connection with an ongoing investigation, I wanted to be able to say one day that we attempted to contact Mr. Thomas and he in fact didn't cooperate with us . . .
> . . . I didn't think Mr. Thomas would in fact cooperate.
> Q. Because there is no reason why he should; correct?
> A. Correct. We really have nothing to offer him.
> Q. And in fact, if he does, he incriminates himself; correct?
> A. True.
> Q. And without any immunity or anything, he is to just be subject to interviews? That is your position in asking for his cooperation; correct?
> A. Well, if he is a rehabilitated criminal, I would expect him to cooperate with law enforcement.
> Q. If he was rehabilitated and cooperative then there would be no need for him to be in the Black Book, would there?
> A. That is correct . . .
> Q. Had he cooperated he would have been . . . a rehabilitated criminal . . . and it would not have been necessary to propose him for inclusion in the Black Book, would it, sir?
> A. I would have second thoughts about proposing him, yes. (pp. 159–160)

Counsel maintained that his argument that Thomas' nomination constituted an equal protection violation was related to the Muhammad Ali boxing case in New York. When Ali refused to be drafted, he received a felony conviction. Then, upon application for a new license to box in New York State, he was denied on the grounds of being an ex-felon. He appealed the decision and, in the process of discovery, found that the New York Boxing Commission had licensed many ex-felons. The court ruled that the New York Boxing Commission's actions in singling him out for treatment constituted a violation of his Fourteenth Amendment right to equal protection under the state's laws (pp. 235–236, 239–241). Commissioner Lockhart was of the opinion that the Ali case weakened what was already a "limited" case for Thomas' inclusion, and that the state needed to expand the bases for that inclusion (p. 234). The deputy attorney general, acknowledging that the Ali case had possible ramifications for the decision regarding Thomas, suggested that, if the commissioners felt the need for more circumstantial evidence, a recess might be called.

In concert with these suggestions and possibly for want of adequate response to some of the issues and questions Thomas' attorney had raised, the commissioners recessed for a month. When the commission reconvened, board member Michael Rumbolz was called to specify the criteria used by the board to select persons who would be investigated for inclusion in the Black Book.[11] He said that, in addition to using the statutory criterion of a felony conviction, the board also relied upon the criteria of incarceration, notoriety and extent of the crimes, role in the crimes, and contacts in the state. He added that notoriety was a major factor in Thomas' selection: ". . . there was a great deal of media attention on Mr. Thomas, both in the State of Nevada and throughout the rest of the nation when he testified in the Argent trial admitting to other crimes and other skimming activities over a considerable period of time . . ." (p. 13). While commission chairman Paul Bible did not allow the state to use the criteria formally, either to compare Thomas with his codefendants or to evaluate their own chances of exclusion, the codefendants were nevertheless discussed informally in relation to the nominee. The gist of the discussion was that he was different from the others and that he better satisfied the criteria for exclusion.

In concluding, the deputy attorney general implied that, if Thomas had received treatment dissimilar to his codefendants, it was because he and his codefendants were not equal. Rather, they were said to have presented different situations for the regulators to consider (pp. 62–65). Some received instruction from Thomas. Some were located differently in the industry. Some were incarcerated. Some were acquitted. And some pled guilty. Having reviewed the criteria and concluded that Thomas fitted all of them, Commissioner Peccole, a lawyer by profession, advocated going forward: ". . . as far as I can see, we got to start somewhere, and if this be it, then I would have to line up with the rest of the Commission and I would have to say that he would have to be included" (p. 99).

In his closing statement, Thomas' counsel responded by going

111

beyond the equal protection and retaliation issues to address what he considered to be the more fundamental issue of what the Black Book actually constituted (pp. 68–69). In refutation of the Nevada Supreme Court's position in the case of Spilotro, Wright maintained that the Black Book was punishment, and punishment that was administered publicly. He said that the regulators were not satisfied that Thomas had been humiliated and penalized in prison, had paid $90,000 restitution, and had been prohibited from coming to Las Vegas during his five-year probationary period.

> . . . [The regulators] want further punishments. They want Mr. Thomas' children, who were born here and live here, to have this book for their father. They want it for the grandchildren. They want him in this book with people named Napi and Ali Baba, Taco Bob. Listed in here just like Hester in the Scarlet Letter, the adulteress right on the front of her shirt. For what purpose?
> I submit it's for punishment. (p. 68)

Finally, Wright reminded the commissioners that his client could not present a contemporary threat to gaming. The federal court, as a condition of his five-year probation, had prohibited his presence within 50 miles of Las Vegas. Wright therefore proposed that the commission wait until that time had lapsed, and then reconsider any threat that Thomas might present. They declined the compromise.

The commissioners voted unanimously to include Carl Wesley Thomas in the Black Book. They did, however, elect to let the inclusion stand in abeyance until Thomas had exhausted his right to appeal. This would appear to have been the regulators' only show of leniency in this case. Finally, in June of 1990, after the U.S. Court of Appeals for the Ninth Circuit affirmed the judgment of the U.S. District Court for Nevada in favor of the state, and Thomas elected not to pursue his case in the U.S. Supreme Court, the exclusion order was finally implemented.[12] Carl Wesley Thomas now officially joined those whom his counsel referred to as Napi, Ali Baba, and Taco Bob in Nevada's "Bible of Infamy."

We nevertheless see in Thomas' case that those who fight their entry into the Black Book are less easily discredited and therefore more problematic for the regulators. In addition to having been able to attain effective legal representation, his former reputation in the community seems to have complicated the denunciation process. He did not fit the mafia image and previously had the respect of the regulators. That respect, however, ultimately came to work to his disadvantage because he was seen as having betrayed their trust.

FINALLY, THE ENTRY OF FRANK LARRY ROSENTHAL

On March 31, 1988, the board put forth the Black Book nomination of Frank Larry Rosenthal, another industry figure who had frustrated the regulators for more than a decade. It was an action that is said to have been initiated soon after the denial of his application for key-employee licensing almost a decade earlier.[13] No questions were raised about the necessity of his exclusion. The members unanimously agreed that he should be entered on the basis of (1) his 1963 felony conviction for conspiring to bribe a New York University basketball player; (2) his notorious and unsavory reputation in regard to gaming; (3) his criminal associations, especially with Anthony Spilotro, who had by then been entered into the Black Book and removed by reason of death; (4) his exclusion from Florida racetracks; and (5) the references to his activities in Chicago Crime Commission and federal congressional reports.[14] A hearing before the commission was set for June but continued on three occasions until November 30, 1988, because his attorney, Oscar Goodman, was involved in protracted federal trial proceedings.[15] By the time the commission finally met, the state had reduced the conditions for entry to the felony conviction ("a crime of moral turpitude") and notorious and unsavory reputation in regard to gaming.[16]

Rosenthal's counsel argued that the felony conviction resulted from a plea of nolo contendere and that his client's civil rights were subsequently restored. He also held to the doctrines of laches and estoppel, in that the board had failed to act on Rosenthal for an inordinate period of time following its knowledge of the conditions, and that because these conditions had become commonplace, the board could not act without new grounds (pp. 61–62). The state's deputy attorney general, Dan Reaser, argued that the laches and estoppel doctrines did not apply to administrative proceedings when the state's action was "to enforce a public interest" (p. 64). He contended further that Rosenthal had indeed been considered for inclusion in the Black Book as early as 1979, but that the state had not acted on the matter because Rosenthal was leaving Nevada and the state supreme court decision in the case of Anthony Spilotro was pending. The latter issue's resolution and Thomas' and Glick's recent linkage of Rosenthal to the skimming activities at Argent were, according to Reaser, the reasons the state was now acting to enter him into the Black Book (pp. 65–67). He stated that

> both the Glick and Thomas testimony indicate that Mr. Rosenthal was an operative for known hoods and mobsters and was skimming casinos on their behalf and delivering money to them through different conduits during the relevant time period of his employment at the Argent Corporation . . . (p. 71)

But, according to counsel, Rosenthal had not left the state until 1983, four years after the board is said to have considered him for the Black Book, and the state supreme court decision in the case of Spilotro occurred five years before the commission's most recent action, also in 1983 (p. 73). Counsel also argued that Glick's testimony was part of a plea bargain in Kansas City, and that Thomas' statement was made under a grant of immunity in which his sentence was reduced (pp. 75–76).

Counsel established that his client had attended college, had served honorably in combat during the Korean War, had opened a legitimate business following military discharge, and cared for his two children, a daughter who was an honor student and Olympic trial qualifier and a son attending the U.S. Air Force Academy (pp. 94–96, 109–110). Interestingly, the state's deputy attorney general objected to counsel's introducing the accomplishments of Rosenthal's children, suggesting that they may have been seen as having a humanizing effect that produced a more favorable image of the nominee than the state wished to acknowledge (p. 110).

Counsel asked Rosenthal also to recount the events that transpired just before his coming to Las Vegas. He told of his sports handicapping and venture into Florida horse racing. His problems with Florida law enforcement and Eli the Juice Man were also rehashed. He explained again that, although he had stopped making book and was devoting all his energies to racing at the time, they had tried to extort money from him as though he were still a bookmaker and that, when he refused to pay, the police searched his apartment. Although he was not charged with an offense, he was nonetheless banned from Florida racetracks as a result of the incident. Then, after coming to Nevada and encountering the licensing problems there, he petitioned for a lift of the ban but was refused because, according to Rosenthal, Nevada gaming authorities sent one of their people to Florida to persuade authorities there that he was unsuitable. They had created a Catch-22, he contended; he was found to be unsuitable for licensing in Nevada, in part because of the Florida exclusion, and now Nevada was acting to prevent his reinstatement in order to sustain its earlier action (pp. 97–108).

Rosenthal once again denied having conspired to bribe the New York University basketball player and explained that he had entered the nolo contendere plea upon the advice of an attorney who had assured him that his Jewish background would disadvantage him in the predominantly Baptist jurisdiction, and because his codefendant, who had also been indicted for attempting to fix sporting events in other states, was prepared to be a witness against him (pp. 111–112). He contended that he had also been the subject of undue police attention following his arrival in Las Vegas. While working at the Rose Bowl race and sports book in 1970, for example, a search and seizure at the establishment resulted in the revocation of his work card (pp. 122–124).

After having his working privileges reinstated in 1971, Rosenthal went to work as a 21 pit boss at the Stardust, which was owned by Recrion Corporation at the time. Following Allen Glick's purchase of the Stardust, Rosenthal quickly moved up through the ranks to become, in 1974, the executive consultant to Glick in his role as chairman of the board of the newly formed Argent Corporation. Rosenthal told of his role as the Stardust entertainment director following the 1977 state supreme court decision upholding his denial of key-employee licensing,[17] and of how he oversaw the highly acclaimed Lido production and obtained illusionists Siegfried and Roy as the show's main attraction.[18] It was also introduced into evidence that he had made substantial contributions to charity, that he was a friend of respected politicians and gaming regulators, and that he had received numerous letters of thanks and commendation from highly prominent individuals while at the Stardust (pp. 145–150).

Rosenthal denied Glick's allegations that he had introduced Glick to reputed mafia figure Nicholas Civella in Kansas City, who Glick said had threatened him and told him that he had to listen to Rosenthal in regard to operations at Argent (pp. 151–152). He also denied Thomas' allegations that Thomas had given him a sum of $60,000 or $80,000 (pp. 165–171, 223–224). He explained that, although he had been questioned several months prior to the indictments being handed down in the Argent case and again after a near-fatal car bombing attack on his life in 1982, he had never been arrested or charged in the case (pp. 152–155).

In addition to asking Rosenthal to rehash many of the issues addressed in the earlier licensing hearings, including his relationship with Anthony Spilotro, the state's deputy attorney general, Dan Reaser, queried him about Glick's Kansas City testimony and the federal investigation into the bombing attempt on his life. Rosenthal was asked: if he had ever had a conversation with Glick at the Stardust coffee shop, wherein he told Glick that he had partners in the skimming operation that he represented and that if Glick didn't cooperate "he would never leave the corporation alive"; if he had telephoned Glick and told him "he was going to make a trip to Kansas City and he didn't have a choice"; and if he had ever met with Glick and Nicholas Civella in Chicago; all of which he denied (pp. 218–220). Rosenthal said that, following the car bombing, federal law officers offered him protection in return for information that would allow them to obtain convictions on "everybody and anybody" (p. 226). He explained: "I think that they felt that . . . when you experience a situation that I did . . . , you'd be vulnerable to just about anybody's help, Red Cross or FBI" (p. 227).

Deputy Attorney General Reaser wanted to know if Rosenthal had provided the federal officers with information that had enabled the prosecutions in the Kansas City case and, in particular, if they had questioned him about Glick or Thomas. He denied any knowledge about the skimming incident and said that he had not been asked about the two men (pp. 226–227).

The state's deputy attorney general nevertheless argued that the Argent case was "replete with accounts that . . . Rosenthal was

the man who was there for the mob, to take the money . . ." (p. 249).
Reaser's depiction of the nominee was especially graphic. Draw-
ing upon Glick's testimony in the Kansas City trial, he said that
Rosenthal was

> . . . a man who doesn't mind telling the owner of a casino you
> have silent partners and you die if you don't do what you're told.
> He doesn't mind ushering those people to dark motel rooms
> with organized crime officials wherein those organized crime
> members tell Mr. Glick he dies if he doesn't do what Mr. Rosen-
> thal says.
>
> He's the type of man who doesn't mind to continue those
> threats. Mr. Glick ultimately was told his children were going to
> be killed if he didn't do what Mr. Rosenthal told him to do.
>
> . . . Clearly, Mr. Glick . . . made deals . . . But the question is
> whether or not the general public who . . . have heard . . . [these
> things] in the press . . . will think very highly of Nevada gaming if
> this man can walk in the door and sit down at a 21 table and start
> gambling if he wants, or if he can get in the elevator and punch
> the button for the executive suite and walk in and maybe make
> the same kind of threat. (pp. 249–250)

Counsel, in turn, reiterated the laches and estoppel arguments
that too much time had passed since Rosenthal had originally
come to Nevada and that there was not a sufficient demonstra-
tion of differences in the conditions that he presented then and
now (p. 261). He argued that there was "not one problem in the
interim, not one arrest, not one conviction, and not one pointing
the finger with any type of meaning" (pp. 264–265). He spoke of
Rosenthal as having been an easy scapegoat and of the stigmatizing effects of placing his client in the Black Book. He referred to
the action as barbaric and uncivilized (p. 254), and likened it to
branding him with a "horrible mark, which he would have to live
with forever, himself and his children, and their children and
their children" (p. 263).

Commissioner Robert Peccole also questioned the state's reliance on the Glick and Thomas testimonies, especially that of
Thomas, given that Thomas himself had been previously declared unsavory and placed in the Black Book. Peccole explained:

> I have a little trouble with the leapfrogging . . . we are playing
> here, in the sense that we put Mr. Thomas in the Black Book . . .

117

and that is supposedly based on the fact that he is unsavory and . . . a threat to the State of Nevada, and then we turn around and use his testimony to put somebody else in . . .

Now are we to believe him as it's been pointed out? Do we take this unsavory man's testimony and apply it now to Mr. Rosenthal . . . ? Do you have a little trouble with that? (p. 292)

Peccole also questioned: (1) whether Rosenthal's conviction translated into a threat to the reputation of gaming; (2) the state's use of the information gathered for his denial of key-employee licensing in establishing a notorious and unsavory reputation when the record did not specify that such was the basis for the denial; and (3) whether Rosenthal's alleged social acquaintances constituted unacceptable associations, since they were not business related (pp. 294–300). Finally, the commissioner raised the issue of the state's delay in acting on Rosenthal a decade after they had decided that he was of a notorious and unsavory reputation when called forward for key licensing. He noted, in particular, the potential prejudice caused by the delay, especially in regard to loss of evidence due to fading memories:

> The fading memories thing sort of hit me . . . [because] all through this hearing every question that was asked of Mr. Rosenthal about . . . [events going back] . . . 20 . . . [to] 25 years, he couldn't . . . pinpoint the times. He couldn't relate to the questions you were asking because he couldn't figure out when . . . [the events] happened or where they happened. (p. 301)

The commission nevertheless voted unanimously to enter Rosenthal into the Black Book on the basis of the factors stated in the bill of particulars, with Commissioner Peccole stating that he supported the entry reluctantly because of his "great concern and reservation with regard to the defenses of laches and estoppel," a problem that he said he also had with the Thomas and James Tamer cases (p. 310). Peccole explained:

> It seems to me that when you take a record that goes clear back prior to 1968, and then you bring that forward in 1988, and try to argue that this is the first time this man has become unsavory and notorious and a candidate for the Black Book, I feel that that is not correct, I don't feel that it should happen . . .

I just want for the record to be consistent in that I felt the same problem in the Thomas case, . . . I felt the same problem in the Tamer case.

But this one even more so. I feel compelled to follow the law in that we have been instructed [by the deputy attorney general] that laches does not apply. Also we have been instructed that the statutes and regulations are constitutional, and so long as they are there, I feel that I am compelled to follow them. But I do so reluctantly. (p. 310)

A year later, however, the same judge who had overturned the commission's 1976 decision to deny Rosenthal licensing as a key employee, district court judge Joseph Pavlikowski, ruled to reverse Rosenthal's inclusion in the Black Book on the basis of the laches doctrine. Rosenthal's attorney, Oscar Goodman, was described as ecstatic over the decision and quoted as saying that his client was now "a man without a scarlet letter on his head" and had every intention now of going to the casinos, of "shooting craps at the Mirage and sipping wine at the Palace Court."[19] But, as one local editorialist surmised, the state had not yet finished its fight.[20] Indeed, the board used Goodman's statements as an indication that the exclusion was all the more necessary, with one of the members quoted as saying, "His lawyer's comments show a pressing need to keep him out of the state. . . . He intends to visit Nevada and that makes him a threat to Nevada's gaming industry."[21] Editorials followed recounting Rosenthal's Chicago connections and long-time involvement with illegal gambling, questions of Pavlikowski's integrity and independence of mob interests replete with rundowns of his earlier decision favoring reputed organized crime figures, and the predictions of gaming regulators that the state would prevail.[22]

However, banning Rosenthal from the state's casinos did not bring an end to perceived threats on the part of major industry figures. There was at least one more individual who, because of his atypicality, presented considerable problems for the regulators: James Tamer.

7

Tamer "The Atypical"

After 17 years of investigation by five separate Nevada gaming control boards, 76-year-old James Tamer became the 28th nominee to the Black Book. While others were denied licensing as early as 1970 because of their business associations with him, Tamer was not entered into the Black Book until 1988. He had been denied licensing as a key employee of the Aladdin in 1978; was convicted of conspiracy to have hidden ownership in the hotel and casino in 1979 and was subsequently excluded from its premises; was nominated to the Black Book first in 1986, only to have that nomination dismissed in five months; was nominated a second time in 1987; and was finally entered on the List of Excluded Persons in 1988.

Tamer was in several ways very different from most of those who have been entered into the book. He was a respected businessman—an owner of a major steel and electronics manufacturing firm, the owner of a country club, and the director of a Las Vegas show. Born of Lebanese parents in Pottsville, Pennsylvania, Tamer was awarded a Statue of Liberty Ellis Island Foundation ethnic achievement medal in honor of his contributions to Lebanese Christians only two weeks before his first nomination to the Black Book. Even experts on organized crime did not agree about his association with certain crime families. He had no felony conviction record when the regulators first sought to deny him licensing as a key employee in the industry. And, when a conviction finally had been obtained against him in 1979, it was only for conspiracy. Adding to the state's problem was his personal decorum and the very competent legal representation that he had throughout his dealings with the regulators.

Because Tamer did not fit the traditional conception of organized crime, there were problems in establishing his threat to the industry. Struggling with the issue, the regulators sought to redefine the factors that constituted such threat. These included issues of ethnicity, what constitutes an official record of criminality, and the very nature of organized crime itself. By expanding the conception of organized crime to encompass Tamer's national origin and business activities, and by viewing as a history of criminality unfounded allegations, indictments that were dismissed, and convictions that were subsequently reversed, the board was able to establish the grounds necessary for its action.

FIRST ATTENTION TO TAMER

Tamer was a subject of board concern as early as 1970. At that time, a friend and business associate, George George, was denied a license for ownership of the Aladdin Hotel because of his association with Tamer. Then in 1976, while executive show director of the Aladdin, he was again under the scrutiny of state regulators while they considered the application of George's wife, Mae Ellen George, to hold an interest in the casino through purchase of its stock. The owners of the Aladdin had given Mr. George an option on the stock and, following his death, said they would honor the agreement with his wife.[1] Her application for ownership was also denied because of her relationship with Tamer, who was viewed even then as a "person of notorious or unsavory reputation."[2] There was never any question of the basis for the denial. Responding to the commission's inquiries regarding her relationship to Tamer, Mrs. George directly inquired of Chairman Phillip Hannifin whether he, too, considered her "tainted" because of the association, a word that the board's investigators had used earlier to refer to her (p. 108).

Of concern to the regulators at the time of Mrs. George's application was not whether Tamer had any association with organized crime, but what the nature of that association was. There was a presumption of guilt. James Ritchie, an attorney with the U.S. Justice Department, Organized Crime and Racketeering Section, was called as an expert witness in the case (pp. 41–66).

121

Ritchie testified regarding Tamer's activities and reputation in the Detroit area on the basis of knowledge from his assignment to the Detroit strike force from 1968 to 1971. The following excerpts from Ritchie's sworn statement cast doubt on Tamer's alleged involvement with organized crime:

> Mr. Tamer was reared in the same location as many of the individuals identified as members of organized crime . . . he knows them through those common maturation experiences, and has on occasion seen them socially . . . [But] Mr. Tamer, contrary to many of his similar ethnic neighborhood associates, was never employed by, nor associated with, organized crime activities in the City of Detroit. (p. 43)

Ritchie's answers when questioned by board member Jeffrey Silver also cast doubt:

> Q. You are guaranteeing to this State that this man has absolutely no connections with organized crime?
>
> A. I am guaranteeing by my offering under oath that evidence that it is the truth, Mr. Silver. I am in a position to know who is and who is not connected . . . (pp. 50–51)
>
> Q. If I asked you if Mr. Tamer was associated with any other organized criminal groups other than the Sicilian Mafia, what would your answer be?
>
> A. . . . If you are asking me, is he an associate of some other criminal concert, I would have to say, what do you mean by that[?] Do you mean by association did he work for them, did he pay tribute to them, was he subservient to them, did he follow their instructions? If those are your criteria, the answer is no. (p. 53)

When questioned by Commissioner Hannifin, Ritchie's answers again cast doubt:

> Q. The only problem I am having . . . with your testimony . . . is that kind of a hundred percent certainty that is bothering me.
>
> A. Well, Mr. Hannifin, while I ran the Strike Force in Detroit and while I ran . . . other government offices, I had the occasion to come into contact with all levels of law enforcement, many gossamer oriented concepts of law enforcement which were

funded by LEAA, which were ineffectual and absolutely un-
reliable, which were compounded by creating information,
innuendo and inference in order for their own self-import. I
became and am very, very critical of information which is
blithely accepted because someone with a badge or creden-
tial says it is so.

I began questioning the basis for these conclusions, and I
have very strong feelings about quality of information . . .

Now, again, you know the respect I have for yourself,
your fellow members, for this Board and this institution. I
offer this testimony very begrudgingly because I sense since I
haven't had, just like a jury that is going to vote against you,
any of you look at me since I have been in this room all
afternoon, and that your minds are made up. I am going to
stand by what I know to be the truth, and I only offer it for
that. (pp. 57, 58)

Ritchie's statement was affirmed by Clyde Pritchard, a former
attorney with the U.S. Justice Department. With knowledge of
the Detroit area from the 1960s through 1976, Pritchard gave a
sworn deposition that Tamer was not a member or associate of
organized crime and, furthermore, that he was not, as was also
alleged, a bookmaker (p. 26).* But these expert testimonies were
not what the board wanted to hear.

The board nevertheless persisted in its conviction that Tamer
was associated with organized crime. The belief was based largely
on their knowledge of two "chance meetings" between Tamer
and Vito Giacalone, a "known . . . enforcer" and brother of Anthony Giacalone, a reputed Detroit organized crime figure (p. 69).
The alleged meetings were said to have occurred when Giacalone
spoke to Tamer at a dinner of over 100 people (p. 11), and when
Tamer, "with too many drinks under him, and on the way home
[from the dinner] had an accident and was . . . picked up and
driven home" by two men in Giacalone's car (p. 65). This illustrates the presumptive evidence with which law enforcement
constructs cases of individual association with organized crime.

---

*Such deposition was later questioned by the regulators when it was learned
that two years later Pritchard represented Tamer before the grand jury in Detroit
(NGCB transcripts, July 12, 1978: 34).

CALLED FORWARD FOR KEY-EMPLOYEE LICENSING

By the next year, in 1977, James Tamer, along with several others, was the subject of possible federal indictment by a Detroit grand jury on charges of hidden control of the Aladdin. Following extensive local and national newspaper coverage of the pending action, the commission began to inquire further into Tamer's relationship to the casino operation at the hotel (p. 97). The Aladdin was accordingly instructed to submit a key-employee-licensing application for Tamer,[3] thus calling for and allowing the regulators to conduct an extensive investigation into his background.

The board's investigation of James Tamer revealed an unusual criminal history. He was convicted of bank robbery in Michigan in 1939 and served five years in the state prison at Marquette. In 1948, he was alleged to have violated parole as a "central figure in a hockey betting scandal" and served five more years.[4] Then in 1957, he was convicted of a misdemeanor gambling conspiracy charge in Florida and sentenced to a year in prison, but was successful in appealing the charge and served no time. In 1959, he was convicted of conspiracy to avoid excise tax in a "layoff book-making operation"* in Indiana and served five years in Leavenworth (pp. 4, 7). And finally, in 1974, he was indicted by a federal grand jury for interstate transmission of wagering, an indictment that was dismissed on legal grounds (p. 4). As a result of the state's failure to provide counsel in his 1939 robbery charge, the conviction was subsequently expunged following the U.S. Supreme Court decision in *Gideon v. Wainwright* (1963). His 1959 conviction was set aside on the basis of the Marchetti-Grosso rule, a rule derived from two 1968 U.S. Supreme Court decisions[5] protecting the Fifth Amendment right against self-incrimination,[6] and subsequently made retroactive in 1971.[7] These expunctions and his success with dismissals and appeals on the other charges meant that Tamer technically did not have a felony record.

Tamer's alleged criminal activities nevertheless received considerable newspaper attention and resulted in his being placed under constant surveillance by federal and state law enforcement agencies.[8] Yet, without an official record of felony convictions, there were limited grounds to forbid his involvement with li-

---

*He took bets and then placed them with someone else.

censed gaming activities. So frustrated was the board at one point that they unsuccessfully tried to have the Michigan attorney general's office appeal the 1939 robbery expunction in an effort to obtain "official" grounds for his removal from Nevada gaming.[9]

The board persisted in its efforts to establish the criminality of Tamer, viewing his lack of official convictions as a result of "legal technicalities," a stance that prompted Tamer's counsel, Gary Logan, to comment: "Mr. Tamer's convictions haven't been reversed because of legal technicalities . . . [but] because of unconstitutional infirmities. There is a difference."[10] Board member John Stratton responded that he was "completely confused" by counsel's explanation of the constitutional basis for the reversals, while Chairman Roger Trounday referred to the explanation as "a lot of legal mumble jumble" (p. 59).

In the absence of an official record of felony convictions, the board further sought to build its case on the bases of Tamer's alleged character and associations. In the words of Chairman Trounday:

> Well, the fact being that we cannot use the convictions in our deliberation, the part that disturbs me about this is the thread that seems to run through Mr. Tamer's life . . . He is constantly flirting with the law . . . he has admitted to us that he was involved in these various activities . . . [And he] does have associations . . . over and above what he has admitted to us . . . based on [the] fact that he is on the fringes of dealing with illegal acts and his associations, I can't find Mr. Tamer a man of good character and integrity . . . suitable to be a licensee in the State of Nevada. (pp. 50–51, 60–61)

The board's argument that Tamer was an associate of organized crime drew heavily from the testimony of FBI Special Agent William F. X. Kane. The testimony of this FBI agent conflicted with that of the attorneys of the U.S. Justice Department in earlier hearings. Kane provided an affidavit which stated that in 1976 Tamer had met repeatedly with Vito Giacalone and others reputedly associated with organized crime to discuss the business activities of the Aladdin. The affidavit was described by the board's chairman as revealing "a startling conspiracy involving Tamer in the violation of . . . [the] State's fundamental gaming licensing laws" (p. 9). He summarized Kane's affidavit as stating that

> Mr. Tamer meets regularly with Vito Giacalone, Charles Gold-farb, Charles Monazym and others at a restaurant called Chuck Joseph's Place for Steak in Detroit, Michigan.
>
> During these meetings they discuss their hidden interest in the Aladdin Hotel.
>
> James Tamer is their man . . . on the scene in Las Vegas and asks for reports on earnings, personnel and other important items about the management of the hotel whenever he is in Las Vegas.
>
> Conversations have been overheard where they discussed concern over the cost overrun of the new construction.
>
> Goldfarb was overheard talking on the phone to Tamer where they discussed the fact that Giacalone wanted to talk to Tamer about the possible loss of Teamster Pension Fund financing of the Aladdin Hotel.
>
> Billy Giacalone was overheard stressing the fact that gamblers from Detroit should utilize the Aladdin for their gaming activity due to the fact that it is controlled by the Detroit "outfit."
>
> Giacalone stated that Goldfarb and Tamer are not taking as much money from the Aladdin Hotel and Casino as the Detroit "outfit" expected.
>
> There are many other conversations listed as well as numerous phone calls made from Chuck Joseph's Place for Steak and from a location called the Goldfarb Bonding Agency, all to the Aladdin Hotel. (pp. 9–10)

Kane's statement was corroborated by a second affidavit from Vincent W. Piersante, director of the Organized Crime Division of the Michigan Department of Attorney General (p. 11). Piersante presented himself as the principal author of the hierarchical chart of the mafia used by the McClellan committee in the Valachi hearings. Relative to his investigation of members and associates of organized crime in Michigan, he explained that one of the individuals he investigated was James Tamer. The disparity between Tamer's image and the traditional mafia image and the inconsistency between his activities and the chart seem to have prompted much of Piersante's testimony. It goes without saying that Piersante had a vested interest in the chart and would also benefit from its expansion. As he said:

A proper definition of Organized Crime cannot be limited to the so-called Mafia or La Cosa Nostra families, which have been identified in various Congressional hearings. These individuals certainly are a part of the Organized Crime picture, however, individuals from all ethnic and racial groups comprise the totality of the problem which we encompass within the definition of Organized Crime. Thus, any individual who participates in the conduct of illegal businesses by providing some personal service which aids and abets these criminal conspiracies to function on a continuing basis within our society has to, of a necessity, be considered a member of Organized Crime.

Such a person is JAMES TAMER, who has a well documented background for aiding and abetting and participating in illegal gambling operations, in conjunction with those recognized and identified Organized Crime figures.

Although JAMES TAMER may be categorized by some persons merely as an accomplished odds-maker and handicapper, I have never known this service by TAMER to have been provided to any legitimate or legalized gambling operation, but rather for the purpose of aiding and abetting illegal gambling endeavors.

Law enforcement surveillances and investigations in recent years have established TAMER's continuing association with known and identified Organized Crime figures.

To categorize a person as a member of or an associate of Organized Crime would be patently unfair if it were based solely on a life-long association with identified and known members of these criminal groups. However, in JAMES TAMER's case, this association stands alongside of a great number of investigations conducted by various law enforcement agencies that established to their satisfaction the fact that TAMER was a participant and a principle in illegal gambling operations. On a number of occasions, JAMES TAMER was indicted and on at least one occasion, he was convicted of participating in illegal gambling. As recently as 1972, a gambling conspiracy charge was dismissed against TAMER because of highly technical reasons rather than on a factual basis and in another case, a long standing conviction expunged from his record. (pp. 12–14)

The difficulty of fitting Tamer within the traditional conception of organized crime led to an expanded conception that included his ethnicity and alleged criminal activities. This expanded model eventually facilitated the board's decision to deny his license.

To establish further Tamer's associations with members of organized crime, the board introduced several photographs which they contended were evidence of Tamer's meetings with Vito Giacalone. But the poor quality of the photographs led to their being challenged by counsel. It was argued that one could not really discern who was in the photographs. Further, the report's description of where the photographs were taken was at odds with what the photographs actually depicted (pp. 30–31). The result was a somewhat humorous, if not informative, discussion involving Deputy Attorney General Hicks, board member Stratton, counsel Logan, and James Tamer:

MR. HICKS:

. . . The photographs are of Mr. Tamer outside of Paul's Chop House . . . [They] portray Mr. Tamer as Subject No. 1—there is a number by his head—speaking with Subject No. 2, who is identified by the Detroit Police Department as Vito Giacalone . . .

MR. LOGAN:

. . . I don't believe . . . that anyone is prepared to say in Detroit that this person in this picture is James Tamer.

Now, . . . if you look at the pictures, one is apparently taken in front of an engineering company, and we know the other one is taken in front of an engineering company because you can see the *E* up here in the corner.

MR. HICKS:

That is correct. Huron Engineering Company is across the street from Paul's Chop House . . .

MR. LOGAN:

Is that true?

MR. TAMER:

I don't know. If it is across the street, how could I be in the Chop House? How could I be coming out of the Chop House? How could I be coming out the door, and the picture across the street shows me across the street?

MR. LOGAN:

And that is what the intelligence reports say, that he was photographed outside of Paul's Chop House.

MR. STRATTON:

The thing is: Is that a picture of you there?

MR. TAMER:

No, it isn't.

128

MR. HICKS:
> You deny that is a photograph of you?

MR. TAMER:
> I can't tell if it is me.

MR. LOGAN:
> Well, I can see. You don't have very good eyes, but it is not you.
> (pp. 30–31)

The board ultimately concluded that James Tamer was unsuitable for licensing as a key employee at the Aladdin. Although he had no record of felony convictions, and his alleged associations with members of organized crime were not conclusively established, the board rendered its decision on the basis of what was described by the board chairman as "that common thread that seems to consistently follow Mr. Tamer. He is always on the fringes of various activities that are illegal" (p. 60).

Two weeks later, a federal grand jury in Michigan returned a 22-count indictment against Tamer, Charles Goldfarb, James Abraham, Edward Monazym, and the Aladdin Hotel Corporation for violations of Title 18, referred to as the Travel Act, of the U.S. Code.[11] The defendants were indicted for using interstate telephones to carry on their alleged unlawful activity of hidden ownership and operation of the Aladdin. Tamer was named in several counts of the indictment.

Within another two weeks, the commission met to consider the board's recommendation for denial of Tamer's application for key-employee licensing. At the hearing his attorney, Gary Logan, contended: (1) that there was lack of due process because he was unable to subpoena out-of-state control board witnesses, including Kane, Piersante, and the two Detroit police officers who were said to have identified Tamer in the photographs (pp. 7–8); (2) that the commission had been prejudiced by the information contained in the recent federal indictment; and (3) that the board's allegations that Tamer had been a "central figure in a hockey betting scandal" were a distortion of the facts (p. 11). Regarding the last issue, he explained, "There was some type of feeling left that Mr. Tamer had been involved somehow in an attempt to fix a hockey game" (p. 11). Yet, the board's own exhibit, a press release by the president of the National Hockey League, stated: "There

129

has not been any charge [of] fixing or attempting to fix a hockey game, although that expression has been erroneously employed several times in recent publicity, and the evidence completely negates that suggestion" (p. 11). Attorney Logan's efforts were futile, however; the commission took only 27 minutes to sustain the action of the board in denying Tamer's application for key-employee licensing.

When the convictions were returned on the federal indictments a year later, Tamer was convicted only of conspiracy, or "attempting to exercise influence and perpetrate or continue . . . hidden ownership" in the Aladdin,[12] whereas the codefendants were convicted of actual hidden ownership. Thereupon, the commission issued an emergency order threatening suspension of the license of the Aladdin Hotel Corporation if certain conditions and limitations were not met, and demanding that the hotel exclude certain persons whose photos were attached. The four convicted felons and the Aladdin's officers and directors, Richard L. Daly, Sam Diamond, Peter J. Webbe, and Mae Ellen George (a formerly denied applicant), were all banned from the hotel's premises.[13] Interestingly, none of the other banned individuals was ever nominated to the Black Book, and James Abraham, one of Tamer's codefendants convicted of hidden ownership, has since been employed in the industry.[14]

Tamer's denial of a license and physical exclusion from the Aladdin did not cease his involvement with the hotel. In 1980, he was said to have been seen at New York meetings in which the stockholders of the Aladdin tried to sell the hotel to the Riviera.[15]

Suspicion of Tamer's role in the sale prompted the regulators to attempt further action against him. Richard Bunker, board chairman, suggested that "the Commission empower the Attorney General's Office to make whatever contact they can with the U.S. Attorney's Office to proceed with any proceedings that they would find appropriate to limit Mr. Tamer's continued association" with the Aladdin (p. 2). The concern and frustration with the situation is reflected in the motion of Commissioner Swarts, a motion that was subsequently approved:

> Mr. Chairman . . . I will make the motion that we provide any information that we have available to the U.S. Attorney and respectfully request on behalf of this Commission that the U.S. At-

torney petition the Court or whoever it may be, whoever should be petitioned, to try to relieve us of the problem of having Mr. Tamer constantly out here involved in our matters when he is a Federal criminal who is out on bail and is harassing us, causing us problems, and possibly maybe we could—I think the State of Nevada at least would be served for him to either stay out, and it may take incarceration to insure that. (p. 6)

While Swarts may have wanted Tamer to be imprisoned to keep him from "harassing" the regulators, whatever action was taken by the U.S. attorney's office as a result of the motion is not clear. However, following numerous attempted purchases of the Aladdin, it was finally sold later in the year, after which time the concern with James Tamer apparently subsided, that is, until 1986 when he was nominated to the Black Book.

TAMER'S NOMINATIONS TO THE BLACK BOOK

On October 2, 1986, the Nevada Gaming Control Board nominated James Tamer to the List of Excluded Persons. The sole basis for that nomination was the federal conviction for his role in the alleged behind-the-scenes ownership and operation of the Aladdin. Though Tamer appealed that conviction, the U.S. Court of Appeals for the Sixth Circuit affirmed it, and the U.S. Supreme Court denied him consideration of it. The board alleged that

> Tamer among others assisted Charles Goldfarb who had been denied a gaming license as owner of the Aladdin in maintaining a secret and illegal role in the ownership and operation . . . ; that . . . Tamer accepted the position of executive show director . . . at a salary and under conditions intended to induce the . . . Board to conclude he was not a key employee . . . ; [and] that . . . Tamer and . . . Goldfarb were allowed to exercise influence and control over the gaming operations of the Aladdin . . . by co-defendants James Abraham and the Aladdin through its officers who knew full well that neither . . . were licensed to do so . . . [16]

Five months after this nomination, on March 19, 1987, the commission, without explanation, unanimously responded to the request of Tamer's counsel, Thomas Pitaro, to dismiss the bill of particulars regarding his client. To our knowledge, this is the only instance in which a nomination to the Black Book has ever been dismissed.

Then a year later, and again without explanation, a new board with a four-volume set of information on Tamer moved to enter his nomination to the Black Book. The basis of the action apparently had not changed, although there were additional items mentioned, specifically: (1) that he was a denied gaming applicant; (2) that he had earlier testified about his involvement in illegal bookmaking; (3) that he had on occasion had lunch with Michael Polizzi, a 1975 Black Book nominee and a man convicted of hidden ownership in the Frontier; (4) that during the mid-1980s he had been seen in various casinos within the state; and (5) that he was suspected of having made a loan to the owners of the Royal Casino in Las Vegas.[17] Yet, the bill of particulars listed only two grounds for his inclusion: his prior felony conviction for conspiracy to violate the Travel Act and his violation of the Gaming Control Act relating to his "failure to disclose an interest in a gaming establishment."[18]

When the commission met to consider Tamer's second nomination, at issue was the discrepancy between the two items in the bill of particulars and the numerous allegations contained in the voluminous material placed in state's evidence following many objections on the part of counsel. Pitaro objected to the commission's constant attempts to enter material other than that contained in the bill of particulars. The result was to question virtually every aspect of the state's case, and ultimately to move the commission itself to doubt the strength of the case.

Pitaro built his case against the entry of Tamer: (1) by questioning the relevance of the state's documents; (2) by making light of the seriousness of Tamer's conviction; (3) by suggesting selective application relative to Tamer's codefendants; (4) by questioning the reality of a threat which was not acted upon for nine years; and (5) by suggesting that the board had not acted within the statute of limitations. Additionally, he presented information to suggest that Tamer had, in fact, not frequented Las Vegas casinos in recent years. While Pitaro dealt with specifics that transpired during the hearing, he also attacked the very hearing itself, saying: "A proceeding like this, based upon the facts that have been presented by the Board, make a mockery of this statute . . . [and] this Commission in enforcing it in this respect" (p. 104).

His opening statement included an objection to the 1,500–2,000 page document the state entered as evidence, presumably in an effort to impute a sinister character and illicit motivations to his client (p. 58), referring to the document as a "monstrosity . . . that deal[t] with investigations, hearings, and whatever mishmash that Board had to put together" (p. 14). He argued that, although Tamer was charged in essence with the "use of a telephone" to commit unlawful activity in regard to the Aladdin, even the federal grand jury saw fit to acquit him of that (p. 33) and to convict him only of conspiracy with a sentence of just 10½ months (p. 78). He also drew attention to James Abraham's subsequent licensing as an employee in the industry, first at the Barbary Coast and then at the Gold Coast (p. 35).

Pitaro's case against Tamer's inclusion in the Black Book also concerned itself with the length of time between his conviction in the Aladdin case and his nomination to the Black Book. Pitaro cited state law, which mandated that certain civil actions be brought within six years, though Deputy Attorney General Ellen Whittemore countered that administrative proceedings are not civil proceedings, and therefore are not subject to statutes of limitation (pp. 92–96). Pitaro questioned further why it had "taken nine years to bring this thing forward?" He went on to argue that it "flies in the face of reason that a person whose mere presence in a gaming establishment is so destructive to the State of Nevada that we had to wait nine years . . ." (p. 10).

Pitaro's "evidence" for Tamer's lack of present threat came from the results of subpoenas served to 28 major Las Vegas casinos, requesting information on his client's involvement with the establishments (p. 11). The various custodians of records at the casinos responded to the subpoenas by telephoning Pitaro's office, whereupon he or his secretary recorded the information requested (p. 120). The responses were construed by counsel to suggest that Tamer had not been in the casinos for some time, a conclusion with which the deputy attorney general took exception:

> [The subpoena] asks for documents or other writings in your possession or under your control concerning James Tamer as it relates to any and all involvement of James Tamer with the operation, management, or control of your establishment as an unrestricted gaming licensee in the State of Nevada since July 9th, 1979, to the present.

He does not ask for any room reservation records, credit card, or any other of the multitudinous documents that a nonrestricted licensee has, and I would be willing to bet at this point that most casinos would not have any records that James Tamer was either operating, managing, or controlling their establishment, and so therefore, I think what he's asked for he was going to get a negative answer. (p. 127)

The dogged efforts of Pitaro did nevertheless seem to prompt the board to amend its bill of particulars.

It took only five minutes on the morning of August 24, 1988, for the Gaming Control Board to amend the bill and, without notice to counsel, to include an additional basis for Tamer's exclusion from the industry—that of having a notorious or unsavory reputation. This reputation, according to the board, was based on his robbery conviction, hockey scandal involvement, (which was never established), illegal bookmaking activities, association with Michael Polizzi, newspaper identification as an associate of organized crime, denial of an application for licensing, and making false and misleading statements during the course of the board's investigation. Further, a confidential exhibit was introduced that was said to indicate that Tamer was registered at the Barbary Coast in Las Vegas in 1985, which implied that he was a present threat.[19] This very short board meeting thus provided the commission the additional grounds believed to be necessary to secure its action against Tamer.

In one month, the Nevada Gaming Commission continued its hearing on Tamer. The hearing lasted four hours, but the vote was unanimous to enter him into the Black Book, though one commissioner, Robert Peccole, voiced reservations.[20] In an effort to overwhelm any opposition in consummating the action against Tamer, the state introduced virtually all the information that they had compiled on him. Thus, in addition to certified copies of numerous court decisions, many other documents were put forward in support of the state's allegations of his notorious and unsavory reputation. The additional materials included transcripts of various other investigative hearings, multiple exhibits and testimonies within those hearings, convicted persons' questionnaires, a Detroit mafia organization chart, newspaper articles (including one from 1948), surveillance logs, special investigations exhibits, internal board memoranda, a SCOPE printout on Irwin Gordon, an FBI printout on Tamer, and, finally, the Las Vegas Metropolitan Police Department's SCOPE record on Tamer (pp. 12–20).

Pitaro, an aggressive and able adversary, took objection to virtually every one of the documents. He said that the Detroit mafia organizational chart was particularly offensive to him as an attorney of Italian-American ancestry, and suggested further that most sensible people would be offended by a chart that appeared to represent whatever those who drew it up wanted to find (p. 35). Regarding the entrance of newspaper articles into evidence, he suggested that reasonable people don't give credence to statements in newspaper articles when making decisions that govern other people's lives (p. 36).

In the main, Pitaro objected to having these documents regarded as official and appropriate for making legal decisions. Deputy Attorney General Whittemore pointed out that such administrative proceedings need not follow the more stringent rules of evidence used in legal proceedings, quoting from the Nevada Revised Statutes, chapter 463.313 (1) (d), which states:

> The hearings need not be conducted according to technical rules relating to evidence and witnesses, and any relevant evidence may be admitted and is sufficient in itself to support a finding if it is the sort of evidence on which responsible persons are accustomed to rely in the conduct of serious affairs regardless of the existence of any common law or statutory rule which might make improper the admission of such evidence over objection in a civil action. (pp. 21–22)

Pitaro was not deterred, however, and again objected to the introduction of materials to be used as substantive evidence in the absence of foundation. He argued that because an administrative body is "not bound by the technical rules of evidence has never meant that . . . [they are] not bound by any rules of evidence" (pp. 26–27).

In order to establish some foundation for these documents, the deputy chief of the board's Intelligence Bureau, Ron Hollis, was called forward. Pitaro challenged the ability of Hollis to speak to either the documents' relevance or their authenticity, arguing that Hollis could say only that he compiled them or knew who compiled them, and then say that they represented something that he relied upon (p. 27). Counsel's objections were overruled, however, and the material was entered, even that which was considered hearsay. On the basis of an earlier Nevada Supreme Court decision in the Rosenthal case, it was decided that "hearsay . . . [could] be admitted in administrative proceedings before the Commission" (p. 58). Further, Whittemore stated that hearsay would not be a problem for the regulators because they had been chosen by the governor for their ability to "weed out what's relevant and what's important" (p. 59). Ultimately, the majority of these documents were entered on the bases that they were "the type of information that is commonly relied upon by the Commission" (p. 39) and were "relevant to the question of whether . . . [Tamer had] a notorious and unsavory reputation" (p. 45).

Of particular note among the information presented is that concerning Tamer's alleged association with several persons formerly licensed in the industry—Morris Shenker, Moe Dalitz, and Irwin Gordon. There was the entry of a confidential report that indicated that Morris Shenker was Tamer's attorney in 1959 (pp. 33–34). A surveillance log on the activities of Tamer in Las Vegas in March of 1983 was said to mention Tamer having a conversation with Dalitz and several conversations with Gordon (p. 88).

It is not clear from the transcript what the intent was in introducing the information about Tamer's associations with Dalitz, Shenker, and Gordon. It may have been merely to establish that he had had communication with those who had held high positions in the industry, and therefore that he himself might be assumed to be influential in the industry. It may have been to suggest that he was connected to those whose reputations included connections with illegal activities, however long ago those activities occurred. However, one thing that is somewhat confusing is the mention of Dalitz here, because he was at that time regarded very highly in the industry. One might ask, Why would conversations with Dalitz be a problem? If as a friend, what would be the harm? If as a business associate, what would be the harm? Dalitz was no longer licensed and had, in 1976, received Las Vegas' Humanitarian of the Year Award.

After all the documents were entered over objections of Pitaro, Chairman John O'Reilly requested that Whittemore present her concluding arguments quickly (p. 126). As part of these arguments, she alleged additional circumstances surrounding Tamer's 50-year-old robbery conviction, allegations that suggest a notorious and unsavory character: "[Tamer] participated in an armed robbery of a Flint, Michigan, bank in 1934. He eluded authorities until 1939, when he was involved in a fatal accident. And it was only through that unfortunate incident that his true identity was discovered and he was returned to Michigan to face the old bank robbery charges" (p. 127).

Pitaro's summation viewed the proceedings in a much different fashion. In fact, he very plainly stated that it was a "hoop-to-do" and similar to the fairy tale about an emperor wearing new clothes when he was actually naked. Pitaro concluded, "I am here . . . to tell you that I think this procedure . . . is nakedness" (p. 134). Further, he suggested that the efforts of regulators in this instance amounted to "sound in fury [sic], signifying nothing" (p. 139) because Tamer presented no present threat and his criminal history was an ancient one. Finally, Pitaro suggested that what they might have managed was to create publicity and set "out a false front that . . . [they were] somehow tough in Nevada" (p. 140). Indeed, they may have accomplished just that when they banned a man who they alleged had harassed them for nearly two decades—a respected businessman of high status and a man who had received national recognition for his civic contributions.

PART 3

The Revitalization Period

8

Renewed Zeal

When the regulation of Nevada gaming entered the mid-1980s, some of the questions that had been raised about the constitutionality of the Black Book had already been resolved in the 1983 state supreme court decision in the case of *Spilotro v. State ex rel. Gaming Commission.* The decision also paved the way for the 1985 gubernatorial mandate to revitalize the List of Excluded Persons. So when the regulators moved to add additional persons to the list, they acted with great fervor. Although they were to ban some who had tormented them for more than a decade—Carl Wesley Thomas in 1987 (entry stayed until he exhausted his appeals) and James Tamer and Frank Larry Rosenthal in 1988—they additionally entered a number of small-time "hoods" and "bookies" and a new category of threat to the changing marketplace, "slot cheats," who presented little challenge to their efforts. Persons in this last category were often nominated while they were in prison for gambling-related crimes and were processed routinely because they often failed to contest their entry or to be represented by counsel. They seem to have been easy targets.

Never before had the regulators been so actively involved in gathering information and preparing cases for exclusion of individuals who were thought to pose a threat to the industry. The acceleration of the process, however, did not mean that the regulators had substantially changed their conceptions of what constituted a threat to gaming. Perhaps even more than before, they held dearly to beliefs about organized crime that by now had

141

become institutionalized both within the national law enforcement community and in the society at large—the mafia myth.

The beliefs about organized crime that were voiced in the Kefauver and McClellan investigations of the 1950s and 1960s became accepted as fact with the "findings" of the 1967 federal Task Force on Organized Crime. The task force concluded that there was a mafia of Italian origins operating in the United States and that this mafia was: structured in a highly bureaucratic manner; governed nationally by a commission; involved rigid rules enforced by violence; engaged in conspiracy to monopolize certain illegal activities; and was composed regionally of families, with members assigned to specific roles within those families.[1] Already wedded to such beliefs, the law enforcement community was quick to institutionalize this "alien conspiracy theory" of organized crime. And the theory has persisted within law enforcement,[2] although it has been regarded by many scholars as built largely on inconsistent and questionable findings.[3] It also merged with popular beliefs as conveyed through the media, cinema, and literature,[4] and has been accepted even by certain social scientists as well.[5] The acceptance of these beliefs by some social scientists seems to have derived from their reliance on the same journalistic and governmental reports that shaped law enforcement practices in the area, presumably because of misconceptions that the secrecy and danger associated with organized crime precludes the collection of data by researchers themselves.[6]*

The U.S. Senate and federal task force conclusions, in combination with popular and certain social scientific conceptions that have evolved in part from them, have also continued to circumscribe the decisions of regulators regarding those selected for inclusion in the Black Book. Regulators seem to select aliens or those of foreign background, view these persons' relationships with others as conspiratorial, often associate them with a specific family of organized crime, and interpret their activity in light of the specific roles believed to exist within the family.

*Reliance on government reports to study organized crime is not dissimilar to the now questionable use of official records to study crime more generally (Galliher and Cain 1974: 73). Neither practice adequately addresses the issues of selective enforcement and the intended uses of the information, the latter being the accusation and prosecution of certain individuals rather than the objective understanding of crime.

THE TRADITIONAL STEREOTYPICAL THREATS

Chris George Petti

The extent to which Nevada regulators continued to be constrained by the mafia myth is especially evident in Chris George Petti's 1987 entry into the Black Book. Court documents (including judgments of commitment, indictments, and probation orders), California crime reports, and newspaper articles made up the large part of the state's case for the inclusion of Petti in the Black Book.[7] The documents, as entered in evidence before the Nevada Gaming Commission, included the mention of several organized crime families and various roles in which Petti allegedly was involved. A 1982–1983 report on organized crime to the California legislature included the testimony of criminal investigator John Armstrong, who described Petti as a "former Chicago loan shark collector . . . [who had become] the top organized crime figure in San Diego as a result of his close association with the Chicago mob through Tony Spilotro in Las Vegas, the Joe Bonanno family in northern California and the Sica gang in Los Angeles" (p. 14). And the following year's report to the legislature (1984) referred to Petti, who had just been released from prison after serving a year for bookmaking, as "among 20 organized crime figures and their associates who were arrested . . . for attempting to establish control over bookmaking in the Southern California area" (p. 11).

Commenting on the differences in the California reports, as well as on the actual behavior of his client, counsel for Petti drew different conclusions. He read into the transcript quotations from the 1984 report in reference to the activities of various crime groups/families in southern California (including the Accetturo–Taccetta crime group), various New York crime families (Bonanno, Lucchese, Colombo, Gambino, and Genovese), the Chicago crime syndicate in Las Vegas, and the southern California crime family. He concluded that the deputy attorney general was unable to link Petti positively to any of these groups (p. 48).

Also in Petti's case, the state concerned itself with the part of the mafia myth that portrays violence as a means of doing business. Thus, court documents were admitted regarding an

Chris George Petti and attorney Oscar Goodman. Petti, *left with hand in pocket,* and Goodman, *right holding papers,* are shown arriving at the federal court house in San Diego in October 1990. Petti is believed in law enforcement circles to have risen to the top of organized crime in San Diego as a result of his close association with Anthony Spilotro and other Chicago organized crime family members in the Southern California area. The magnitude of such involvement, however, was questionable at the time of his Black Book entry, as was his threat to Nevada gaming. Photograph from the *San Diego Union-Tribune* / John Gibbons.

incident in which Petti was charged with assault with a deadly weapon.[8] The incident was an interesting one. An altercation apparently ensued following a young man's early-morning demand that Petti and three other older men break up their condominium pool party. Counsel for Petti described what followed:

> This young man that yelled out at two o'clock in the morning gathered up three of his friends and started chasing Mr. Petti and the three friends that he was with. Mr. Petti is up in years. His friends were up in years. These four charging young men were in their early 20s. And attempted to start a fight . . .[9]

The older men, who had been drinking, tried to protect themselves from the younger men, who were under a similar influence, when "Mr. Petti grabs a [baseball] bat, which is about two feet long, and tries to protect himself" (p. 43). The young

144

man who was hit by the bat was examined at a local emergency room, released, and went to work at seven o'clock that morning (p. 43).

This incident, though apparently a minor one, was seen as very relevant to the state's case for placing Petti in the Black Book. Deputy Attorney General James Chamberlain explained that, while "it might be asked why this [crime] has been introduced, . . . we believe that it shows propensity towards violence that can be used at times to enforce other efforts, including organized crime efforts" (p. 28).

What is the witness to this Nevada Gaming Commission hearing or reader of its transcript to conclude? Is Petti presently or has he ever been a top organized crime figure, a loan shark collector, or a bookmaker? Is he or has he been a person likely to resort to the violence said to be used by "strong-arm enforcers"? And, to which crime family does he belong—the Chicago mob, the San Diego mob, or one of several other mobs in southern California? The state's failure to provide definitive answers regarding Petti's criminal affiliation or roles seems clear in light of various statements of the deputy attorney general. After the documents were introduced and the exhibits were accepted, he absolved the regulators of any burden of proof or legislative mandate for proof regarding the allegations in documents entered as evidence of the criminal activity and associations of Petti. Rather, Chamberlain suggested that it is only required that people believe that Petti engaged in these activities and had these associations for him to cause potential damage to the Nevada gaming industry. He stated:

> Whether or not you assume there is a mafia, whether or not you assume that Mr. Petti is involved with organized crime, was involved with Anthony Spilotro, is involved with Chicago crime families, we have to believe out there there are people who do believe that and who if they saw him in a licensed gaming establishment would be concerned because of the reputation. (pp. 22–23)
>
> Again, I would note that we are not trying to prove the underlying allegations necessarily, only [that] the reputation exists. (p. 26)

In his closing statement, Chamberlain said:

We don't need to prove whether there is a Mafia. We don't need to prove whether there is a Cosa Nostra . . . [And, the legislative statute does not require that proof.] The statute just requires that we hold people at bay. (p. 69)

Michael Anthony Rizzitello

Michael Anthony Rizzitello was brought to the attention of the board in connection with his alleged attempted extortion of two long-time industry leaders, Benny Binion and Moe Dalitz.[10] His nomination came within a month of his release from prison following conviction of the charges, and he did not contest that nomination. He is said to have had his dinner interrupted at a California restaurant when he was served notification of his nomination, however. Rizzitello had an extensive record of crime dating back to 1947, including convictions for robbery, kidnaping for ransom, and defrauding an insurance company (p. 28). He was also indicted, but not convicted, in connection with the murder of Frank "the Bomp" Bompensiero, a mobster turned informant (p. 28).

Rizzitello was said to be an associate of alleged California organized crime figures Jack Lociero, Louis Tom Dragna, Samuel Orlando Sciortino, Dominick Phillip Brooklier, and Jimmy "the Weasel" Fratianno.[11] He was variously identified in numerous publications "as . . . a mob associate, a member of the Mafia, a reputed member of the Mafia, [a] leader of the Mafia, [an] organized crime associate, or other synonymous phrase[s]."[12] The allegations were made in *The Last Mafioso*, Ovid Demaris' (1980) book about Rizzitello's alleged associate Fratianno, in a report of the California Crime Commission (May 1978), in some 146 newspaper articles, and in an unidentified number of national magazine articles. One of the more amusing of Fratianno's allegations of Rizzitello was that he was "one of the five leaders of the . . . 'Mickey Mouse' . . . Mafia in the State of California," having been "made a member . . . in a motor vehicle."[13] What threat he posed to Nevada gaming is unclear, however.

Frank Joseph Masterana

Frank Joseph Masterana was a bookmaker. He took bets and placed them over the phone. That was his crime. In November

146

1978, 10 years before Masterana's name was added to the Black Book, the Nevada Gaming Commission denied his application for a work permit. Prior to that denial, he had worked as a bus boy, shill,* and dealer at virtually all the major Las Vegas casinos. A history of gaming-related crimes dating back to 1951, including "three convictions . . . relating to illegal gambling activities,"[14] was given as the reason for the denial. Louis Wiener, counsel who appealed Masterana's denial of a work card to the commission, also admitted to being his friend and lending him money, though he characterized him as stupid:

> If I were to characterize . . . [Frank], as I have on occasion characterized some of my clients in front of juries, in front of courts, I wouldn't say that he was not a man with evil intent. I'd say he's probably stupid. I'm not only saying that to you in public, I've told him that in private and I just think he's a stupid man. (p. 108)

Irrespective of this defense, Commissioner Clarence Haycock adamantly condemned Masterana's behavior, characterizing him as having "cheated everybody in the State of Nevada" (p. 113). After this he misquoted the biblical story of Esau selling his birthright for some pottage and confused the story as one of Aesop's fables, saying: "In the words of Aesop, . . . [Frank] sold his work right for some pieces of silver" (p. 113). Just prior to the vote that made visible the commission's designation of Masterana as an unsuitable person and therefore not worthy of a work card, Chairman Harry Reid informed Masterana's counsel, "You're wasting your time" (p. 114).

A month later, and with the same apparent level of objectivity, the commission denied the application of Masterana's former wife for a 100 percent interest to operate 15 slot machines at the Burger Hut in Las Vegas, where she was the manager.[15] Although Stella Masterana was divorced from Frank, the commission's denial was based on the Masteranas' alleged continued association. Stella probably had no intention of condemning Frank when she

---

*Shills are employed by casinos to pose as players to get games started, usually poker and baccarat. When legitimate players are attracted to the games, the shills then drop out to make room for others.

Frank Masterana and his attorney, Stephen Stein. Masterana, *left,* was a Las Vegas bookmaker. He took bets and placed them over the phone. His threat to gaming in Nevada was alleged to be the receipt of monies that would have otherwise been part of legitimate sport books and therefore subject to state revenues and taxes. A Las Vegas fixture for several decades, his Black Book entry is probably his major excursion into the public eye. Courtesy *Las Vegas Review Journal.*

appeared before the commission, but in the stress of pleading her case she said, "He is a lousy husband—he was, but he's an excellent father" (p. 23). Then, when it became clear that her application would be denied, she queried in frustration, "Would it make any difference if . . . [Frank] were dead?" To which, commission chairman Reid responded, "I'm sure it would make some difference." Then Commissioner Haycock facetiously countered, "Not to be taken as a suggestion" (p. 28). The decisions on the part of the regulators and perceptions of Frank Masterana by those who knew him in 1978 seem to have cast a spell of doom on the decisions and perceptions of a decade later.

In nominating Masterana to the Black Book, the Gaming Control Board of 1988 argued that he was "the largest bookmaker in Las Vegas, and if not, the West Coast," and that he had been identified as an associate of Chris Petti and Anthony Spilotro, and was allegedly paying Spilotro protection monies to operate in the state.[16] Masterana was also described as having an "extensive criminal record" (p. 17), as a "notorious and unsavory character which . . . [was] supported by his inclusion in the 1984 Sheriff's Report on Crime for Southern Nevada" (p. 11), and as a "wonderful candidate for the List of Excluded Persons" (p. 16). It was only on the basis of Masterana's criminal record, however, that his nomination was ultimately put forward to the commission.

In her opening statements to the commission, Deputy Attorney General Lisa Miller argued that Masterana's convictions spanned a time period of 15 years and several jurisdictions.[17] They were said to have been for "conspiracy to violate interstate gaming laws, interstate travel in aid of racketeering, use of a facility in interstate commerce in the aid of unlawful activity, that is gambling, use of a wire communication facility in interstate commerce to transmit bets and wagering on sporting events, attempts to evade wagering excise taxes, and aiding and abetting in interstate transmission of wagering information" (p. 4). Some of these activities were legal until the passing of the Omnibus Crime Bill in 1971, which made the placing of bets over the phone a crime in Nevada. Telephone bets were then made legal again in the state in about 1983. It was during the interim that Masterana had accrued a substantial part of his record.

Masterana's threat to the state and industry was described

largely as a monetary one. The state argued that monies that Masterana was taking in from his bookmaking activities were monies that would have otherwise gone to legitimate sports books and ultimately to state revenues (pp. 21, 22). The nominee, on the other hand, argued in his own defense that, since he placed his bets at the legitimate books, his activities actually benefited the industry and state revenues. He was almost an "innocent" here, telling them what he did, defending it before those who were bound to see it, in any terms, as unethical and illegal. His words were:

> I was what you would call a sports service man. What I would do, if you lived in Tennessee, you call me up and say, "What's the price of the game?"
>
> I would say, "Pittsburgh Steelers are a seven point favorite."
>
> And he would say to me, "Well, bet me $3,000 on Pittsburgh minus seven."
>
> I would take the gentlemen's 3,000 and bet it at one of the legal books that had it six and a half, Pittsburgh six and-a-half. So what would happen is I couldn't do—I couldn't lose. I would take your money and place it with a legal book. The player says he's got minus seven, but I bet it off at minus six and-a-half. If the game falls seven, the player gets a tie, but I win his 3,000, with no risk.
>
> And that's how I have done it the majority of my life, because to be as big a bookmaker as the federal government thinks I was, I would have to have a billion dollars. But what I was was a sports broker.
>
> Like I had a gentleman in Reno and I explained it, I bet on one side of the game and bet on the other and go for middles, which you can't lose. One of the games has to win.
>
> So I have always tried to earn with other people's money. And that's why I explained to the State that I have created a market and put revenue into the economy. I have not taken anything out of the economy of Nevada. (pp. 41–42)

Masterana stated that he had even provided valuable advice to the Gaming Control Board regarding the operations of legal books:

> I can't remember the year, but it was when Phil Hannifin and Shannon Bybee were on the Board. I received a call from Mr. Shannon Bybee, and I am sure you don't have a record of this,

but Mr. Bybee called me to his office and he asked for my opinion of why a citizen of Nevada would bet with an illegal bookmaker instead of a legal bookmaker.

And I explained to him that the laws that you gentlemen have passed made it impossible for a player to bet a legal book. They had a 10 percent tax that you had to pay to the federal government, and you had no telephone accounts. I mean, a person would have to walk in to bet. And it was absolutely impossible for a legal bookmaker to make any money, because of the restrictions. And I explained this to Mr. Bybee.

So if my intentions were to harm the State of Nevada, then why would I give Mr. Bybee the benefit of my expertise in gaming, which I am? But I did that. (p. 29)

During the commission proceedings, Masterana also commented on the law enforcement evidence that the board had gathered in their case against him as being "10 percent truth and 90 percent exaggeration and distortion" (p. 28). He voiced feelings that he had been "singled out and discriminated against" and that others who had been involved in some of the same activities had not been as harshly dealt with as he had been (p. 33). His first conviction for transmitting wagering information over the wire was an instance of giving information on "the price of a football game" to an old school friend who called him from Ohio. Masterana said that, out of about 50 people involved in the incident, including Ohio bookmakers, he was the only one fined and that it had "just snowballed since then" (p. 33). This snowballing process was epitomized, according to Masterana, when "a few years ago the State of Nevada charged . . . [him] with being an habitual criminal and wanted to put . . . [him] in jail for life . . . for gambling, transmitting wagering information, taking a bet . . ." (p. 34). For an individual who 10 years earlier had been described as stupid by his attorney and seemingly poked fun at by the regulators and even his former wife, Frank Joseph Masterana seemed exceptionally insightful about the circumstances that had led up to his entry into the Black Book.

Gaspare Anedetto Speciale

In December of 1988, the board nominated reputed bookmaker and loan shark Gaspare Anedetto Speciale to the Black Book. Three months later, he was entered. Speciale had previously been denied a license to operate a sports book in Las Vegas and, at the time of his nomination, was operating a sports betting information business there, J and J Sports Service.[18] His felony convictions included interstate transmission of bets in 1965, loansharking and racketeering in 1976, obstructing investigations by refusing to testify before a federal grand jury in 1976, and conducting an illegal sports bookmaking business in 1983 (pp. 2–5). One might question why he was seen as a threat at this time. An additional 19 arrests, 11 dismissals, and 8 convictions for bookmaking had resulted in fines of $10–$350 for each offense (p. 3). He had been described by the investigations subcommittee of the U.S. Senate Committee on Governmental Affairs as a New York mafia loan shark who was doing business out of the Tower of Pizza Restaurant in Las Vegas (p. 6). He was also alleged to have been an associate of a number of Las Vegas' more notorious figures, several of whom had recently been placed in the Black Book: Frank Larry Rosenthal, James Tamer, Michael Rizzitello, and Frank Joseph Masterana. The local newspaper attention given to his alleged associations and bookmaking and loansharking activities was said by board chairman Michael Rumbolz to have "brought a black eye" to Las Vegas (p. 10). It took only a few minutes to nominate Speciale to the Black Book. He was an easy target.

Speciale's hearing before the commission was likewise brief, leaving only a 12-page record in comparison to the same year's hearings of James Tamer and Frank Rosenthal, which compiled several hundred pages each. The only issue of question in Speciale's entry came when his attorney sent a letter to the commission explaining that his client's physician had his offices in Caesars Palace on the Las Vegas Strip, and that his exclusion from casinos might pose a personal hardship. Discussion of how the issue should be dealt with consumed the majority of the hearing. The regulators questioned whether they were obligated to consider the letter as information, and whether acting against Speciale without considering it was likely to become a basis of subsequent legal challenge. The regulators were also unaware of the location of the doctor's office in relation to the general layout of Caesars Palace and of whether accessing the office required entry into the casino. It is surprising that the regulators did not know the layout of one of their industry's largest businesses or that

Gaspare Speciale. Speciale was a reputed bookmaker and loan shark who was alleged to be soft. He is said to have been operating such illegal activities out of his Tower of Pizza Restaurant in Las Vegas for two decades before being placed in the Black Book. His entry was uneventful, except for its implications for his failing health. His physician's office was in Caesars Palace, which meant that once he was banned from casinos, his access to his doctor would be affected. He died within three years of his entry. Courtesy *Las Vegas Review Journal.*

they did not seek to find out just where the doctor's office was located in the complex. We are also patients of Speciale's doctor, and even we could have told the regulators that there is no apparent entrance to the office other than through the hotel lobby, which adjoins the casino.

Commissioners Robert Peccole and Kenneth Gragson did nevertheless express the need to consider the information, even though Deputies Attorney General Wilson and Stendari argued against its appropriateness. Yet, commission chairman John O'Reilly pushed through the vote for exclusion, suggesting that, even if the information were introduced, it would not necessarily preclude Speciale's doctor from seeing him elsewhere.

MR. WILSON:

It is my legal advice . . . that this particular letter not be admitted as evidence for [Speciale] . . .

COMMISSIONER PECCOLE:

Well, we have already received this [letter] and everybody has read it, and now we have to close our mind to it, is what you are saying?

MR. WILSON:

Well, . . . while this is here, it is not evidence . . . for you to consider . . .

COMMISSIONER PECCOLE:

The only problem I have with that, any judge in his right mind, if he all of a sudden had some evidence like this in front of him before he passed sentence, would obviously say, well, I want to take . . . [these circumstances involving Speciale and his doctor] into consideration . . . Can we send this thing back to the Board for the Board to consider this?

MS. STENDARI:

. . . I am informed . . . that the Board . . . does not wish to consider this . . . I think [writing a letter] . . . is not the way to put evidence before this Commission . . . This is completely inappropriate . . . An attorney should know better than this . . .

COMMISSIONER PECCOLE:

What happens if this takes place? Let's say the scenario goes this way: What if Mr. Speciale goes into this doctor's office and we arrest him or somebody arrests him or Caesars Palace kicks him out of there based on the Black Book?

I mean, are you prepared to defend whatever kind of civil actions might come down the road?

154

MS. STENDARI:

I don't think there would be grounds for a civil action against the Board or Commission.

COMMISSIONER PECCOLE:

I can frankly, myself, see a civil rights action in a federal court.

MS. STENDARI:

I disagree . . .

COMMISSIONER GRAGSON:

. . . I just think that we ought to consider that if a man has his doctor in a casino, . . . I think it should be checked out, and I know he is a very respected doctor, one of the top doctors in town. But I don't know for sure if this is his only office. But if it is and that is his doctor, are we going to have him cut a hole in the outside?

CHAIRMAN O'REILLY:

Let me handle it this way procedurally. First of all, we have an issue of evidence . . . [and] an objection to the consideration of the . . . letter as evidence.

I am going to sustain that objection based on the advice of counsel and discussions we have had here today, and therefore, the letter will not be considered as evidence by the Commission . . .

[Further], . . . it would appear to me that the treating physician is one who also has access to and has patients in a hospital and could see this individual as part of his rounds at a hospital or a waiting room or a meeting room off the premises of the property, if in fact the doctor's offices are located in what is legally defined as a gaming establishment . . .

COMMISSIONER PECCOLE:

We don't have any evidence to that effect. (pp. 131–138)

Without further incident, the commission unanimously entered Gaspare Anedetto Speciale into the Black Book. Within less than three years, Speciale died and was removed from the book. One may dare pose the question of whether his death might have been related in any way to lack of access to his doctor.

ENTER THE SLOT CHEATS

The Black Book was officially created to deal with those who, because of their association with organized crime, posed a threat to gaming. That was the public message that had been put forth as early as 1960 by the press and various regulatory boards, and its accompanying vocabulary of threat included *mob, conspiracy, enforcer, loan shark, bookmaker, associate,* and the like. By the 1980s, however, the industry was no longer dominated by the blackjack, poker, and baccarat tables. Slot machines occupied an increasingly important portion of the marketplace—over 50 percent by the 1990s. Hence individuals were now able to cheat machines. Hence individuals were now able to obtain money that should have gone to the state by causing machines to pay off in other than the preprogrammed fashion, and even in the absence of repeated insertion of money. With the new technology, new images of threats to gaming developed. So, how do you create a new vocabulary of threat? You rely, to some extent, on the old.

John Joseph Vaccaro, Jr.

For eight years, since the 1978 entry of Anthony Spilotro, no one was nominated to the Black Book. When the board resumed this major task again, in March of 1986, it nominated a "slot cheat." John Joseph Vaccaro, Jr., was referred to as "the mastermind of a slot cheating ring," which included his wife and 10 others, a ring that was involved in the rigging of and the attempt to rig jackpots at major casinos in Reno, Stateline, and Las Vegas between 1980 and 1982.[19] Vaccaro was named the ringleader, a term which conveyed the image of conspiracy. He was said to have been listed in a 1984 report on organized crime to the California legislature, a listing which served to taint him.[20] Thus, the one who paved the way for subsequent slot cheats, including his own wife, was one whose criminal activities and associations were described in terms somewhat similar to those of earlier Black Book nominees. Though the regulators' attempt to pattern this image of threat was in its formative stages, Vaccaro was nevertheless entered unanimously into the Black Book like the majority of the nominees before him.[21]

The generally tenuous basis for assigning formal organized crime roles to nominees and the role of the media in this process are thus especially evident in the case of Vaccaro. While the board suggested that he was associated with traditional organized crime interests at the time of his nomination to the Black Book, the media later took it upon themselves to award him a "lieutenancy" in the mob. The influence of such media depictions on the thinking of regulators is evident in the following dialogue from a subsequent case:

COMMISSIONER:
> . . . It is my belief . . . that John Vaccaro . . . was supposedly a lieutenant for organized crime . . . in California . . .

BOARD CHAIRMAN:
> . . . The allegations of his involvement as a lieutenant, as a member of organized crime, were actually aired first in the media after the Nevada Gaming Commission put him on the List of Excluded Persons . . .[22]

Vaccaro had been convicted of several gaming related felonies: illegal gambling (bookmaking) in California in 1974, slot cheating in New Jersey in 1984, and "masterminding" a slot cheating ring in Nevada in 1985, the last of which he was appealing to the U.S. Court of Appeals for the Ninth Circuit when the board nominated him.[23] Because his slot cheating activities in Nevada amounted to over $1 million, the board viewed him as posing a major threat to gaming. Counsel argued that the board's action was premature because his client's major conviction was under appeal. He also held that the action involved "selective enforcement" because being charged with cheating at gambling was so common in the state's district courts and because the board hadn't nominated any of the codefendants in the case, two of whom were also "ringleaders" (pp. 15–21). The deputy attorney general countered, "Well, you have to start somewhere, don't you?" He went on to say that, should Vaccaro's conviction be subsequently overturned, a clear mechanism was in place for him to petition to have his name removed from the book (pp. 31–33). Of the seven others, only Vaccaro's wife was eventually added to the book.

Sandra Kay Vaccaro

Sandra Kay Vaccaro, John's wife, was nominated and entered within a year. Although she had been part of the slot cheating ring, others who were convicted were never nominated, including two whose culpability was equal to her husband's, according to the prosecutor in the case (p. 21). It is indeed surprising, if not remarkable, that her counsel never introduced the selective enforcement argument in Sandra Vaccaro's case.[24] Her arrest in 1980 for attempting to insert a "cooler deck" (a deck of prearranged cards) into a blackjack shoe at the MGM Grand was given as an additional reason for her nomination, although the charge had been dismissed upon her pleading guilty to trespassing.[25] Ultimately, the state's Final Order of Exclusion for Sandra Vaccaro named only the four counts of the 1985 violation of Title 18 of the U.S. Code: illegally setting up and collecting jackpots on slot machines and transporting monies taken by fraud over state lines.[26] Apparently, the federal trial court viewed her as only a minor figure in the cheating ring, at least in comparison to her husband, John, who was convicted on 17 counts of violation of Title 18 of the U.S. Code. Perhaps the threat she posed was her association with her husband. Recall that Stella Masterana, even though divorced from Frank, failed to obtain licensing by the regulators.

During the commission hearing on Sandra Vaccaro's nomination to the Black Book, the state suggested that her threat was serious and immediate.[27] Deputy Attorney General Jim Guidici attempted to persuade the regulators that Vaccaro would be recognized by patrons of casinos, who would believe, when they saw her, that cheating was taking place.

> What is that patron going to think if Sandra Kay Vaccaro walks in, sits down next to her and starts playing? It seems to me that patron is immediately going to think, Sandra Vaccaro is helping somebody set up this slot machine and I am going to get out of here. (p. 29)

Guidici himself said that, if he "saw Sandra Vaccaro playing a slot machine, . . . [he] would figure something is going down" (p. 23).

There were some who were not convinced by this line of reasoning. Counsel for Vaccaro doubted whether anybody would recognize her client. Commissioner Peccole expressed similar doubts, and also raised the issue that the real threat that Vaccaro posed—that she could rig machines to pay off—couldn't be dealt with by placement in the Black Book, because it would not bar her from places that had only slot machines. He responded to Guidici's comment:

What if she was totally disguised and you didn't even know who she was, which probably close to a hundred percent of the public do not know who this woman is? I don't conceive of that as a threat. I do conceive the fact that she knows how to cheat and she knows how these schemes are set up as posing a threat . . . (p. 24)

Again, Guidici maintained:

The threat, the presence Sandra Vaccaro poses is the threat to public confidence and trust that the gaming is free from criminal corruptive elements. To me, it is as simple as that, Commissioner Peccole. (p. 26)

Just minutes before the vote, Peccole raised a critical issue:

Mr. Chairman, could I make an observation? It is sort of interesting that our law dealing with . . . people . . . who are put in the Black Book for exclusion seems to indicate that these people can go in any place where there . . . [are] slot machines only, and yet, the crimes that Mrs. Vaccaro . . . [has] been convicted of deal with slot machine cheating. So she can just go in any establishment that doesn't have live games and possibly go about doing what she knows how to do. And there is nothing we really can do about it. Just an observation. (p. 34)

The vote was taken, and Sandra Vaccaro followed her husband into the Black Book. As of this date, the issue that Peccole raised has never been resolved. This is especially interesting in light of the fact that, since the Vaccaros were entered into the Black Book, a number of additional slot cheats have been added, and machines now contribute over 50 percent of the revenues of the gaming industry.

Harold Travis Lyons

Harold Travis Lyons' criminal history consisted of convictions for burglary, grand theft, slot cheating, and, most recently, drug related charges.[28] He was described by the regulators as "worse than being a career criminal, [in that] he . . . [was] a career slot cheating criminal."[29] He was also depicted as indiscriminate in his choice of targets, having carried out his crimes at various locations throughout the United States, as "an equal opportunity thief and slot cheat" of sorts (p. 20). The regulators expressed doubt that he could ever be rehabilitated, pointing out that he had even engaged in slot cheating while on parole (p. 26).

Although Lyons was indeed a felon and repeat offender, he was at the same time dissimilar to most of those who had been entered into the Black Book before him. He was a slot cheat but not reputed to be a member or associate of organized crime. To resolve this inconsistency, the regulators sought to draw parallels between his criminal activities and those of others with whom they were more familiar. This was accomplished by the use of the vocabulary they were wont to use on those they were accustomed to entering into the book, a vocabulary that more clearly established the nature of the threat that such an individual presented. Lyons' collaboration with others in crime was especially useful to the regulators in this regard, because it allowed them to characterize his offenses as conspiracies against the state (p. 19).

However, Lyon's nomination was not without question. Board member Gerald Cunningham called attention to the limited effectiveness of the legislative statute that governed the Black Book in keeping Lyons away from slot machines. Cunningham reminded his fellow board members that Lyon's Black Book entry would not prohibit his entry into gaming establishments that had slot machines only. The industry had a substantial investment in slot machines in recent years, both in terms of their numbers in the larger casinos and in their placement in establishments that lacked table games. But the legislative statute that governed the Black Book was not applicable to the latter establishments, because they included airports, grocery stores, bars, laundromats, convenience stores, and the like. Cunningham thus held little hope for the efficacy of the proposed exclusion of Lyons, because the nominee presented as much a threat to establishments with only slot machines as he did to casinos.

MEMBER CUNNINGHAM:
. . . there is an interesting aspect that we might talk about, and that is that the orders that we normally issue prevent . . . [excluded persons] from entering a variety of places except those

areas that have slot machines only, and this seems to be extremely inconsistent with our concerns [in this case].

CHAIRMAN RUMBOLZ:

Unfortunately, that is statutory.

MEMBER CUNNINGHAM:

I recognize that, and I wondered maybe we could condition
his license.

[DEPUTY ATTORNEY GENERAL] STENDARI:

You are stuck with the statute.

CHAIRMAN RUMBOLZ:

Condition his inclusion? I agree with you, Mr. Cunningham. It
is a shame we can't keep him away from all slot machines or at
least make his activity in getting close to them criminal in and
of itself . . .

It is a question of whether slot machine only locations are
what . . . [the legislators] were considering in the amendment
or were they more concerned that they not be excluded from
restricted locations, which might stop you from . . . purchasing
food or in this day and age getting your car lubed.

MEMBER CUNNINGHAM:

Or your clothes washed.

CHAIRMAN RUMBOLZ:

. . . I think that . . . we may want to suggest to the legislature
they simply be excluded from all Group I and Group II casino
operations.

MEMBER CUNNINGHAM:

Or III.

CHAIRMAN RUMBOLZ:

Except for airports or transportation centers.

MEMBER CUNNINGHAM:

You don't have a taste for letting him walk?

CHAIRMAN RUMBOLZ:

Yeah. Unfortunately, the Supreme Court in the Spilotro case
said that might be going just a little too far when you stop them
from getting on a train . . . or taking a plane. (pp. 21–23)

Regardless of this rather light, but meaningful, repartee among
the board members, Lyons was entered into the Black Book with
little additional attention to the inadequacy of the legislative statute. At that time, he had another conviction, for illegal drug activity, and neither he nor counsel on his behalf made an appearance.[30] He, too, was an easy target.

William Gene Land

Not all of those who were considered for inclusion in the Black Book at the time had the kinds of backgrounds that fitted with either the regulators' old or new conceptions of persons who presented a threat to the industry. This is especially evident in the case of William Gene Land. Land's is the only case in the 35-year history of the Black Book in which the commission failed to render a unanimous decision; two of the five members voted against his entry. This occurred because he was able to establish some legitimacy and humanity, his crime did not quite fit their criteria of threat, and he was not associated with organized crime.

Land's "crime," and the basis for his 1988 entry into the Black Book, was marking cards from the Riviera in Las Vegas for the purpose of cheating at blackjack there in 1984. The board alleged that they had learned from a confidential informant that Land was seeking the cooperation of a casino pit boss or floorman who could supply him with cards that could be marked and inserted into a game in which he was to be a player.[31] Upon obtaining this information, the board arranged for one of its undercover agents to phone Land, who was residing in Arizona at the time, indicating that he could supply such a contact (p. 39). Posing as a casino employee, and with the cooperation of the Riviera, the agent delivered the cards to Land at his home in Arizona, where he observed Land mark the cards chemically (p. 40). When the cards were then put into play at the Riviera, agents of the Gaming Control Board were on hand to arrest Land for cheating (pp. 4, 5).

Land's record showed one other arrest, an arrest for burglary in 1961 in his home state of Kentucky.[32] Although the board said that he had admitted to being previously involved in an attempted card cheating scam at Circus Circus in 1982, and suspected him of having been involved in similar scams at other Las Vegas resorts,[33] he denied these allegations and admitted only to having observed the Circus Circus scam (p. 41). The board also was unable to establish that Land had ever derived any financial benefit from the alleged previously attempted cheating.

Land appeared before the commission on his own behalf and without benefit of counsel. He told of his cooperation with law enforcement in the plea bargaining process (pp. 19, 73), and of having paid his fine and served his sentence of probation and community service (p. 16). He explained that he no longer gambled, only infrequently went to casinos for dinner and entertainment (p. 73), and that he came to Nevada only for the purpose of his wife's cancer treatments and because his two sons worked in the state:

> My only question in being here today is that why I am being selected for this book of all the hundreds of people that have been convicted of cheating at gambling . . .
>
> In 1984, when I was convicted, I had had no connection whatsoever with the gaming business. I lived in Arizona until the past six months when I moved back to Nevada. My wife is a terminal cancer patient and her doctors are here, and that is why I am back in the State of Nevada now.
>
> If and when the time comes, I am going to leave the State of Nevada again. I have family here. I have two boys that are working in the State of Nevada. That's the only reason I am here is for them, not for myself.
>
> . . . Why after four years they are bringing this up again, punishing me again for something that I have already paid for, I don't know . . .
>
> The only thing that putting me in this book is going to do is create a hardship on my kids that live here in this state, that are going to live here probably for the rest of their life. (pp. 15–16)
>
> I will always regret the mistakes I have made, and while that guilt remains with me, I feel that I have given sufficient restitution to the state for my crime . . . I . . . did my sentence and I paid my fine. The action that you are now taking I believe is tantamount to double jeopardy and cruel and unusual in regards to my situation.
>
> . . . For you to continue moving towards entering my name into the List of Excluded Persons is putting me in the same category as the other organized crime related individuals that are currently in the Black Book . . .
>
> I have never been connected with organized crime. I do not pose a threat to the gaming industry.
>
> . . . I cannot help but think that your actions are like using a shotgun to kill a mosquito . . . (pp. 18–20)
>
> I am just a little guy. Why was I selected? And then after the four year period . . . (p. 72)

At issue in Land's case was whether or not he was associated with a group that had been involved in several card cheating scams in and outside Nevada, including one that netted $149,000 at the Las Vegas Tropicana. In the nomination of Land, the board's chairman, Michael Rumbolz, stated: "Mr. Land has been a moving force behind card cheating rings in the State of Nevada . . . I believe that . . . [he] has admitted to hundreds of thousands of dollars being stolen as a result of his activities at various locations."[34] Also, at the commission hearing, the deputy chief of the board's Intelligence Bureau, Ron Hollis, gave this testimony: "[Mr. Land] was an integral part of this group, and without him and without his participation in it it would not have worked successfully."[35]

In response to Land's questions regarding what proof there was for his involvement in the group's activities, however, Hollis said: ". . . that was not my testimony. My testimony was a group in which you operated, a group in which you were a member had the occasion to cheat a number of casinos . . . So, again, I am implicating the group, Mr. Land" (p. 41). Then, in response to further questioning from the commission chairman, John O'Reilly, Hollis stated: "I have no direct evidence relative to the extent or lack of extent of Mr. Land's involvement in those other criminal activities. I will say that he was associated with and knew very well those individuals who perpetuated those acts, those activities" (p. 42). Commissioner Kenneth Gragson then asked Hollis "whether [Land] knew the people or was associated with [them] at the time the Tropicana was [cheated]—or . . . [if] he was more or less personally involved" (p. 44). Hollis responded: "It's difficult to answer, Mr. Gragson, because there were no charges ever brought there. There was no successful prosecution. I cannot affirmatively say if—first of all, I can't positively identify who exactly was involved" (p. 44). In spite of these apparent contradictions to the original allegations, Commissioner Betty Vogler, just minutes before the vote was to be taken, stated: ". . . the fact that monies did not go to organized crime, I don't think lessens the principle or the severity of the crime at all. The crime was committed. There was a conspiracy" (p. 85). All this made evident the need on the part of the regulators to force the circumstances of Land's case into their existing categories of perceived threat to the industry.

Land's case presented considerable difficulty for some of the commissioners. In addition to their having to consider the more personal issues of family and children, there was the question of whether Land's case fitted the intent of the law and the issue of justification for the four-year interim between his conviction and nomination. Responding to Deputy Attorney General Lisa Miller's presentation of the state's case, Commissioner Robert Peccole raised several questions:

COMMISSIONER PECCOLE:

... He came to the attention of the Board in 1984. I am having the same concerns Mr. Land is having. Why all of a sudden out of the blue four years later do we say that he is a person we should be putting in the Black Book?

MS. MILLER:

I think it's been the policy of the Board not to pursue the actual Black Book until the sentence has been completed ... it hasn't been the practice of the Board to go forward with individuals who are incarcerated or in his case were on probation.

COMMISSIONER PECCOLE:

I assume he was off probation before '88. In fact, I thought he only served two years of probation.

MS. MILLER:

His probation was completed in February of '86. But there is an investigation that has to be done and paperwork and the Board has to take action.

COMMISSIONER PECCOLE:

I am not buying all of that. I mean, myself, I am having a real problem with the idea that we pick somebody four years— who has committed a crime four years ago, all of a sudden we are saying he meets all the requirements of this statute, and I don't think in my mind this statute was ever set up to do what we are doing right now.

I think the intent at the very beginning was to get the people like the Spilotros and the organized crime people out of these casinos ...

I haven't seen any evidence in the record that you presented that Mr. Land has even been in the casinos since 1984 ...

MS. MILLER:

We also don't have any evidence that he has not been in any casinos.

COMMISSIONER PECCOLE:

You are the one that is selecting him for the book. You are supposed to be proving to me that I should put him in the book. And you are supposed to be proving that he poses a present threat ...

But there is no evidence in this record to indicate he is any part of a ring or any part of a conspiracy presently. I am having a lot of trouble with this. (pp. 24–28)

Before the vote of the commission was taken, Peccole argued further:

. . . it is really important for us to understand that the stigma that goes with the Black Book doesn't apply only to the person who is in the Black Book. It applies to his family.

And obviously, Mr. Land's children had to go through the stigma of his having been convicted of a crime in 1984, and now once again they have to face the possible stigma that their father will be in the Black Book. I don't think that that's proper at all . . .

I would have to say that I don't feel that the Black Book statutes and regulations were meant to be applied in just every case that comes down the road. This is one of these instances where I don't think it should be applied.

I think that we should be looking towards the Civellas . . . the Vaccaros. That's what the Black Book was all about in the first place.

And if my memory serves me correctly, I believe that what happened when the Black Book came into play was there was an idea that we would try to keep the mafia-connected organized crime out of the casinos, and the reason that was was because there were hidden interests and these people were hanging around the casinos . . . (p. 78)

In addition to the lapse of four years between Land's conviction and nomination (pp. 24–27), it was also established that Land was not involved with "traditional" organized crime (pp. 67, 80). Thus, when the vote was taken, it reflected the many concerns raised. In the entire history of the Black Book, it is the only instance in which the nominee's entry did not receive unanimous support of the commission.

166

9

Cusumano "The Typical"

Joseph Vincent Cusumano, an alleged loan shark, was known on the streets of Las Vegas as Anthony Spilotro's replacement for Chicago organized crime interests in town.[1] Recall that the Nevada Supreme Court had upheld Spilotro's Black Book entry in 1983, so for a little while Las Vegas seemed free of his imminent threat. Nevertheless, there remained a concern on the part of some that Chicago might still be around, and that concern focused on the person of "Joey" Cusumano. Cusumano was an easy target of concern—he was Italian, his personal manner seemed consistent with the stereotype of organized crime, and he was from Chicago—and could be said to be typical of most who have been seen as posing a threat to the gaming industry. Indeed, even the attorney who represented Joey recognized the likelihood of his being seen as disreputable, referring to him as an easy target, a "good scapegoat," a "person who fits the stereotype."[2] What makes the case of Cusumano unique is its explicit attention to the issue that has ever so subtly appeared in other cases: differential selection, especially toward Italians. His being so typically Italian illustrates the selection process.

In 1985, Cusumano thought that he was to be nominated to the Black Book. He claimed there were reliable accounts that such a nomination was imminent, and on this basis he filed a federal lawsuit challenging the book's constitutionality and calling for an "injunction prohibiting his inclusion."[3] His action may have been precipitated by the Las Vegas Metropolitan Police Department's gathering of the names of 100 persons to submit to the Gaming

167

Control Board for recommendation to the Black Book, and the likelihood that his name was among them.[4] It was also at a time when he was undertaking a career as a line producer in motion pictures, most notably for the movie *The Cotton Club*.[5] Although the lawsuit was dismissed, being held to be "premature" in that the board had taken no action at that time,[6] what Cusumano had anticipated did come to pass.

It was in December of 1989 that Joseph Vincent Cusumano was indeed nominated to the Black Book.[7] Two years earlier, when he already suspected he would be nominated, he acquired a felony record. He was convicted of conspiracy, interstate travel in aid of racketeering, and aiding and abetting in violation of Title 18 of the U.S. Code for his 1980 role in a kickback scheme involving the skimming of $315,000 from a life insurance policy for culinary union members.[8] It was this three-count federal conviction, his being named by the Chicago Crime Commission in 1983 as an affiliate of organized crime, and his alleged association with organized crime figures, including three Black Book members, that formed the bases for the board's decision to nominate him.[9] Cusumano served two years of a four-year sentence, and was released from prison just three days prior to the board's hearing.[10]

Once the formal bases of his nomination were read into the proceedings, two board members engaged in a facetious discussion of the candidate. They contended that Cusumano had had contact with the law beginning at age 17, contact involving bookmaking, bribery, burglary, fencing, labor racketeering, and receiving stolen property,[11] but entered no evidence in support of those contentions. What followed was this dialogue:

MEMBER CUNNINGHAM:
> . . . I couldn't help noting, it took him 22 years to drop out of school in the 11th grade. I don't know that that had an effect on his subsequent social activities. But it's there to be noted.

CHAIRMAN BIBLE:
> He probably wasn't devoting his full time and attention to his studies.

MEMBER CUNNINGHAM:
> Possibly that's true.

CHAIRMAN BIBLE:
> At least that curriculum. (p. 585)

The vote to nominate Cusumano to the Black Book was unanimous, with William Bible and Gerald Cunningham the only board members in attendance.

Within six months, the Nevada Gaming Commission met to consider the board's nomination of Cusumano.[12] It was a meeting that illustrated how images of threat and of good and evil are created and maintained. The Las Vegas newspapers played a major role in creating the perception of the man in the proceedings that day. The newspapers had printed his photo, but their verbal images of him as someone who was "as cool and polished as a soap opera gigolo" and who "look[ed] and act[ed] like a wise guy" were painfully stereotypical.[13] They are the images commonly associated with the Italian male and, even more so, a member of the mafia, and they raise the question of the extent to which the press dramatizes issues and creates threat.

We had the occasion to attend the commission hearing that was held at the offices of the Gaming Control Board in Las Vegas, and were able to view the dynamics of the proceedings and the interaction among those who were involved. Inside the meeting room there was the appearance of a solemn and official proceeding. The furniture was arranged in a fashion similar to that in a courtroom. The commissioners (as judges) were seated at a long table in the front of the room, flanked by the United States and Nevada State flags. At two smaller tables to their right were Gaming Control Board members and deputies attorney general representing the state's case. To the left of the commissioners was the court stenographer. Between the table and the audience was a podium for those who were appearing before the commissioners. Perhaps the only items which stood out as somewhat atypical were two large video monitors. Members of the audience gave respect to the proceedings, most being attired in suits and ties regardless of the 105-degree weather. It was to be an all-day affair.

The monthly review of applications for licensing consumed most of the morning, and when the commission recessed briefly, we went outside toward the parking lot. Standing on the steps of the building were two well-tanned and smartly dressed men—one thin, average in height, immaculately groomed, and dressed in an Italian suit; the other tall, muscular, younger, with longer-length hair, dressed similarly, and talking on a cellular telephone. They faced the parking lot. A dark-colored Mercedes pulled in and a rather distinguished, slightly gray-haired man approached. Without actually knowing who these three men were, we surmised they might be the Black Book nominee, his "bodyguard," and his attorney.

We soon discovered that we had correctly identified two of the men. Indeed, the first was Joseph Vincent Cusumano, and the man driving the Mercedes was Oscar Goodman, his attorney. Once inside the meeting room, the men sat to the left of the commissioners. Goodman, obviously known to many in the room, joked and talked. Photographers approached and took pictures of them. These activities added to the appearance of a media production. Goodman, leaning over a massive set of documents—those in support of his client—said to a woman he apparently knew: "This will put Nevada on the books . . . [It's] a black day for Nevada." Again, apparently cognizant of a larger audience, we heard him go on to say: "There will be two separate votes today—one for Cusumano and one for Goodman." Several seated nearby laughed. The woman next to me leaned over and commented, "[This is] going to be the best show this month"—an interesting comment in light of the city's reputation as the entertainment capital of the world. Individuals returned to the room from the recess. The chairman of the commission, John O'Reilly, called the meeting back to order.

Cusumano's case began at 2:40 in the afternoon and ended only shortly before midnight. Those who remained until the end witnessed, in addition to the general manner of regulatory proceedings, the videotaped testimonies of two movie producers, Francis Ford Coppola and Barrie Osborne, in support of Cusumano's character and work in the motion picture industry. Unable to attend the hearing, Coppola was "finishing up the editing . . . of Godfather III."[14] One might query, Why a videotape rather than a sworn affidavit? Photographers, major motion picture figures, videotaped testimonies—these hearings had all the earmarks of a Las Vegas production.

Attorney Oscar Goodman had a theme that he pursued throughout the hearing. The theme was one of discrimination on the part of the regulators, in that they had selectively targeted Italian Americans for inclusion on the List of Excluded Persons. One of his statements in reference to the Italian-American background of those on the list is classic:

170

... when you look at the List of Excluded Persons ... you see that ... with the exception of a chunk of Hawaiians who went in there who throw the skew off, just about everybody in the book is Italian. Starting back with Marshal Caifano, Nick Civella, Corky Civella, Tom Dragna, Sam Giancana, Joe Sica—Tony [Spilotro] is not in the book anymore. He is dead. So that makes some people happy. One way to get out of it, I guess. The Vaccaros, husband and wife. And those poor Hawaiians who I can't figure out how they got in the book ... (p. 302)

The road to establishing discrimination (in regulatory terms, "selective prosecution") was paved with a 300-page document (p. 409) that had been part of the earlier Black Book case of Carl Wesley Thomas, a document that showed that persons who had felony records had been issued gaming licenses (pp. 204–215). Goodman argued that it was incongruous and selective for the regulators to allow convicted murderers, child molesters, drug users, rapists, bookmakers, and robbers to work in the gaming industry in a gaming capacity without objection (pp. 223, 420–435), but not allow someone with a "white collar conviction" into a casino (p. 234). One may question to what end Goodman discussed the Thomas exhibit at length. The information apparently accomplished little in the case of Thomas, and because it did not specify the ethnicity of those felons who were licensed, it would seem inadequate in addressing the thesis of ethnic discrimination in the case of Cusumano. Yet ultimately, the document served to illustrate that, while having a felony conviction is a basis for nomination to the Black Book, it is often overlooked when gaming licenses are issued.

Responding to Goodman's charge, Deputy Attorney General Neil Friedman affirmed that, on the basis of the federal appeals court ruling in the Thomas case (694 Federal Sup. 750), "selective prosecution" could be proved only if the board acted on an "unjustifiable standard such as race" (pp. 208–209). At the same time, Friedman was willing to stipulate that

... there are individuals with felony convictions who hold workcards ... But it is entirely irrelevant, as there are no other Joey Cusumanos except for the one presently here before you. They do not have Joey's reputation. They do not have Joey's convictions, and they do not have Joey's mob associations. (p. 211)

These initial issues having been presented and sides taken, Chairman O'Reilly suggested they proceed with the hearing. It was to have the semblance of legitimacy, with its order and decorum. Exhibits were entered into evidence and opening statements were made. And, for much of the time, the proceedings were to be conducted almost ritualistically, that is, until the actors appeared to have wearied at the end of the day.

The ritual—to maintain the legitimacy of the industry and the efficacy of its regulators—included the introduction of materials to establish the nominee's notorious reputation: 45 newspaper articles, editorials and opinions, and a novel, *On the Edge: The Life and Times of Francis Coppola*.[15] Goodman objected to these materials on the basis of hearsay (p. 242) and lack of foundation (p. 247), as well as sensationalism and editorialization (pp. 262–264). In return, the state's attorney maintained: (1) rules of evidence are not applicable to administrative hearings; (2) the Nevada Supreme Court had ruled that hearsay is admissible in such hearings (pp. 253, 261); (3) newspaper articles had been relied on in the past and were "probably the best evidence . . . of . . . Cusumano's reputation . . . in the community" (p. 261); and (4) the novel's descriptions of him as a guy who had Anthony Spilotro as a friend and as the "favorite gangster" of the cast and crew of *The Cotton Club* constituted additional support.[16]

The case against the entry of Cusumano was based on Goodman's contentions about his client: (1) that he had not been a criminal since age 17;[17] (2) that he was not an associate of organized crime (pp. 219–220); (3) that he had a legitimate career in motion pictures, one vouched for by notable motion picture producers (p. 298); and (4) that the regulators' selection of him for nomination constituted discrimination against Italian Americans (pp. 220–221). How could a man with a rap sheet that included only the failure to appear on a traffic warrant in 1980 and the federal conviction in 1987 (pp. 218, 300) be a career criminal? Indeed, why, when Cusumano had been under surveillance for 15 years, hadn't he acquired a more substantial official record (p. 369)? And, how could the state accept the statements of novelist William Roemer, author of a new novel on the mob (1989), and an undocumented chart of the structure of organized crime in Chicago even though it was part of the 1983 Chicago Crime Commission report (p. 257)? Friedman affirmed that acceptance of the chart

172

was possible because "being a government publication is itself authenticating . . . [The chart] . . . appears as though it has been in a Chicago Crime Commission crime report. It was accepted by the United States Senate. As a result, it's fairly reliable" (p. 259).

The large part of Goodman's case alleging the selective prosecution of Cusumano hinged on the testimony of two individuals who were said to be authoritative in regard to Italians and Italian Americans in southern Nevada. Dominic Gentile, a Las Vegas attorney extensively involved in national organizations for Italian-American lawyers, was first to testify regarding the ethnic composition of the Black Book. Goodman questioned him:

> . . . did you make any type of evaluation as to whether or not any of . . . [the names] were of Italian derivation?
>
> GENTILE:
> . . . Based upon . . . [the fact that] I have been an Italian longer than I have been a lawyer . . .
>
> Based upon my life experience, it appears to me that 13 of the 20 people that are in the book or have been in the book bear what are clearly known to me to be Italian surnames.
>
> GOODMAN:
> . . . do you have any opinion as to why there would be such an overwhelming . . . [percentage] of Italian entrants into the book as . . . [opposed to] white Anglo Saxon protestants?
>
> GENTILE:
> . . . I think there is evidence of an institutional bias . . .
>
> . . . it is just simply not believable to me that 13 out of 20 people could bear Italian surnames because while there are many people of Italian extraction that we are not particularly proud of that are genuinely bad guys . . . it is impossible for this book to have acquired . . . that high a percentage of Italian Americans without the focus having been on people of Italian American extraction. (pp. 312–313)

Under cross-examination by Deputy Attorney General Friedman, Gentile made light of Friedman's very deliberate approach. The exchange between the two men is humorous, to say the least.

> Q. . . . Mr. Gentile, I am going to go down the list of those people on the List of Excluded Persons and would you tell me, one, whether you know these individuals?
> Marshal Caifano?

A. The last time I saw Marshal Caifano I was 12 years old . . .

Q. In what capacity do you know him?

A. He used to eat at the same pizzaria that I did.

Q. Is that in Las Vegas?

A. No. It was in Chicago.

Q. And how is it you know—I am assuming that you are of the opinion he is Italian.

A. I know that he is Italian because . . . his nephew is a very good personal friend of mine.

Q. Do you know Carl Civella?

A. No, I never met Mr. Civella.

Q. . . . You are assuming from the name spelling that he is Italian.

A. That is correct.

Q. Do you know Louis Dragna?

A. No, I do not.

Q. So again, you are assuming from the spelling that he is probably Italian?

A. That is correct . . .

Q. . . . Joseph Sica, are you familiar with him?

A. No.

Q. Are you asserting that he has an Italian surname?

A. Well, I know a lot of people that have the surname Sica . . . and they are all Italian . . .

Q. Are you familiar with John Vaccaro?

A. Yes.

Q. In what capacity are you familiar with . . . [him]?

A. I have been . . . [his] lawyer for 10 years.

Q. And is it your knowledge that he is Italian?

A. Yes.

Q. On what do you base that?

A. Ten years of being his lawyer.

Q. Has he expressed to you he is Italian or are you saying that from an assumption?

A. I am saying it from observing his family, himself, his father. He's Italian . . .

Q. Has he ever told you he is Italian?

A. He hasn't needed to . . .

Q. Are you familiar with Chris Petti?

A. I have met Mr. Petti.

Q. Do you know of your own personal knowledge that he is Italian?

A. No, I don't . . .

Q. Are you familiar with Mike Rizzitello?

174

A. I don't think I have ever met Mr. Rizzitello.
Q. So you have no personal knowledge that he is in fact Italian?
A. Nothing other than the spelling of his surname . . .
Q. Are you familiar with Frank Masterana?
A. No, I am not.
Q. Are you assuming that he is Italian?
A. Yes, I am.
Q. On what basis?
A. By the spelling of his surname . . .
Q. And do you know Gaspare Speciale?
A. Yes.
Q. And are you personally familiar with . . . [him]?
A. Yes.
Q. In what capacity . . . ?
A. . . . [He] eats in my restaurant.
Q. And is it your opinion that . . . [he] is Italian?
A. Yes, it is.
Q. And what leads you to believe that?
A. Because he likes to eat spaghetti.
Q. That seems stereotypical . . .
A. I know of his Italian heritage the same way as I know of the Italian heritage of all of those other people that have Italian surnames. I was not there when they were born or conceived. (pp. 316–324)

Friedman had proceeded in methodical fashion to name each and every one listed in the Black Book and, by way of concluding with Gentile, said: "Thank you, Mr. Gentile. Let me count this up. Out of the 16 people presently on the List of Excluded Persons there . . . [are] 14 . . . [who] you have no personal knowledge as Italian; isn't that correct?" (p. 324). These regulatory proceedings had the appearance of maintaining the proper protocol of questioning witnesses but, as this dialogue suggests, in the absence of anything of substance.

Goodman's second expert witness was Professor Alan Balboni, whose recent research focused on Italian Americans in southern Nevada (pp. 340–341). According to Balboni, Italian Americans constituted less than 10 percent of the state's population (p. 342) and less than 5.5 percent of the nation's population, which made it "extraordinary" that "60 to 70 percent of the Black Book entries . . . [had] Italian surnames" (p. 346). When asked to explain this extraordinary finding, Balboni credited popular

175

opinion, newspapers repeating information, and certain "mythic proportions that the Mafia has assumed" (p. 347).

Nevertheless, the state was unwilling to concede that these surnames were indeed Italian, even though they had been identified as common Italian names by Gentile and Balboni, who were qualified to make such determinations, as most intelligent people are. The state's deputy attorney general even suggested that the Black Book members could be subpoenaed to answer to the commissioners whether or not they were Italian (p. 344). The humor of his statement was met by laughs from several spectators. Yet, the scene was more than humorous; it was ludicrous. In all fairness to the regulators, we wondered if some of the nominees had indeed changed their names. Then we were struck by the unlikelihood that few persons born with names such as David Jones would change them to Anthony Rizzitello or Frank Masterana, although as diehard positivists, we do not completely rule out even this remote possibility on the part of nominees to the Black Book.

The audience appeared to relax amid the entertainment provided by the videotaped statements next entered into the record. Francis Ford Coppola was full of praise for Cusumano for how during the production of *The Cotton Club* he was able to bring the movie to its conclusion. Coppola admitted that he had been "aware of . . . [Cusumano's] reputation" initially, but that Joey had brought "harmonious resolve to situations" on the set, and that he had grown to "admire [Cusumano] very much." In bright, dazzling color, Coppola announced to the entire hearing room that he was "unhesitatingly in . . . [Cusumano's] praise." No other Black Book nominee had had an entrepreneur of this notoriety formally enter accolades into the record. Then, Goodman read the letter of Michael Daly, a contributing editor of *New York Magazine,* wherein the editor admitted that Cusumano was his friend, and that he hoped this admission wouldn't mean he himself would be banned from casinos in Las Vegas (p. 364). Finally, Barrie Osborne, executive producer of *Dick Tracy,* again by means of videotape, credited Cusumano with "salvaging the situation" on the set of *The Cotton Club,* having a "charismatic personality," and being a man of his word.

What happened to the proceedings as the evening wore on? Tempers began to flare, the facade of the ritual began to fray, and other obligations took precedence. One of the commissioners, William Curran, had another commitment for that evening. The following is the dialogue that transpired prior to Curran's recess:

CHAIRMAN O'REILLY:
. . . Commissioner Curran has a commitment about seven o'clock.

MR. GOODMAN:
For the rest of the evening, may I ask?

CHAIRMAN O'REILLY:
It would probably take about an hour to an hour and a half.

COMMISSIONER CURRAN:
Four innings . . . About two hours, I would think.

CHAIRMAN O'REILLY:
Two hours?

MR. GOODMAN:
As I say, I think we can wind this . . . [testimony] up at . . . 7:30. But if you have a prior commitment, I can understand that and we can come back . . .

CHAIRMAN O'REILLY:
Let's press on . . .

COMMISSIONER CURRAN:
I want to swear him. I want to swear him, and I want you to know who you answer to and it's not me. It's my son who is playing in a Little League championship game at seven o'clock.

MR. GOODMAN:
Well, if you want to . . . we can come back tomorrow morning, and I am serious. I wouldn't want you to miss a Little League championship game. (pp. 370–371)

The entire episode raises the question of the importance that such proceedings hold for certain of the regulators. Curran's priorities were obviously to his family, rather than to the hearings that involved the life chances of Cusumano. Thus, the hearings were in recess from 7:24 to 9:39 P.M. (pp. 406–407).

Cusumano's current employer, Jerry Shafer, owner of International Video Communications, was called to testify regarding the line production responsibilities the nominee performed for him and the necessity of his being inside casinos for the filming of some of the productions (pp. 372–379). One of those productions was a video of a "lingerie party" by the girls of Crazy Horse II (*sic*), a topless bar in Las Vegas. Chairman O'Reilly asked Goodman if he intended to show that to the audience, and Goodman responded: "After Commissioner Curran leaves for the [Little League] softball game" (p. 379).

The closing statements had less flair and drama than what had occurred earlier. Nevertheless, at 10:44 in the evening, Deputy Attorney General Friedman warned, in words that could have been excerpted from a movie or a novel about the mafia:

> Time is of the essence. As a result of Spilotro's premature demise there now is a void in the control of the Chicago Mob's business ventures here in Las Vegas. As the evidence shows, Joey Cusumano had been groomed to step in and fill Spilotro's shoes as the overseer of Chicago's interests in Nevada.
>
> Cusumano has proven himself to the boys in Chicago that he can be trusted . . . (p. 452)

Finally, Friedman maintained that selective prosecution of Cusumano, a man who was "tailormade" for the Black Book, could be illustrated only if the actual percentage of organized crime associates who were Italian was known and compared with the percentage of those in the Black Book who were Italian (pp. 454–455). On the other hand, Goodman argued that Joey was a gentleman, decent, and honest, and that to put him in the Black Book was to do "harm to society," because he had a valuable contribution to make (pp. 461–462).

The vote to enter Joseph Vincent Cusumano to the List of Excluded Persons was, of course, unanimous. And although Goodman asked that the entry be stayed pending judicial review, and that Cusumano be allowed to enter casinos in the interim if only on a professional basis, the stay was denied (p. 484). At a few minutes before midnight on June 21, 1990, the Black Book gained another member. The ritual had ended. The show was over.

Cusumano was not out of the headlines for long, however. In three months, his request that the conditions of his parole be changed so that he could travel out of state to make a documentary series was captured in the local newspapers.[18] Within four months' time, he was the victim of an attempted murder. Upon entering his garage, Cusumano was shot three times in the left shoulder by two men wearing ski masks. He managed to activate the garage door opener, drive away in his Mercedes Benz convertible, and admit himself to a local hospital emergency room. The attempt was described as a possible mob hit,[19] and whether it was or not, it again served to confirm in the minds of the public and the regulators his associations with organized crime. Next, he was in court claiming that a local attorney had failed in his promise to split his cut from a multi-million-dollar legal judgment, a split that amounted to $1.7 million.[20] And, in November of 1992, Cusumano married for the fifth time. He remains a colorful individual, and one not likely to "lay down and play dead," as he once said. Could this really have been Spilotro's replacement?

10

Contemporary Moral Crises

When Nevada gaming entered the decade of the 1990s, it faced yet two additional crises. They both involved allegations of corruption that were of scandalous proportions. One raised questions about the integrity of the state's race and sports books, and the other questioned the legitimacy of the regulation of gaming itself. In each instance, grave concerns were raised about the morality of the industry and its corrupting influences on legitimate institutions. Because there was widespread publicity given to the problems, there also developed deep concerns about the problems' effects on the reputation of gaming.

The more serious of the problems centered around the board's acting chief of Special Investigations and Intelligence and one of his agents' allowing an illegal bookmaker to operate in Las Vegas in return for intelligence information. Both the agents and the bookmaker contended that the activity had been carried out with the consent of the board chairman. The chairman denied the allegations, however, and the agents were forced to resign. Various state efforts to investigate and resolve the matter were protracted over a period of almost three years and received considerable publicity. Because the affair did not result in indictments of the agents, and the illegal bookmaker pled to a minor state tax violation just prior to the scheduled criminal trial for the activities, further doubt was cast on the efficacy and integrity of the state regulators.[1] It was, to quote a Las Vegas editorialist, a "fiasco" that would leave many questions unanswered regarding the role of the board in the undercover operation.[2]

180

Compounding this problem was a crisis that erupted almost concurrently in the area of collegiate athletics. The University of Nevada, Las Vegas, men's basketball program became linked to a reputed sports fixer, Richard Perry. Rumors of the association had circulated for more than two years, then, shortly after the national champions lost to Duke in the final game of the 1991 NCAA tournament, the rumors erupted into a national scandal when photos of Perry with three of the players appeared on the front page of a Las Vegas newspaper. Although Perry had been in Las Vegas for several years, was known to have been a convicted sports fixer, had been in contact with the players as early as 1989, and local editorialists had called for his exclusion from Nevada gaming, it was not until his ties with the team received widespread national publicity following the publication of the photos that the state moved to enter him into the Black Book.

REGULATORY CORRUPTION

The problem of regulatory corruption surfaced during federal congressional hearings into a mid-1980s' failed undercover bookmaking operation dubbed Project Layoff, in which the bookmaker involved in the present 1990s crisis, Matis Marcus, was said to have been a lead operative for the United States Internal Revenue Service. Operated from a Las Vegas storefront by two IRS undercover agents, the project was a highly successful bookmaking operation, taking in more than $22 million in bets, but a highly *un*successful undercover operation, costing taxpayers almost $600,000 without any significant prosecutions, and having to be abruptly shut down following threats on the agents' lives.[3] It was said that during the hearings a Nevada representative spoke of Marcus' illegal bookmaking operation, and board chairman Bill Bible asked his acting chief of Special Investigations and Intelligence, Ron Hollis, to look into the matter. Hollis then allegedly staged a phony raid on the operation on June 3, 1990, and, according to Bible, "tricked" the board chairman into putting out a false news release about the incident.[4] The news release said that, following a month-long investigation, agents had arrested six people, including Marcus, and seized the equipment and records of an illegal bookmaking operation which took in a million dollars a week in wagers on horse racing and sporting events.

181

Hollis was quoted as saying, "It turned out to be a bigger operation than I anticipated . . . They had 11 phone lines, plus three toll-free 800 numbers . . ."[5]

Bible said that he became suspicious about the raid when he learned that no money had been confiscated, and none of the arrested men were booked into jail; two of the men turned out to be his own undercover agents. It was later learned that the illegal bookmaking operation had been in business under the sanction of the board's Special Investigations and Intelligence Division since January 1, 1987.[6] Marcus, or Fat Mat as he was called, was described in the newspapers as "a fast talker who had gambled away his place in society in seedy bookie joints from coast to coast. A law school dropout, . . . [he was said to be] a scammer and a braggart with an ego as big as his 300-pound frame." It was said that "if you listened [to him] long enough . . . , sooner or later you'd believe him," and that "everyone who has had dealings with him . . . [has] been stung and . . . [has] come to regret it." Black Book inductee Frank Masterana was no exception. After reportedly bankrolling a soon-to-be-found-out San Diego bookmaking operation of Marcus', Masterana said that Marcus turned him over to authorities in order to save himself. Masterana was quoted as saying of his partner in the brief venture that "he's probably as low a human being as you can get."[7]

Consistent with his image, Marcus was able to get the backing for his Las Vegas operation from an unassuming Las Vegas maître d', Daniel Murphy, whom he befriended at a local AA meeting and who just happened to have a $30,000 inheritance. They became partners in what must have looked to them like an opportunity of a lifetime: "a [state] sanctioned illegal bookmaking operation."[8] And it was said that the way they ran their operation was indicative of the protection they must have enjoyed. Marcus reportedly even advertised, handing out business cards and openly greeting those whom he would meet with a "Hey, how ya doin'? We're bookin' all the games."[9] He and his partner also were said to be soft on "welchers," not seeming to care if they did not pay, as though the two were simply playing with other people's money. An employee of Murphy's said, "If you didn't pay Dan Murphy–the–bookmaker, after two weeks he wouldn't take your bets anymore."[10]

For a while some at the Gaming Control Board seemed to

Matis Marcus. Marcus was an acknowledged informant for agents of the Special Investigations and Intelligence Division of the Nevada Gaming Control Board, a role which he was believed to have also performed for the FBI and IRS. In exchange for being allowed to operate an unlicensed sports book in Las Vegas, he provided gaming authorities with information about other illegal bookmaking. When his involvement with the Board became public, it created a major crisis of confidence in the regulation of Nevada gaming. Although recommended for the Black Book by the state's attorney general, Marcus ultimately left the state and was never entered. Courtesy *Las Vegas Sun*.

justify the Special Investigations and Intelligence Division's relationship with Marcus. The papers reported that sources there had indicated that his information had led to the shutdown of a multi-million-dollar illegal gambling operation only six months earlier.[11] Giving further reason to condone the arrangement, the press reported that this earlier operation had been backed by

Buffalo mob interests that were currently under investigation by federal authorities in Las Vegas. An attorney representing several of the men arrested in that raid took issue with this depiction however, contending that the links of the bookmaking operation with Buffalo mobsters were "part of the disinformation campaign being conducted by disgruntled agents of the Gaming Control Board."[12]

If this justification was unacceptable, yet another was offered by the press itself. Hollis, a dedicated 10-year veteran agent, was seen as doing what he had to do in light of his understaffed and underfunded office. The very nature of the work was said to require going "inside." One Las Vegas editorialist said: "When the subjects of the intelligence search are illegal bookmaking and organized crime, then the inside means dealing with the likes of Fat Mat." It was said that Hollis' mistake was that he hadn't obtained written approval and, therefore, could be set adrift when the operation failed.[13]

Said to be concerned for his safety, Marcus quickly left Las Vegas and, according to newspaper sources, sought admittance to the federal witness protection program. Obviously not as fearful as at first believed, he was soon after reported to be running a wide-open illegal bookmaking operation back East, again, it was thought, with the protection of law enforcement. In the meantime back in Nevada, documents related to his operation and undercover relationship with the Special Investigations and Intelligence Division became public, complete with reimbursement vouchers and receipts for his expenses paid by the board. Reportedly, the documents had been circulated among the offices of the Gaming Control Board over the two-and-a-half-year period of the operation, which raised further questions of the board's knowledge and involvement in the affair.[14] Not only was Bible's role in the matter questioned, but eventually so was that of previous board members, including the other two board chairmen under whom Hollis had served during the span of Marcus' operation— Barton Jacka and Michael Rumbolz.[15]

Adding to the already scandalous situation was a document produced by Marcus himself. While Hollis may not have been a very good bureaucrat when it came to leaving a paper trail, his bookmaker informant was. Two days before the phony raid, Marcus prepared a notarized statement that Bible, with the endorsement of the FBI and Nevada gaming agents, had himself decided to stage the raid. He said that the decision was made after the FBI had been tipped off about illegal phone-betting services in Las Vegas and after a call from local news columnist Jeff German to Bible informing him of Marcus' operation. Marcus further contended that his sports book was operating with the sanction of not only the FBI and Nevada Gaming Control Board but also the criminal investigation division of the United States Internal Revenue Service and the Las Vegas Metropolitan Police Department. He said, "I have cooperated completely with the above mentioned agencies in preparing for this staged mock raid and arrest, and have provided them with information, inaccessible to them otherwise, without which a real raid and arrest would have been impossible to perform."[16] Unidentified gaming sources confirmed part of Marcus' allegations with their contention that the board chairman was given advanced details of the staged raid and participated in the cover-up. Backed by fellow board members, Bible denied the allegations, contending that he thought it was a legitimate raid at the time.[17]

When the state attorney general's investigation into the Marcus affair was just getting started, additional concerns began to surface. First there was the concern that Marcus might have used his relationship with gaming agents to put his competition out of business; he reportedly had supplied the agents with information that resulted in busts of rival sports books. Then there was the suggestion that he was being bankrolled by the government and that "hundreds of thousands of dollars" had been lost and a couple of agents almost killed in the process.[18]

However, it was allegations of the board chairman's involvement in planning and covering up the raid that continued to loom like a dark cloud over the integrity of Nevada gaming. Concerned that the investigation into the matter was "hampering the daily operation of gaming control," the governor urged the attorney general to resolve the matter.[19] Newspaper editorials likewise called for a more intensive investigation, and columnist Jeff German, who had reportedly informed Bible of Marcus' bookmaking operation, called for the "stingman's" entry into the Black Book.[20] District court judge Earle White, Jr., who had signed the search warrant affidavit for what he reportedly thought was a legitimate raid, also urged investigation of the issue by the district attorney as well as the attorney general, and requested that the matter be turned over to a grand jury.[21] But the investigations seemed to drag on according to many observers, including editorialist German, who wrote:

> Back in the late 1970's, Nevada underwent a serious credibility problem . . . a series of startling disclosures in FBI wiretaps . . . revealed that top Midwestern Mafia bosses had been wielding hidden influence at several of the biggest casinos on the Strip . . . eventually, with the help of the federal government, the mob was forced out . . . and Nevada restored its integrity.
>
> Today . . . the state faces another gaming crisis, and some are suggesting it is moving too slow to clean up its image . . . Unless the attorney general acts soon, the federal government again may be forced to do the state's job . . .[22]

Regardless of the calls for an accelerated investigation, it was 16 months before the grand jury looked into the Marcus affair.[23] At that time, the attorney general's office determined whether to indict the agents and Marcus and his partner for running an unlicensed sports book and failing to pay state gaming taxes.[24] Hollis contended that he was being used as a scapegoat, as a "sacrifice on the altar of Nevada politics," to protect the board's chairman, Bill Bible.[25] The acting chief held that Bible had asked him about Marcus a year before they had staged the phony raid and that he had told Bible about the undercover arrangement, including the agreement not to investigate Marcus' activities as long as he was supplying information. He contended further that Bible had been involved in the planning and cover-up of the raid, and that he had even joked in a meeting with Hollis and the agent that "if we pulled it off, we ought to get an Academy Award" (p. 4A). Bible denied the claims, saying that the conversations never occurred and that the operation was without the board's knowledge. The other board members and two former chairmen came to his support.[26]

The agents were never indicted but, almost two years after the raid, the bookies were. Then just two days before his scheduled trial almost a year later, Marcus pled to a charge of conspiracy to evade state taxes; soon after, the charge against his partner was dismissed. Marcus was required to pay a $1,000 fine and was sentenced to two years' probation, during which time he was to stay out of the state's gaming establishments.[27] There was also the suggestion that he might be nominated to the Black Book. "I assisted the state in putting other people in the Black Book," he said to the idea. "What would they do, put me in . . . for that?"[28] But, in an unprecedented action on March 30, 1993, the attorney general indeed called for Marcus' entry into the Black Book and moved to prepare the presentation of the case to the board following sentencing. Of the proposed nomination, Marcus said, "It makes more sense to nominate Chairman Bible for the entry into the Black Book than it does me."[29]

As recently as June 1993, the board chairman indicated that he has no plans to nominate Marcus, and the attorney general's office seems to have reversed ground, issuing a statement that the matter might be reconsidered if Marcus moves back to Nevada or fails to complete his probation successfully.[30] As of this writing, Marcus has not returned to the state, and Bible remains chairman of the Nevada Gaming Control Board.

PERRY AND THE RUNNIN' REBELS

Adding to the crisis of confidence in the regulation of gaming in the early 1990s was a problem that developed almost simultaneously at the University of Nevada, Las Vegas. The university's already highly controversial men's basketball program received widespread publicity over alleged ties with a convicted sports fixer. The affair once again focused national attention on crime and corruption in Las Vegas. Concerns quickly followed about the effects that this might have on public confidence in gaming and in particular on the perceived legitimacy of the sports and race books. Others wondered what it might mean for the reputation of the university, which gave the city at least a modicum of respectability.

It is evident throughout this work that the reputation of Nevada gambling is a paramount concern of the state. Maintaining an image of a legitimate and tightly regulated industry is viewed an essential to the state's economic well-being. However, even under the best of circumstances, this has been a difficult task. The far-reaching public association of the industry with organized crime and the plethora of vices thought to be connected with it mitigate against such efforts. The job becomes all the more difficult in a place where there are thought to be few conventional organizations to buttress a legitimate reputation. Las Vegas, more than any other part of the state, seems to be faced with this problem. Although it struggles for legitimacy, claiming to be among American cities with the highest number of churches per capita and recently marketing its gaming industry as family entertainment, it remains in the minds of many a place without conventional institutions and the traditions that accompany them. Rather, it continues to be viewed as a city of vice, a place where the pursuit of hedonistic pleasures is the driving force of social life.

Thus, the prevailing legitimate institutions, whatever they may be, become exceedingly important to Las Vegas and its gaming industry. One sees almost a starvation for something cultural, for some kind of traditions to hold on to. Indicative are the new housing developments which advertise that they are family communities and the many groups struggling to organize civic activities. At the hub of this group struggle is southern Nevada's only four-year institution of higher education, the University of Nevada, Las Vegas (UNLV). Most of the city's cultural activities are held at the university, making it the center of alternative community life (alternative to gambling, that is). This is no more evident than in the area of athletics, especially in regard to the university's men's basketball team, the UNLV Runnin' Rebels. One of the most winning teams in the nation in recent years, the Rebels won the NCAA championship in 1990 and were well on their way to winning it again when allegations of their connections with a sports fixer were rumored in 1991.

The success of the UNLV basketball program has brought considerable notoriety to the university. The team's national identification with Las Vegas has also meant that it has become a major source of civic pride. So, as with a particular gaming activity, when things go wrong with the Rebels, it is believed to reflect on the entirety of Las Vegas. It could have been predicted, then, that when a picture of three of the team's players in a hot tub with a reputed sports fixer appeared in a local newspaper, it would result in local hysteria over what it would mean not only for the image of the university and its athletic program but for the city and gaming as well. A national magazine described it as "a grappling over the very soul of a city long presumed to have sold it off."[31] There were rumors of point shaving and federal investigations into the matter, accusations of political witch hunts and counterclaims that critics of the basketball program had been physically threatened. The goings on in an assistant coach's training class were surreptitiously videotaped, coaches were said to be forced to resign, and, most important from the standpoint of this work, people were consequently put in the Black Book. These were some of the problems that surrounded Richard "the Fixer" Perry's entry into Nevada's List of Excluded Persons.

Born in Brooklyn of Jewish background, Perry, a former youth basketball coach himself, was said by some to have had a genuine interest in helping athletes. Also a professional gambler, he was said to be an astute bettor with an impressive intellect and mathematical skills. But Perry was said to be best known as a mob bookmaker with ties to New York's Lucchese crime family. Having been convicted of horse race fixing in New York in 1974 and again in a point shaving scandal at Boston College during the 1978–1979 season, he was said to have a special aptitude for corrupting harness drivers and college basketball players.[32]

There had been a concern about Perry's involvement with the UNLV basketball program as early as April 1989. It was then that *Time* magazine reported that in October 1988 he had met for a poolside lunch at Caesars Palace with two of the players and had given them money. The players were said to have known Perry as a former coach who went by the name of Sam Perry; one of them had formerly played on Perry's summer league team in New York City.[33]

Head coach Jerry Tarkanian, like the players, contended that he knew Perry as Sam Perry. Many doubted this, however, pointing to what they considered to be information to the contrary. Some of this contradictory information was itself unconvincing. One editorialist implied that the coach must have known Perry's true identity, since Perry was reported to have been wearing a shirt with RP monogrammed on it when he once met with the coach several years earlier.[34]

Then in February 1991, Las Vegas newspaper editorials rehashed the *Time* article and reported that Perry was seen at several Rebel games.[35] It was later suggested that one time during the 1986–1987 season he had used tickets that had been authorized by coach Tarkanian.[36] The editorials chided that the players should not be permitted to associate with Perry. They also accurately predicted that Perry's presence could cost the coach his job and suggested that Perry was a good candidate for the Black Book. The coach adamantly denied that Perry had any association with UNLV or that any of his players were aware of Perry's reputation as a sports fixer. Tarkanian also contended that his signature was forged on the document authorizing tickets for "Sam Perry." The concerns nevertheless intensified when the undefeated and heavily favored Rebels lost to Duke in the final game of the 1991 NCAA championship tournament.

However, it was not until photos of Perry and three of the players sharing a hot tub and playing basketball at Perry's home appeared on the front page of the *Las Vegas Review Journal* on May 26, 1991, that a national scandal erupted. Among the many questions raised by the photos was, of course, who had given them to the press. Tarkanian accused the interim athletics director, who he believed was at the center of an administrative conspiracy to get rid of him.[37] It was eventually learned, however, that the press had obtained the photos from a man who was said to be a friend of Perry's wife. Employed as a landscaper and stonemason, the man had reportedly been hired to design a driveway for Perry and, in the course of the work, had become involved with Perry's wife, who gave him the photos.[38]

Following the appearance of the photos, the team's coach resigned, and Perry was banned from entering the casinos of Mirage Resorts, Inc., the parent company of the Mirage and Golden Nugget hotels and casinos, and eventually from Caesars Palace and Harvey's at Lake Tahoe.[39] Rumors circulated of a federal investigation into point shaving when an organized crime task force subpoenaed documents thought to be part of the university's probe into Perry's involvement with the basketball program. Although the Department of Justice denied in a letter to the Nevada regents that it was conducting such an investigation, the suspicions continued.[40] Newspaper editorials argued that the federal authorities did not deny that they had asked whether points might have been shaved or that they had subpoenaed information from the university about Perry and the players. The Justice Department's denial of an investigation was a matter of semantics, they said; ". . . to the bureaucrats, asking questions does not constitute a formal investigation."[41]

Then the papers reported that Perry would be nominated to the Black Book. The nomination was officially based on an alleged notorious and unsavory reputation in regard to gaming and on his 1974 and 1984 convictions for fixing harness races in New York State and conspiring to bribe a Boston College basketball player. Of particular concern was the effect that his presence would have on public trust and confidence in Nevada gaming, especially regarding the race and sports books. As evidence of his reputation, the regulators pointed to the numerous newspaper and magazine articles chronicling his alleged involvement with the UNLV basketball program, and mention of his activities in the reports of the President's Commission on Organized Crime.[42]

Said to be out of the country on vacation at the time of the board's action, Perry could not be found for notification of his nomination. Failing to serve notice to him personally or by certified mail, the state sought to inform him by public notice in the Las Vegas and Reno newspapers. Although his attorney, Oscar Goodman, had indicated earlier that they would fight the inclusion, Perry declined to appeal the nomination, partly out of his concern, it was said, that the players would be further drawn into the matter.[43] Instead they considered challenging the constitutionality of the law by Perry's paying a visit to a casino and subjecting himself to arrest. The law has never been challenged in this respect, and, Goodman argued, "It would never pass constitutional muster if challenged criminally."[44]

In the absence of an appeal, the commission proceeded to meet on its own on October 27 and 28, 1992, to hear the board's arguments for entering Perry into the Black Book. During the hearing the state's deputy attorney general for gaming, James Rankl, explained that Perry had had a leading role in a conspiracy to fix superfecta races at the Yonkers and Roosevelt harness tracks in New York. It was said that he had conspired with others to bribe drivers to keep their horses from winning and then bet on combinations of other competing entries. Emphasizing the gravity of the nominee's threat, the deputy attorney general pointed to a statement in the parole and probation report for the offense that said Perry was an addicted gambler whose behavior required "companionship with criminally oriented individuals,"[45] an ironic concern in the context of an industry that thrives on "addicted gamblers."

Richard Perry. Richard "the Fixer" Perry was seen as threatening the image of Las Vegas as free from corruption when a photograph of him in a hot-tub with UNLV basketball players was brought to national attention. He is said to be pictured here at a party in honor of attorney Oscar Goodman at the Desert Inn a few months earlier. The black-tie affair was attended by an estimated 1,000 guests from the casino industry, the news media, the entertainment industry, and reputed organized crime. Courtesy *Las Vegas Review Journal*.

The deputy attorney general also reviewed the events surrounding Perry's involvement in the Boston College point shaving scandal. It was said that he and his associates had bribed players to shave points in order to affect the point spread in the outcomes of the games (p. 288). Excerpts introduced from a report given in the President's Commission on Organized Crime suggested that the conspiracy to bribe the players had been orchestrated by members of the Lucchese crime family with the advice of Perry (pp. 290–293). References to the incident in the printed media were also introduced. Identifying Perry as a "business partner" in the caper, an article authored in part by co-conspirator and friend Henry Hill in *Sports Illustrated* told of how the group contacted and bribed the players to fix the games, and then placed the bets in a manner that would not reveal that the group had inside information.[46] Excerpts from Nicholas Pileggi's *Wiseguy* (1986), on which the movie *Goodfellas* was based, was also said to have identified Perry's involvement in sports fixing and to have described how the Yonkers and Roosevelt harness races were fixed.[47]

To establish Perry's notorious and unsavory reputation further, numerous additional newspaper and magazine articles were also introduced (pp. 298–305). It was said that a computer search using Perry's name had generated a 121-page document consisting of 261 stories in all. A large number were AP and UPI news service releases that repeated the stories of his alleged involvement with the UNLV basketball program and prior sports fixing activities and the subsequent resignation of the coach. These releases had appeared in virtually all the major national newspapers, including the *New York Times*, *Los Angeles Times*, *Chicago Tribune*, *Washington Post*, and *Boston Globe*, and in some foreign papers as well. That these same stories had originally brought to public attention Perry's involvement with the players and called for his entry into the Black Book, exemplifies the self-fulfilling effects of media accounts in the creation of public concern with the problem and then the use of those same accounts to substantiate the extent of the problem. It accordingly raises questions of the use of such accounts as a basis for establishing a notorious and unsavory reputation.

It is not surprising that the state concluded that Perry is precisely the type of individual who should be excluded from race and sports books in Nevada. Should he become involved in another such scandal, the commission argued, it would receive publicity equal to that in the UNLV case. The commissioners agreed unanimously in their move to enter Perry into the Black Book. Three years later, as this book goes to press, Perry has not yet tested the constitutionality of the criminal aspect of the law.

11

Return to Morality

In the early 1990s, the Gaming Control Board's credibility was called into question, and the integrity of Las Vegas' major institution of higher education was damaged by adverse publicity. The state and the city were suffering from a lack of public confidence. It thus greatly behooved the regulators to do whatever they could to renew the gaming industry's image of integrity and morality. In the process, they nominated a number of additional persons to the Black Book. Those who were chosen to be banned from the industry were, again, easy targets: those who were visible and engaged in relatively small-time criminal activities. They included a number of persons who cheated at gambling and others who were seen as linked to the nefarious and notorious Chicago mob, as well as to New England mobs, which were relatively new to the streets of Las Vegas.

GAMBLING CHEATS

Douglas Joseph Barr, Jr.

When the regulators entered the new decade, they continued to focus their efforts on the industry problem of slot cheats. Thus, in 1990, Douglas Joseph Barr, Jr., a second-generation slot cheat and repeat felon in cheating at gambling, was nominated and entered into the Black Book. Scheduled for parole within a few months, Barr was serving time in a Nevada state prison for the manufacture of a cheating device when his case was acted upon.[1] Although he had retained counsel sometime following his nomination, it goes without saying that he was not present at the hearings (p. 557).

The board saw Barr as an appropriate candidate because his record included three gaming convictions, all related to cheating at slot machines (pp. 560–562). The convictions were for conspiracy to cheat at gaming, conspiracy to manufacture a cheating device, and manufacturing a cheating device. In addition, he had been arrested 16 times since he was released from prison in 1984, had worked in several casinos, and was said to have "used slot cheating as a way of support because it was the only thing that he knew."[2] His record's inclusion of violations related to controlled substances was seen by at least one board member as a related motivation for the cheating and as further reason that he should be entered into the Black Book (p. 878).

Barr was said to have admitted to manufacturing and cheating with slugs and "top joints," and was thought to be a major source of their supply in the state.[3] Needless to say, the regulators were very curious about his operation, especially regarding the top joint, which is used to affect the circuitry of electronic machines. A board member knowledgeable of the device explained:

> . . . it looks sort of like a big comma . . . [cut out of steel] and they insert it down in the coin acceptor . . . and they make contact . . . then they insert a bottom joint which is a wire . . . [Then] they get up and they rub the contacts where I think they are called wipers . . . With the creation of the contact at the top in the coin acceptor, and then the activation of the crossing of the contacts down where the wipers run, it will cause the machine to pay out . . . (pp. 562–563)

There was a concern among the board members that Barr's entry into the Black Book would not preclude his going into restricted locations, places that have only slot machines. Such places constitute a large and growing segment of the industry, and, as we've discussed, include airports, supermarkets, convenience stores, bars, restaurants, laundromats, and even car washes. The courts have held that to restrict accessibility to such services is a violation of individual rights. The regulatory mechanism's inability to prevent slot cheats from entering restricted locations has, however, raised questions of its efficacy in controlling their threat to the industry. The concern has led to consideration of expanding the Black Book exclusion to 24-hour tavern locations, where, the argument is made, there is no necessity of the individual's presence. With no such restrictions at this time, the regulators seem to resolve the dilemma with the hope that the notoriety surrounding the entry of such individuals as Barr will at least alert restricted locations of their threat.[4]

Some of the commissioners also expressed concern about proceeding with Barr's entry while he was still in prison. The deputies attorney general held that he had been properly notified, however, and that he probably could have appeared at the hearing had he chosen to do so. Because he would soon be eligible for parole and again present a threat to the industry, the state felt it was important to act now.[5] With no apparent further concerns, the commission voted unanimously to enter Barr into the Black Book. Three years later, his father, Douglas William Barr, the self-acclaimed world's greatest gambling cheater, received yet another dubious distinction when he too was nominated to occupy a page alongside his son in the same book of infamous gamblers.[6]

Timothy John Childs

Only a month after Douglas Joseph Barr, Jr., was nominated to the Black Book, another alleged slot cheat was nominated. He was Timothy John Childs, a man who boasted of making $4,000–$5,000 a month cheating the machines, usually by "handle popping." The method, most often applied to older mechanical machines, involves pulling the handle down only part of the way until the payoff symbols are aligned, and then giving it a jerk in an effort to stop the reels from spinning farther.[7]

Also incarcerated at the time of his nomination and entry, Childs, like Barr, was said to have a long history of criminal activity, including numerous violations of gaming laws, and additionally to be a person of notorious and unsavory reputation.[8] As an adult, he had been arrested 36 times for alleged offenses related to burglary, grand larceny, and cheating at gambling. His record of pertinent convictions dated back to 1975 and included attempted grand larceny, felony slot cheating, felony attempted cheating at gambling, felony cheating at gambling, cheating at gambling, and burglary, offenses for which he had received sentences totaling 21 years in prison. He had been arrested for gaming violations six times in the 15 months prior to his nomination, and just the day before his nomination was convicted of several offenses relating to slot cheating, with charges pending for two additional alleged violations.

Not surprisingly, the board saw Childs as "a career offender and accomplished slot cheat who . . . [could] not be rehabilitated" (p. 698), and there was the hope that he might eventually be adjudicated as such. Noting in the investigative report that Childs was repeatedly arrested even when on probation for cheating, the board's chairman, Bill Bible, was moved to comment that ". . . the only time he is not cheating slot machines is when he is in jail" (p. 692). Observing that the nominee had even identified his occupation as a slot cheat on an automobile loan application, the chairman commented further, "This individual *belongs* in the Black Book" (emphasis added). The other board members concurred, unanimously nominating Childs to the state's List of Excluded Persons.

When his case went before the commission, it was handled in a perfunctory manner, with almost no discussion of the nominee himself.[9] The state's deputy attorney general simply noted that, since the initial bill of particulars had been drawn up, the nominee had been convicted of two additional felony gaming violations: attempted fraudulent slot machine manipulation and slot machine manipulation (p. 210), presumably the charges that were pending at the time of his nomination. He also noted that Childs had appealed several of his convictions for handle popping to the Nevada Supreme Court and predicted that the nominee's chances of prevailing were "all but nonexistent" (p. 215). He added that, even if the lower court convictions were reversed, there remained sufficient grounds for Childs's exclusion (pp. 215–216). The commissioners agreed, voting unanimously to enter Timothy John Childs into the Black Book.

In light of his extensive record of gaming law violations, Childs may indeed appear to be a man who "belongs in the Black Book." Contrary to the deputy attorney general's prediction, however, the Nevada Supreme Court ruled on November 24, 1993, that handle popping is not a crime. In a decision written by Justice Thomas Steffen, the court held that "the handle-popping player merely takes advantage of what a slot machine with a misaligned stop bracket will accommodate by a skillful manipulation of the handle." One of the justices had indicated in hearing the appeal that he himself may have tried handle popping as a youth, but without much success.[10]

Although Childs's other offenses may have been seen as sufficient reason for his entry into the Black Book, the fact that so many of his "crimes" were for handle popping could mean that this case has not yet been concluded for the regulators.

Brent Eli Morris

While already excluded from New Jersey casinos and only two weeks away from being released from a Nevada state prison, Brent Eli Morris was nominated to the Black Book.[11] He had eight felony convictions between 1986 and 1989, primarily for "past posting" of wagers (placing bets after dice are thrown or cards are dealt) at crap, roulette, and baccarat tables, and primarily in New Jersey. Although the board members described him as a professional gambling cheat and habitual criminal and as being "drawn to the tables like a moth is drawn to a flame" (pp. 166–167), they awarded him little of their time, and the local press responded similarly, with only minimal coverage. In like manner, when the commission met to consider the board's case for Morris' nomination to the Black Book, Deputy Attorney General Joe Ward estimated that he would need only 5–10 minutes for the presentation. Morris' arrest in the Bahamas within two weeks of his release from prison, again for past posting of wagers, seemed to cinch the unanimous consent of the commissioners that he should be added to the List of Excluded Persons.[12] Again, one who would appear to be relatively small time, and whose threat to Nevada gaming was neither imminent nor evident, is used to illustrate that the regulators are about what they're supposed to be about.

SOUTHERN CALIFORNIA LINKS TO CHICAGO

The Chicago mob is still thought to threaten gaming. Francis Citro, Jr., a 45-year-old Italian from New Jersey, was seen as associated with Chicago's tentacles in Los Angeles. With past employment as a card dealer at several Las Vegas casinos, Citro was nominated to the Black Book on December 6, 1990, while incarcerated in Boron Federal Penitentiary. His stay in Boron was occasioned by a 1986 California conviction for extortion, racketeering, and aiding and abetting. The bases for the board's nomination of Citro to the Black Book were the common ones: (1) his felony conviction record: for extortion in 1980; for racketeering, aiding and abetting, and conspiracy to conduct extortion in 1986; and for conspiracy to use and attempting to use counterfeit credit cards in 1987; (2) his alleged association with the infamous Anthony Spilotro; and (3) his being named as an associate of organized crime in a 1985 report on Organized Crime to the California legislature. In addition, Deputy Attorney General Lisa Miller maintained that Citro had an extensive arrest record, including arrests for "attempted robbery, murder, shoplifting, assault and battery, theft, rape, extortion, aiding and abetting, attempt to use counterfeit devices . . . attempt to receive stolen property, possession of a controlled substance, conspiracy to conduct racketeering, and possession of a firearm by an ex-felon."[13] Although Citro himself denied the arrests for murder, possession of a controlled substance, possession of a firearm, and attempting to receive stolen property,[14] the discrepancies between his and Miller's accounts were not clarified, even at the commission hearing. In commenting on Citro's present threat, Chairman Bill Bible warned that, given Citro's relative youth, "one could . . . safely assume that he would employ himself during the years remaining in his life engaged in some kind of criminal or crime related activities,"[15] probably in Las Vegas because he had lived there previously. It sounded like a familiar tale of threat.

Interestingly, just prior to their vote on Citro's nomination, Gerald Cunningham and Bill Bible discussed another individual; it was a discussion that took on meaning only because we had witnessed the individual in interaction with them earlier that day.

CHAIRMAN BIBLE:
. . . [Citro] represents a very clear threat to gambling in the State of Nevada.
Questions or comments . . . Mr. Cunningham?

199

MEMBER CUNNINGHAM:

> . . . there certainly were other people involved in . . . [the 1986 indictment], and I don't know whether we ought to suggest follow-up with some of the other individuals also . . .

CHAIRMAN BIBLE:

> I think it would be appropriate that we follow up on a number of other individuals. One of the individuals . . . that was named in the indictment . . . appeared before us this morning . . .
>
> He . . . indicated that he would file an application with this agency . . . So we will have a chance to look at him . . . [and] to conduct an investigation [on him] . . . (pp. 775–777)

Who was named in the indictment along with Citro, and why did they want to follow up on him? As fate would have it, we were able to attend the hearing for much of the day and knew to whom they referred. The board's review of an application for sole proprietorship of a delicatessen with slot machines focused on the landlord of the delicatessen—a Mr. B, as we will refer to him, a man whom they questioned for considerable time. Indeed, Mr. B had been indicted along with Citro and five others (four of whom had Italian surnames and one of whom had a Jewish surname) in the 1986 racketeering and extortion case in southern California, though the indictment against Mr. B was dismissed. He had followed family members some 20 years earlier from New York to Las Vegas and made several million dollars in real estate investments there.[16]

Mr. B's reputation in Las Vegas was not necessarily always good, however. He said it was because he was Italian. "When you are Italian in this town, and you know anybody, you have that stigma. I will tell you right now. You have that stigma" (p. 427). Ned Day, a former Las Vegas newspaper columnist, had apparently written several articles alleging that Mr. B had various associations and criminal activities, allegations that, according to Mr. B, may have emanated from Frank Citro (p. 435). Day had alleged that Mr. B was "a boss . . . taking over Spilotro's position" (pp. 415–416), which is interesting, given that Mr. B was from New York, not from Chicago. Yet, it did not improve his image when he admitted under questioning: "I knew Tony [Spilotro]. I knew his brother John, I know his wife Nancy. Like that. Just like anybody else would know them" (p. 421).

There was an apparent need in the Las Vegas community and

on the part of the gaming regulators to assign someone to the position of Spilotro's replacement for Chicago mob interests in Las Vegas. The phenomenon is truly amazing. Joseph Vincent Cusumano, who was placed in the Black Book in 1990, was alleged by the regulators to have been that replacement. Mr. B was alleged by Ned Day to be the one. And another codefendant in the 1986 federal indictment in southern California was said by a Las Vegas editorialist to be the one.[17]

There were additional allegations regarding Mr. B. Ned Day was also said to have implied that Mr. B was somehow linked to what might have been foul play in the auto accident of another man, a man under indictment himself, prior to this man's call to testify against Mr. B.[18] The man owned a gold mine from which very little gold had ever come and was indicted for activities related to his gold company. Mr. B apparently loaned money to the man, and the man apparently gave Mr. B an office suite (pp. 422–423, 430–431). The most interesting part of this scenario was the alleged involvement of a national television talk show host who was described by Mr. B as a stool pigeon and FBI informant who was "fleecing" the gold company by writing checks and telling the other man that he needed the money to pay Mr. B (pp. 421, 423). The actual involvement or extent of involvement on the part of any one of these individuals is not clear from the transcript. It is not even indicated who was ever indicted or convicted in the gold company case. Yet, the story is one that the regulators had heard bits and pieces of and about which they wanted to hear more.

There were other incidents about which the regulators were more curious, however. Of particular concern was a reference in the newspaper to certain FBI wiretap information, wherein two of Mr. B's co-conspirators in the 1986 extortion case talked about "breaking legs and killing people."[19] Upon questioning by board member Gerald Cunningham, Mr. B, by way of explanation of some of the wiretap information, discussed how Italians like him who have known each other for a long time are accustomed to conversing. While his explanation raises the question of the extent to which law enforcement cases are built on misconceptions about conversations and assumptions of guilt, he did not address the specific question related to muscle techniques. Rather, Mr. B elucidated, [the FBI] . . . talk[ed] about cheese. We had a restaurant. We talk about cheese. We talk about sauce.

It was the prosecutor's interpretation of what 10 cases of sauce was and what "soldi" means in Italian, which is money. He had to go through the whole thing and he was saying cheese, 10 cases of cheese is $10,000, or five cases of tomatoes, and we had a restaurant . . .

. . . [A man who was also indicted in the case] was a friend of mine before this indictment.

He has 63 pizza stores. That is why it was a joke. He used to buy pizza sauces and cheeses wholesale, and pass them on to us when we needed them here.

So . . . [the FBI] had to do something. They didn't have exactly what they needed so they fabricated the pizzas and the cheeses and the sauces, and whatever they had actually looked that way. And then people that were raised on the street like . . . I was, have ways to talk that they don't even say the whole thing. And they took those excerpts, and it sounded like whatever you wanted it to sound like . . .

This little prosecutor, he could hardly understand English, and he is trying to decipher what slang Italian is. You see? And that's it.

When we talk, we don't have to—if you are talking to people that you know well and for a long time, you don't have to even finish the total conversation. That's maybe a matter of habit . . . (pp. 429, 432–433)

His explanation—that talking about cheese and sauce is routine if one is the proprietor of a restaurant—seemed to be variously received. But still, and sometimes following few directives, Mr. B continued to talk. This seems to be a common process. Apparently, when an individual presents his case before those in authority, even absent a defensive manner, the presentation itself is interpreted as an indication of guilt. Talking dramatizes issues and lends credibility to the very questions the authorities are apt to ask and the issues they are apt to raise, even if the questions or issues are not always verbalized. Further, this board of authority was specifically engaged in the business of obtaining information. They seemed to structure the interaction in order to obtain as much information as possible, asking leading questions and appearing to be uninformed and open to the viewpoint of the applicant. Not uncommonly in such circumstances, applicants talk, talk excessively, and say things that will tend to incriminate them. Mr. B introduced episodes that tended to make him look bad. Witness Mr. B talking about his altercation with a board agent following what was apparently an unauthorized, but innocent, purchase of slot machines (p. 442):

> ... one of your agents ... accused me of being muscled from New York and got in my face to the point where I really had to tell him off, period. And I asked him if what I did was wrong, then arrest me.
>
> He said, Well, I can.
>
> I said, Well, then arrest me. If I did something wrong, then arrest me. But, don't talk to me like this ... And this you will find in your files. (p. 444)

To set the stage, when the regulators inquired why he had never applied for licensing himself, it seemed as if they led him to believe that such application in the future would have as much chance as that of any other person. The following dialogue with Chairman Bible, member Cunningham, and Mr. B is illustrative:

CHAIRMAN BIBLE:
... would you have any difficulty submitting applications for landlord suitability?

MR. B:
... I don't think I would ... if I was to go that far, ... would you people look at it without prejudice and say, well, let me judge him on what he did or didn't do instead of innuendos and background of hearsay? ...

CHAIRMAN BIBLE:
I would like to give you the opportunity to submit those applications.

MR. B:
... Now I asked you before, if I make an application ... would you fairly look at it? ...

CHAIRMAN BIBLE:
Sure, I would look at it ...

MR. B:
... If you rejected me for a particular thing, not for association or unsavory character, ... I will accept it. But if you turn me down for a silly technicality, ... then I would feel real bad.

CHAIRMAN BIBLE:
We will take a look at it like we do any other application.

MR. B:

Would you do that?

CHAIRMAN BIBLE:

Sure.

MR. B:

Then I would really like to do that.

MEMBER CUNNINGHAM:

I would just indicate . . . some of your associations do pose a problem . . . [At the same time], I am not satisfied . . . that there is evidence of an extortive means . . . I think it is those things that will be key to whether or not your explanations are accepted. But . . . they do have to be clarified.

MR. B:

I respect that . . . Like I say. I could appreciate if you find me doing something wrong, then I will understand it. I am a man. But by innuendo, give me a little edge at least. Not even an edge.

CHAIRMAN BIBLE:

We will give you consideration like we give everybody else.

MR. B:

That is exactly what I want. Not because of anything, being Italian, association or anything. I would really appreciate that as a man.

CHAIRMAN BIBLE:

You would certainly not be judged because you are Italian. You may be judged because of your associations . . .

MR. B:

. . . then I will make application . . . I don't believe in Santa Claus either, but I will take a shot with you just as a man.

CHAIRMAN BIBLE:

That is what I told you we'd do. Okay . . . (pp. 441, 445–446, 448–449, 451)

Mr. B was encouraged to apply for licensing. The board members promised to give him a fair shake and certainly not discriminate against him because of his ethnicity. The chairman in particular seemed reassuring, while his fellow board member did express some skepticism. Long after Mr. B had left the hearing room, the two men discussed what his application would allow them to do. (In accordance with the gaming regulations, the board could not officially conduct a thorough investigation until such time as an individual formally applied for licensing.) The chairman then concluded: "So [now] we will have a chance to look at him as an individual . . . [and] to conduct an investigation" (p. 777).

At the time that the board encouraged Mr. B's application for licensing, they were already aware of certain incriminating information against him. They had discussed with him the indictment in which he was named along with several others, including Francis Citro, as an associate of organized crime. And that information would again be raised that same day when the board moved to nominate Citro to the Black Book. Thus, while they questioned Mr. B, they considered him an associate of organized crime. Under these circumstances, it is highly unlikely that they would look favorably upon, much less approve, his application for licensing. As of this writing, we have no knowledge of whether he actually paid the fee and applied subsequent to their invitation, however.

When the commission convened in September of 1991 to rule on the board's earlier nomination of Francis Citro, Jr., the nominee, with apparently few monetary resources, had very recently retained counsel. William Watters requested a continuance in order to prepare his client's case. Watters was new to the nuances of regulatory hearings, and his client appeared distinct from all others in the room. Citro was dark-complexioned, moustached, and muscular, and he was dressed in a tuxedo.

When Citro did appear before the commission in November of 1991, he accounted for his formal attire by explaining that he had "never been nominated for anything [before],"[20] and "not to show disrespect," but to have them look at him differently (p. 496). Citro was also distinct in being one of only four Black Book nominees who testified in their own behalf. The others were William Gene Land, Frank Joseph Masterana, and Frank Larry Rosenthal. Also, he was the only one to appear before the regulators with his family in attendance. He brought his pregnant wife, married daughter, and young son with him, perhaps to gain sympathy, perhaps to gain legitimacy, and perhaps to demonstrate his differentness. He said, "I'm a family man. A family consists of a wife and child to me. Not a mob. I don't belong to a mob" (p. 497).

The deputy attorney general in the case, Lisa Miller, prefaced her opening remarks with the statement that the mechanism of

Frank Citro, Jr. Citro was nominated to the Black Book in anticipation of his release from federal prison, where he was serving time for racketeering and conspiracy. Although he pleaded in his own behalf that he had paid his debt to society, had been rehabilitated, and was trying to get his life together, the commission nevertheless saw fit to exclude him from Nevada gaming. Even the presence of his pregnant wife and children at the hearing, and evidence of his efforts to start up a local lawn service business could not dissuade the regulators. Courtesy *Las Vegas Review Journal*.

the Black Book was implemented in the name of "strict regulation," which is essential to public confidence and trust in gaming, especially so in light of the proliferation of gaming elsewhere (p. 469). In summation, she wanted it to be clear that things such as "knuckle therapy" and loan-sharking, part of Nevada's old image, are no longer tolerated (p. 520). Thus, the commissioners were made aware that their contemplated action was very important to public trust and the image of gaming, especially in light of marketplace competition. The state's case for banning Citro from licensed gaming establishments seems predicated primarily on the 1986 federal conviction alleging his role in a conspiracy on the part of an organized crime family to take over various bookmakers and loan sharks in southern California and to expand those activities to the Las Vegas area; it was also alleged that this family was "operating with the consent of the Chicago Crime Syndicate" (pp. 483–484, 487).

As was commonplace in these hearings, the state presented both public and confidential documents as evidence. The public documents generally included certified copies of convictions or indictments, excerpts from reports of commissions on organized crime, and newspaper articles. Those records which would remain sealed from public scrutiny, after being viewed by the regulators and sometimes the nominee and his counsel, were said to be confidential. In Citro's case, the confidential records included a board intelligence report and an intelligence bulletin from the California attorney general's office.[21] Thus, although the nominee and his counsel were said to have had the opportunity to review the materials (p. 519), and though attorney Watters said the two agreed ahead of time not to object to anything that was presented at the hearing (p. 476), the bases for the board's decision were never subjected to open question or evaluation. Confidentiality, which amounts essentially to secrecy, benefited the regulators, not the nominee.

It was also because of Citro's desire to be cooperative with the regulators and to answer any question that they should have that his counsel called him forward. And he additionally took the opportunity to explain why he should not be in the Black Book. The following excerpts show how he pled his case:

. . . I'm having difficulty right now really expressing myself because I've gone over this thing a hundred times in my head, how I'm going to present myself. I'm not a public speaker. I'm doing the best I can. (p. 499)
. . . I'm a family man . . . I'm not a gangster.
. . . I've done some bad things in my lifetime. I'm not coming here as an altar boy . . . [But] I've changed my life around . . .
And I've done my best not to even get a parking ticket. (p. 498)
. . . I've never had a problem in a casino. You'll find no testimony anyplace, written or verbal, that I even yelled at somebody, forget about beating them up, or brass knuckles therapy that was written in the newspaper. (pp. 499–500)
. . . [But] you see what happened, somebody put my back against the wall so I have to fight.

. . . because if I go on that list, I can't go any place . . . I'm through. And send a legacy to live on for my son and possibly my other child. (p. 501)

. . . [And my wife is] my biggest problem, you understand. She wants to live a little bit of a normal life. (p. 502)

. . . I've been to prison and still come out and become a good person. Not a problem, haven't thrown a cigarette butt on the ground, and I'm being crucified now. This is the last step for me. This puts the nails in the coffin for me. (p. 505)

. . . Please consider this thoroughly before you make a decision . . . Show a little moxie, let somebody else show a little moxie besides me. (p. 506)

There was also a point of dispute with regard to Citro's record of criminality, one that was never resolved. While he was alleged to have pled guilty to a felony of extortion in U.S. district court, he contended that the charge to which he had pled had been subsequently dismissed. At the time of the commission hearing, no one was able to produce records referable to the support of his contention. Consequently, Citro volunteered to explain, in his own words, the circumstances of the dismissal. He stated that a plea bargain had been arranged with the government for which, in exchange of a plea of guilty, he would receive a very light sentence, not to exceed 90 days. Thereafter, at the time of sentencing, and much to his surprise, he was sentenced to five years— and by Judge Harry Claiborne. Citro said he then attempted to withdraw his plea, whereupon the government decided to dismiss the charge. And the case was, according to Citro, dropped (pp. 509–510).

There was little discussion following Citro's testimony, and the closing statements on the part of the state and counsel were rather short. It goes without saying that the commission voted unanimously to place Francis Citro, Jr., on the List of Excluded Persons.

ENTREE OF THE NEW ENGLAND SYNDICATES

The press continued to pressure the state subtly to resolve the Matis Marcus affair. It was within this slightly hostile environment which the media had helped to create that the regulators during a one-month period in 1993 nominated five individuals to the List of Excluded Persons. The first was Albert Anthony Corbo, a man who had within the previous year purchased a sports information service in Las Vegas. Already having been placed on New Jersey's excluded persons list in 1983, and with gambling-related convictions, including bookmaking, conspiracy to promote gambling, and conducting an illegal gambling business in Atlantic City, Philadelphia, and Miami Beach, Corbo was seen as a viable candidate for exclusion from the industry.[22] Further, certain street sources had suggested that there were links between his sports information establishment and Black Book member Frank Masterana, who was seen frequenting it, as well as certain bookmakers in the Dominican Republic and Jamaica.[23] Corbo was not entered, however, until July of 1994.

Within a month of Corbo's nomination, in May of 1993, the Gaming Control Board nominated four men as a group, three of whom were alleged bookmakers said to have ties to organized crime in the New England states. They were Dominic Spinale, Edward Lawrence DeLeo, Anthony Michael St. Laurent, Sr., and Samuel Filippo Manarite. Spinale and DeLeo, alleged associates of the Boston crime family, shared a common felony conviction as well as association with the infamous Anthony Spilotro. St. Laurent, also a reputed bookmaker, but one said to have ties to the Patriarca crime family, had been recently indicted in what was referred to as the largest bookmaking operation uncovered in Rhode Island.[24] The fourth, Samuel Manarite, with convictions for extortion and loan-sharking and with alleged membership in the New York Genovese syndicate, was apparently seen by law enforcement officials talking to DeLeo at a local casino.[25] Although the four may have been viewed as posing a common threat, their nomination also may have been precipitated by a national rumor, which began to surface as early as 1991, that the New England syndicate was under onslaught by federal law enforcement on its home turf, so was migrating to Las Vegas.

Dominic Spinale and Edward DeLeo were indicted in 1986 and convicted in 1988 for relaying betting information from Las Vegas to Boston. They had been Las Vegas locals for nearly a decade, having been imprisoned for short intervals during that time, and were considered on the street to be small-time bookies. Spinale, who was thought to be the leader of the two, had convictions for bookmaking and conspiracy to defraud, had been seen meeting with Boston organized crime figures by FBI surveillance, and had recently patronized sports books in Nevada.[26]

Of the two men, the commission acted on DeLeo, who was imprisoned at the time of his nomination.* The 1986 bookmaking indictment, to which he entered a guilty plea for conspiracy to conduct an illegal gambling business, reads: "Edward DeLeo at the direction of and assistance from . . . Spinale provided regular line information to . . . [a man] by calling . . . [that man] from . . . the Stardust Hotel and Casino."[27] Also convicted for conspiracy to use counterfeit credit cards, DeLeo in concert with Herbert Blitzstein, Spilotro's reputed former lieutenant, apparently joined with a fur store sales clerk who aided in DeLeo's receipt of furs that were then fenced (p. 248). FBI wiretaps describing him as an associate of Boston La Cosa Nostra members and newspaper references to him as a professional strong arm seemed to cinch a unanimous vote by the commissioners for DeLeo's inclusion in the Black Book (p. 251).

The third nominee on May 6, 1993, was Anthony Michael St. Laurent, Sr., another alleged illegal bookmaker, but one whose home base was Rhode Island. Of the four, he was the first to be moved on by the commission and entered into the book.[28] When the commission met, Deputy Attorney General Charlotte Matanane presented evidence supporting why St. Laurent should be excluded from licensed gaming: (1) a 1987 conviction for running an illegal gambling operation from Rhode Island to Las Vegas; (2) a 1985 conviction for possession of cocaine and racketeering, which followed an arrest for possession of marijuana and gambling paraphernalia in Atlantic City; (3) a 1971 indictment for bookmaking in New Jersey, which was subsequently dismissed; (4) a 1990 indictment for extortion in Rhode Island, which was about to go to trial; (5) a 1993 indictment, wherein he and 26 others were charged with racketeering, conducting a gambling business said to handle $42 million a year, and conspiracy to conduct gambling; (6) an extensive number of arrests for illegal gambling, racketeering, counterfeiting, and extortion; and (7) his reputation as a "made member" of the Patriarca New England crime family (pp. 217–223). The 1987 illegal bookmaking operation involved his son and two others, one of whom, Allen D'Andrea, relayed

*The commission has yet to take action on Spinale.

line information from the Las Vegas Stardust and took bets and wagers from St. Laurent in Rhode Island.

The specifics of St. Laurent's membership in the Patriarca syndicate were embedded in various documents, both confidential and public (pp. 223–233). A Rhode Island state police captain wrote a letter. A corporal submitted an affidavit. U.S. Attorney General Dick Thornburgh's statement to the press regarding the 1990 indictments in Boston and Hartford against 21 alleged associates of the Patriarca family, charging them with various racketeering offenses, was entered as evidence. Also, as was common, newspaper articles describing various criminal activities and associations were relied upon, except in this case the articles were from Rhode Island and New York in addition to Las Vegas.

However, by far the most interesting material in support of St. Laurent's alleged organized crime affiliation and involvement was the testimony of Phillip Leonetti. An admitted Philadelphia La Cosa Nostra underboss of his uncle Nick Scarfo, Leonetti provided testimony regarding the Philadelphia and Patriarca crime families. This testimony of an underboss against other organized crime figures was classified as "expert," "valid," and "reliable" by Deputy Attorney General Matanane (pp. 225, 236). Matanane read certain excerpts from Leonetti's testimony. One excerpt dealt with his being introduced by a member of the Philadelphia crime family to a man who was said to be a Patriarca soldier or made member nicknamed the Saint, and that when they met they talked about fixing games (pp. 227–228). While a made member or soldier is considered the lowest of the actual members in the hierarchy of the syndicate, the intent of the questioning in this instance was to establish that, regardless of the level of membership, such a person is fully initiated (p. 229).

The state's case for entry of Anthony Michael St. Laurent, Sr., seemed well-documented, and in support of the presentation of that case, the commission unanimously approved the motion to place him on the List of Excluded Persons.

The final nominee at the May 1993 board meeting was the gray-haired Samuel Filippo Manarite. Age 74 at the time, Manarite was said to have a rap sheet listing "criminal activities [that] span over seven decades,"[29] suggesting that his earliest arrest would have been when he was four years old. His felony convictions were for collection of credit by extortionate means, making threats of violence to collect an extension of credit, and the sale and distribution of pornography (pp. 225–226). At the time of the nomination, Manarite, his wife, and son were under federal grand jury indictment in Las Vegas for "conspiracy, money laundering, aiding and abetting, wire fraud, interstate transportation of stolen property, and receipt of stolen property" (p. 227), crimes for which within a few months they would be convicted and sentenced to prison. Identified in crime commission reports as a member of the New York Genovese crime family, Manarite was depicted by the state as a man who threatened people with maiming, disfigurement, and great bodily harm (pp. 225–226). In one instance, he allegedly "pled guilty to . . . soliciting an associate of his to pour . . . acid into the eyes and mouth of another associate who had cooperated with the FBI and the Department of Justice" (p. 225). While said on the streets to be a "capo,"[30] Manarite was viewed by the regulators as a loan shark, and a very dangerous one. Nevertheless, because the aging Manarite was shortly to begin serving a 10-year prison sentence, he must have been of little concern to the regulators. Within six months of his nomination to the Black Book, the nomination was dismissed.[31]

Of particular note regarding these four nominees is that, while official court documents associate only two of the men with each other, the Las Vegas press, beginning two years prior to the nomination hearing, linked three of them. Spinale, DeLeo, and St. Laurent were alleged by certain reporters to have been involved in the "Boston–to–Las Vegas" bookmaking case.[32] Now, the 1988 felony conviction for bookmaking between the Stardust and Boston named DeLeo and Spinale, and the 1987 felony conviction for bookmaking between the Stardust and two cities in Rhode Island named St. Laurent and others, none of whom were DeLeo or Spinale. Court records present them as two separate incidents, although in St. Laurent's commission hearing, the cases are called sister cases.[33] While both bookmaking operations did have a connection at the Stardust, that connection involved a different individual in each operation, and none of those involved were named in both indictments. Of course, the several Las Vegas reporters may have had information that was not part of the court indictment and conviction records that were included in the hearings. Also, on the streets of Las Vegas, the men may have associated with one another. DeLeo was said to have been observed meeting for a few minutes with Spinale on one occasion and with Manarite on another.[34] Their association with one another in criminal activities, however, was never established in the records of the regulatory hearings. Again, the issue of the media's role in creating the threat is raised.

FATHER OF A SLOT CHEAT

The year 1993 saw one additional man nominated to the Black Book, an alleged slot cheat and the father of a slot cheat who had already been excluded from the state's casinos. Douglas William Barr was said to have some 64 arrests, 30 of which were gaming related.[35] Three of the latter arrests resulted in convictions, two of which were for cheating at gambling. His primary method of cheating the machines was to use a coin with strings attached, although he is said to have also used a top joint. During the early years, his crimes were considered gross misdemeanors. Then, in 1988, for essentially the same activity, he was convicted of burglary—a felony. The crime was described as "entering a Las Vegas casino with a quarter with clear scotch tape attached to it and some monofilament line attached to a hook device, sometimes referred to as a yo-yo or . . . stringing device."[36] Convictions for conspiracy to transport forged securities (1962), sale of obscene items (1981), and misuse of food coupons (1988), as well as associations with other excluded slot cheats, including his own son, were put forth as additional reasons to suspect his threat to the industry.

The only question raised during the hearing was why the state had not acted earlier to place Barr in the Black Book. After all, he had a long history of slot cheating, and his most recent conviction was on the burglary charge five years ago. Although it was suggested that he had probably spent much of the past 30 years going through the justice system (p. 167), it was evident from the discussion that the regulators were really unaware of his whereabouts during that time. The exact nature of his present threat to the state's industry was not established, and whatever threat he presented in the past seemed relatively insignificant and inconsequential. In reality, the senior Mr. Barr was not a very sophisticated slot cheat and his methods were somewhat primitive, to say the least. Indeed, the description of Douglas William Barr as "playing slot machines by simply holding onto a string inserted into the coin acceptors with his fingers and moving the string up and down without putting any coins in" is reminiscent of a child's behavior (p. 164). Nevertheless, and not surprisingly, the commissioners voted unanimously to add Barr to the List of Excluded Persons.[37] He was another easy target.

PART 4

Denunciation and Inequality

12

Righteous Indignation and the Mark of Cain

We have traced the development and application of the Black Book to perceived threats to Nevada gaming. These threats have emanated from both within and outside the industry, and from legitimate as well as illegitimate sources. They have included, among others, federal threats of intervention, problems of skimming and hidden ownership, and moral crises within regulation itself. A common thread to all such threats is that they have been surrounded by extensive and widespread publicity. More than any objective qualities of the problems themselves, it is this notoriety which seems to be the driving force behind the Black Book and, thus, the real threat to the industry. Without public confidence that the state has effectively eliminated crime and corruption from gaming, the probable outcomes would be a declining patronage, federal intervention, and a loss of state revenues.

During earlier years, there were also members of the industry who derived great benefit from keeping competing groups out. The Black Book's service to their interests may have been an additional factor, if not a major impetus, in its development and earlier enforcement. Although no longer concerned with the Black Book as a means of excluding competing interests, these industry entrepreneurs and their individual and corporate descendants have also benefited from the clean image and public confidence that the industry has come to enjoy. Therefore, they have not been without selfish motivations in their support of the means by which these ends have been achieved.

So the Black Book indeed has served a purpose, though it be largely a symbolic one. It has helped convey a public image of gaming as a legitimate industry and of the state as capable of keeping it free of crime and corrupting influences. Neither the possibility that the stated threats are not the real ones nor the continued existence of numerous other threats to gaming is as important as the belief that all is well in Babylon.

An integral part of this symbolic process is the sharp distinctions that are made between those who are to be placed in the Black Book and members of legitimate society. These distinctions are accomplished in part through the selection of individuals who are external and foreign to established groups as well as to the regulators who represent these groups. By additionally constructing public identities of such individuals as essentially evil persons, as notorious and unsavory types with few or no claims to legitimacy, the regulators are able to set them further apart from others in the industry and to validate the necessity of their exclusion. The overall process reflects patterns of dominance and subordination that have led to a disproportionately large number of Italians being entered into the Black Book.

ALIEN THREATS

We indicated at the outset of this book that there has been a historical antagonism between Las Vegas and the more established northern parts of Nevada, including Reno, Lake Tahoe, and the state capital of Carson City.[1] This antagonism is deeply rooted in social and economic differences between the two regions, which have until recently been manifest in the greater concentration of political influence in the north. The north's issuance of the law and its tendency to view Las Vegas in negative terms may explain the state's focus on Las Vegas in regard to the Black Book. During the 35-year history of the book, no one has ever been entered for posing a threat to gaming in the northern part of the state. All those who have been placed in the book have been described as a threat to the industry in Las Vegas. They either resided in Las Vegas at the time of their entry, or were frequent visitors to the city, or were seen as having undue influence on Las Vegas gambling, or were employed in the city's casinos. None were residents or frequent visitors in the northern part of the state, nor were they said to have had employment or behind-the scenes influence in northern casinos.* Yet, the Kefauver committee hearings suggested as early as 1951 that Michigan organized crime interests with ties to Meyer Lansky were operating casinos in Reno and Lake Tahoe.[2]

The externality of perceived threat to Nevada gaming is also reflected in the origins of Black Book nominees. More than half were not residing in Nevada at the time of their nomination (see appendix C, table C.1). None were natives of the state (see appendix C, table C.2). They came, for the most part, from outside the continental United States and from heavily ethnic-populated midwestern and northeastern regions of the country, especially from Chicago, Kansas City, and the New York–New Jersey area. The majority of those who were born elsewhere in the United States were from the South, and as a group were alleged cheats at gambling, not associated with organized crime, and were of Anglo-Saxon background. Only one such individual was thought to be associated with organized crime, and he was Italian. As we have noted, gambling cheats are a more recent target of regulatory action, not the one for which the Black Book was originally developed.

Historically, socially and politically dominant groups in the United States have been Anglo-Saxon and Protestant. Nevada has been no exception. The distinction is the sizable and influential portion of its Anglo-Saxon population that is Mormon. These influences have been felt specifically in the regulation of gaming, as well as in government more generally. Anglo-Saxons (and seemingly Protestants) have dominated the regulation of Nevada gaming, and for several years during the 1970s, Mormons themselves composed a majority of the Nevada Gaming Commission.

As regulators, Mormons have been said to satisfy certain symbolic functions in establishing the legitimacy of the industry. "The appointment of a Mormon [to a regulatory body] symbolizes integrity," and the Mormon projection of "moral purity" serves to cleanse the industry.[3] In addition, however, Mormons

---

*Although John and Sandra Vaccaro were convicted of slot cheating that also involved Reno and Lake Tahoe casinos, they were residents of Las Vegas, and the major part of their alleged criminal activities was carried out in Las Vegas.

bring a special kind of cultural experience and morality to the regulatory process. Their presence appears to have had an influence on the culture of regulation itself. Together with the more general separatist and conservative Anglo-Saxon and northern views, it seems to have contributed to a tenor of decision making that is very much attuned to cultural differences and issues of morality. The regulatory process thus reflects a preference for commonality and a suspicion of out-groups,* the latter having seemingly inclined regulators to be especially receptive to the mafia myth of organized crime.

Such preferences and suspicions are evident throughout regulation. For example, in reviewing the background of an applicant for licensing, the board chairman stated that the investigation was "quite favorable" and that the applicant was "a Mormon bishop." When told that the applicant was "not a bishop . . . [but] a saint" (as all Mormons are called), the chairman, seemingly determined to establish the man's credibility, told of the applicant's assignment to a mission to England.[4] It was as if the man's religion and status within his church were sufficient indication of his worthiness to be licensed.

This incident is in sharp contrast with one surrounding the same board's discussion of an out-group member. A gaming control agent could not recall the man's name and said it was "an Italian sounding name." On the basis of this statement, a series of inquiries followed. First the board members suggested that they should have more information, then that a personal history form be completed, and finally that a fingerprint check be done.[5] The mere Italian sound of the man's name generated considerable suspicion. The episode is indicative of the more general "suspicion awareness context"[6] in which regulators seem to operate in cases of members of this out-group.

These are not isolated examples. Assessments of applicants for licensing often extend beyond issues of financial solvency, criminal history, and the like to more personal matters and moral issues. Thus, as recently as 1987, commissioners expressed grave concerns regarding the granting of licenses to persons involved

---

*Galliher and Cross (1983: 123–124) have observed that such an attitude of suspicion seems to pervade Nevadans generally, and that they tend to see the state's problems as produced by outsiders.

in the ownership of houses of prostitution, suggesting that they are not worthy of having gaming licenses. We additionally find applicants being denied because of mere association with prostitutes, approved on the condition that they not drink on the premises, and admonished for being late in child support payments. There are also drawn out discussions of whether nude entertainment is or is not offensive, complete with references to naked girls and statements such as "some nudes offend me more than others."[7] These are intriguing concerns in light of the social context—a place where drinks are free and sex can be legally purchased—and reflect the extent to which the morality of the regulators is at variance with many of the members and patrons of the industry.

Because so many of the applicants for licensing have had histories of criminality and of illegal bookmaking in particular, the regulators have been forced to make somewhat fine distinctions among them. These distinctions are made largely in terms of judgment of whether the applicant is, for example, an ethical or unethical bookmaker.[8] While on the surface this is a reasonable approach in light of the context, it is one that encourages and justifies a greater latitude of moral judgment in assessing the suitability of applicants. Thus, those with problematic backgrounds who are or are not licensed may not be significantly different from each other in terms of objective criteria but simply more or less acceptable in terms of the morality of the regulators.

This cultural context of regulation might explain the state's response to Howard Hughes in the late 1960s and 1970s. Hughes's employment of so many Mormons would seem to be predictive of the regulatory deference shown him and the absence of a perceived threat to gaming while he was in Nevada. As we have seen, he was personally attended by a Mormon entourage, and by 1971, a powerful Mormon became second-in-command of the parent company of Hughes's Nevada holdings and appointed other Mormons to various positions in the top echelons of the corporation.[9]

Most important from the standpoint of our analysis, the in-group–out-group orientation of Nevada regulation appears to be an important contributing factor to the disproportionately large number of Italians nominated to the Black Book (see appendix C, table C.3). Indeed, almost two-thirds of those nominated were

Italian. Further, almost two-thirds of the associates who were named to discredit the nominees were Italian (see appendix C, table C.3). Although Jews numbered as few of the nominees, they constituted a substantial number of the associates. Thus, while Jews are not often nominated to the Black Book, others are nominated because of their associations with Jews. Anglo-Saxons accounted for only seven of the nominees and four of the alleged associates. The disproportionate selection of Italians for inclusion in the Black Book raises important legal questions regarding regulatory compliance with the 1989 law stating that entry may not be based on ethnicity.[10]

We have seen that the issue of selective application of this regulatory procedure has been raised since the time of the first official hearing to enter a person into the Black Book (Anthony Spilotro) and in several subsequent cases, but with no apparent success. Thus, when counsel for Spilotro questioned the basis for his client's selection and charged that he was "being singled out," the chairman of the commission, Harry Reid, responded, ". . . everyone that is a candidate for the black book is being . . . singled out; and the reasons for their being singled out are not important as far as we're concerned."[11]

The social characteristics of those who make the choices of whom to exclude are not nearly as discernible. Assembled information is simply not available for the regulators. While a thorough search of the Division of Archives and Records of the Nevada State Library and Archives and the Nevada Historical Society on our part and on the part of the employees and librarians of these institutions resulted in much information, data on the regulators were largely incomplete. Even gubernatorial records were lacking in biographical data on the appointees to the Gaming Control Board and the Nevada Gaming Commission over the years. What information we were able to glean came from various historical sources, newspaper articles, and obituaries.[12]

A total of 47 individuals who have served on the Gaming Control Board and the Nevada Gaming Commission have made decisions to nominate and enter persons in the Black Book. Their place of residence was roughly divided between the north and the south in the state, with more of the early appointees being from the north. We were able to locate the birthplaces of slightly more than half of the regulators, and of those, 71 percent were native to the state. Their occupations were relatively equally distributed among law, accounting, law enforcement, and business more generally. Although we were able to locate religious affiliation for only half, of those, more than a quarter were Mormon. Furthermore, Mormon regulators appear to be even more influential in decision making than these numbers suggest, and several have been dominant in regulation over the years. The surnames, which were available for all the regulators, also reflect their overwhelmingly Anglo-Saxon heritage (see appendix C, table C.4). Only three board members and five commissioners did not have Anglo-Saxon surnames. Of the 47 regulators involved in this procedure over the 35-year period, only 2 were Italian and 2 were Jewish.*

Finally, confirming the regulators' primary allegiances to the industry and the opportunities provided in regulatory appointments, almost two-thirds of those on the Gaming Control Board have entered the industry following their tenure. About one-third of the commissioners have also gone into the industry or represented gaming interests in their law practices. Even Mormon regulators have subsequently taken positions in the industry.

DRAMATIZATION OF DISREPUTABILITY

We now turn our attention to the more specific means by which the image of a clean industry is created and maintained. Here we focus on the denunciation process itself as it symbolically affirms the legitimacy of gaming and the efficacy of the bodies responsible for its control. By setting apart and emphasizing the evilness of those who are said to present threats to gaming, the regulators cleanse gaming of its corruptive elements and assert their ability to effect the controls necessary to achieve those ends. The dramatization includes attention to the nominee's alleged criminal associations, activities and reputation, and aliases, and a lack of attention to any ties that he might have to conventional society.

---

*Five of the regulators were Catholic (all commissioners) and three were Basque (two board members and one commissioner), who themselves may also be Catholic. One would expect, therefore, that there might be some degree of identification on their part with Italians who are also Catholic. The appearance that this has not been the case leads further credence to the saliency of ethnicity and the mafia image.

Especially evident in this regard is the extent to which nominees to the Black Book are said to be associated with organized crime, as part of a larger force in opposition to a legitimate industry. When the names of other notorious and unsavory individuals are entered into the record as associates of the nominee, the regulators establish the disreputability of the individual, and build their case for the magnitude of his threat to the industry and therefore the necessity for his entry into the Black Book.*

In only six cases of placing persons in the Black Book was there no mention of criminal associations; five of these were cases of individuals convicted of cheating at gambling, all but one of whom was Anglo-Saxon. Almost two-thirds were said to be associates of organized crime or other Black Book members, of which Anthony Spilotro was the predominant "contaminating" member. Over half were reputed to be organized crime figures themselves, three-quarters of which were Italian. The figures were said to be affiliated with major crime syndicates, especially with the Chicago–Kansas City–Los Angeles syndicate. Most were reputed to be bosses, lieutenants, enforcers, and loan sharks (see appendix C, table C.5). The only bosses to be entered since the original 11 were Pulawa, who may have never been in the state, and Rizzitello, who was reputed to be one of the five bosses of the Los Angeles Mickey Mouse mafia.

Not all those who have come before the regulators are as easily connected to organized crime. As we have seen, some appeared to have little organization to their activities at all, let alone have mafia or syndicated crime associations. There remains, even in these cases, however, an apparent need on the part of the board to build its case on the basis of some notion of conspiracy. Thus, when the board has had difficulty establishing its argument, it has forced existing information into categories that might be interpreted as supporting the nomination.

A notorious and unsavory reputation and a felony conviction

---

*Yet, as we have seen, some with alleged connections to organized crime have not been nominated to the Black Book, and have even been licensed in the industry. The regulators have acknowledged this, mentioning on one occasion that a licensed individual had a definite relationship with the head of one of the 12 major La Cosa Nostra families (GCB transcripts, May 19, 1976, agenda item #76-21).

were the most frequently given bases for nomination to the Black Book. Only three individuals were nominated because of their exclusion from gaming activities in other states. Other stated threats of the nominee centered around implied behind-the-scenes influence on the industry and proximity to Las Vegas. Court records, crime commission reports, and newspaper and magazine articles served as the major sources of evidence for the nominations. Other sources of evidence were FBI affidavits, wire-taps, and nonfiction literature and fictionalized accounts.

It appears that most of those nominated and entered into the Black Book do in fact have notorious and unsavory reputations and extensive records of crime. Indeed, all were said to have been convicted of a felony, and more than 90 percent were convicted of a gaming violation. It is questionable, however, that these records have accrued without the influence of the constant surveillance over such individuals by local, state, and federal law enforcement agencies. If suspicions of crime have self-fulfilling effects of con-tributing to such records, as well as to the reputations of individ-uals, objective bases for the strength of allegations of serious fel-onious behavior and notorious and unsavory reputations may be drawn into question in some of these cases. As we have seen, this is evident even in the case of the most notorious and unsavory member of the Black Book, Anthony Spilotro, the board's socio-metric star.

In the denunciation process, officials also seem to ignore or seek to suppress any bases on which a nominee might claim a legitimate public identity, such as occupation and family ties. Yet, the occupations of those for whom information is available has included ownership of large corporations or casinos, production and direction of entertainment concerns, and ownership and management of medium-sized businesses (see appendix C, table C.6). The board's lack of attention to such matters conveys an image of the individuals as those with few ties to conventional society, and thus affirms the label of disreputability. Indeed, we have seen that attention to family ties has complicated the ap-plication of this label. This was apparent in the cases of William Gene Land, whose family circumstances were seemingly critical factors in his entry not receiving the unanimous support of the commission, and Frank Larry Rosenthal, a case in which the

225

state's deputy attorney general for gaming objected to Rosenthal's counsel questioning Rosenthal about the accomplishments of his children.

Further affirming the disreputability of the nominee is the extent of regulatory attention to the issue of aliases. They are mentioned routinely in hearings, and are listed in the Black Book as part of the identifying information on the individual (see appendix B). The procedure has the effect of amplifying the criminal character of the individual and of creating an image of a more extensive threat to the industry than is presented by the individual alone. The board now has before it, not merely one person with specific deviant acts, but an individual with as many as a dozen aliases who conceivably has committed numerous other acts under those or other names. The use of aliases also provides evidence of unsavoriness by projecting an image of the individual as one with intent to deceive and to hide his true identity. Ultimately, the attention to aliases further removes the individual from past and present legitimate identities by associating him with the allegations at hand. Again, the result is to set the individual apart from conventional society symbolically and to convey a public image of him as an essentially deviant type.

A careful reading of the aliases, however, suggests that many, if not most, of the names are simply nicknames (possibly acquired as early as childhood), shortened versions of the individual's full name, names prior to Anglicization by the individual or his family, and misspellings of names (largely Italian), possibly resulting from mispronunciations by others unfamiliar with them. Thus, we see that Marshal Caifano is also Marshal Cafano and Marshall Califano; Francis Citro, Jr., is Frank Citro; Carl Civella is Corky, Cork Civella, and Corky Civella; Joseph Vincent Cusumano is Joey and Joey Cusumano; Sam Giancana is Mooney Giancana, Sam Gencani, Sam Giancaco, Sam Giancano, Sam Giancanno, Sam Gincana, and Sam Gincani; and so on. It is as though many of the "aliases" were obtained from the registration lists of hotels where the desk clerks had difficulty with the spelling of the names.

A recent case also suggests that aliases might be given to the individual by law enforcement officials themselves. Addressing the offense for which his client was being considered for inclusion in the Black Book, the attorney of Francis Citro, Jr., stated that his client had nothing to hide. He argued that the only alias that his client had, Little Frankie, was the "one . . . the government gave . . . him to distinguish him from another Frank in the indictment."[13] If most of the aliases were creations of the men themselves, their remarkable similarity to the original names certainly raises questions about any intent of deception.

CONCLUSION

We have seen that the Black Book originated and has been implemented in response to perceived threats to the image of legalized gambling in Nevada. Further, given the potential for problems within such a large industry, a relatively small number of individuals have been placed in the book, many of whom themselves would appear to have presented little threat to the industry. These observations suggest that the functions of the regulatory mechanism are indeed symbolic. The very existence of the Black Book and public attention to its ceremonial processes serve to affirm the legitimacy of gaming and the efficacy of its regulatory body to control organized crime in the industry. By drawing attention to those who are to be entered into the book and publicly establishing their disreputability, regulators create an imagery of the state's commitment and ability to deal with corruptive elements in gaming. Critical to this process are the sharp distinctions that are drawn between those selected for the Black Book and legitimate members of the community. By creating a public identity of the individual as generally disreputable, a notorious and unsavory type, regulators set him apart from others and give his exclusion legitimacy.

We have seen that the Black Book also serves to illustrate patterns of dominance and subordination in Nevada: certain groups make the selections, and other groups are selected. Dominant groups in Nevada are typical of those elsewhere in that they tend to be Anglo-Saxon. In addition, the state has a historical tradition of political and civic involvement on the part of its Mormon population. Further, the state has been divided along regional lines, with the north playing a more active role in law and regulation. The relatively minor role in state governance that Las Vegas in the south has played until recently is due to its relative youth and its population of persons from the Northeast and Midwest—

groups viewed as alien to those longer settled in the state. These patterns are reflected in the social backgrounds and morality of those who regulate gaming.

Those selected for inclusion in the Black Book stand in marked contrast to the state's dominant society and culture. Their origins are external and their ways are foreign. In several respects they represent an alien threat to the interests of the state. Their threat has emanated entirely from Las Vegas in the south. None were born in the state. They have been largely from the heavily ethnic urban areas of the Northeast and Midwest. But most important, the large majority has been Italian, and a substantial number have been alleged members or associates of the Chicago mob (which is said to include also the Kansas City and Los Angeles groups). Interestingly, few have been linked to the predominantly Jewish New York, Cleveland, and Detroit groups (also thought to be affiliated) that gained an early stronghold on Nevada gambling. The stereotype that organized crime is the exclusive domain of Italians seems to have been particularly seductive to the social backgrounds and moral orientations of the regulators. The stereotype evolved out of federal congressional investigations, was elaborated by the federal Task Force on Organized Crime, became institutionalized in the law enforcement community, and was reinforced by mass media and social scientific accounts. This made it an especially powerful imagery in guiding regulatory action in an industry highly sensitive to public opinion.

Given that Jews are also alien and subordinate to the established society, and additionally represented half of Las Vegas' original investors with illegal backgrounds and were about a quarter of those mentioned as associates of the nominees, in concluding interest we might ask, Why has the regulatory reaction to Jews been somewhat at variance with that to Italians? Part of the answer may lie in the fact that the institutionalized stereotype of organized crime does not encompass Jews to the extent that it does Italians, possibly in part because it was codified at a time that the American public was becoming sensitized to the persecution of Jews. When Jews are identified with organized crime, they are often believed to be "fronting" for Italians. It has even been suggested, for example, that Bugsy Siegel and Moe Dalitz were fronting for Italian organized crime interests in Las Vegas,[14] which is remarkable in light of their reputations, but nonetheless confirms the persuasiveness of the stereotype. Additionally, Jews are popularly stereotyped as good investors and businessmen, a stereotype that may over the years have inclined the regulators to look upon them more favorably. This image, along with the pejorative one that Italians are dumb as well as criminal and violent, may also explain why it is popularly believed that Italians use Jews to make their rackets profitable. Finally, Mormon influences on the regulatory process may explain this finding. As we have noted, Mormons doctrinally identify with Jews. This identification may also incline them to look more favorably upon individuals of Jewish background, much in the same way that the regulatory process might favor Mormons themselves. Jews may thus be buffered from the more negative assessments that members of out-groups face more generally. As we have seen, they have tended not only to avoid entry into the Black Book but also to have obtained major interests in the industry.

Epilogue: Where Are They Now?

The extent to which a largely symbolic mechanism such as the Black Book can accomplish a degree of control in the gaming industry is an interesting issue. One might comment on that through a look at the present circumstances of those who have been listed on its pages over the years. Without question, some of the individuals, although indeed colorful and possibly even notorious, appear to have presented little real threat to the industry.

Where are they now? The dreaded Civellas, Frank Masterana, Chris Petti, and even Anthony Spilotro? When were they last seen? Only 3 of the original 11 are alive: Marshal Caifano, Louis Tom Dragna, and Joseph Sica. In 1991, Caifano was released from prison at age 80 following a 1979 conviction for dealing in stolen securities. Dragna, now 74 years old, is imprisoned following a 1980 conviction for racketeering and conspiracy. Sica, 83, is retired in Los Angeles County. And Carl Civella only recently died in prison, where he had been serving time for skimming in the Tropicana case. His death is said to have left the Kansas City mafia without a boss.[1]

The situation of the nominees in the mid-1960s and 1970s is not as discernible. Of the three men who were placed in the Book in 1965, Kolod died shortly thereafter, and the whereabouts of Alderisio and Alderman are unknown. The two Hawaiians are still living, apparently in Hawaii; as far as we have been able to discern, they have never come to Las Vegas, either before or after their exclusion from casinos. Whether Giordano and Zerilli, who were nominated in 1975 and removed from nomination in 1976 because they were imprisoned for hidden ownership in the Frontier, are free in the community, still imprisoned, or deceased is unclear. Because DeLuna had received 16 years for skimming from the Stardust and 30 years for skimming from the Tropicana, the regulators dismissed his 1979 nomination to the Black Book in 1989. Agosto, known for his "staying power" with the regulators, was in the news almost a decade after his fatal heart attack in the federal penitentiary in Leavenworth, Kansas. Because he was said to have been linked to the collapse of the Mineral Bank in Las Vegas, the Federal Deposit Insurance Corporation asked for a judgment in bankruptcy court against monies that his production company obtained in a judgment against the operating company of the Tropicana. The FDIC won over $2 million.[2]

The Black Book's sociometric star, Anthony Spilotro, although dead now more than eight years, continues to generate local attention. Black Book members Rosenthal, Citro, Cusumano, Masterana, Petti, Spinale, Manarite, and DeLeo were discredited and continue to be discredited because of alleged links to Spilotro. One should not forget the infamous Hole in the Wall Gang, a Las Vegas burglary ring allegedly masterminded by Spilotro and run by his lieutenant, Frank Cullotta, now under protection as a government informant.[3] Although the ring was said to have taken merchandise amounting to millions of dollars, one is compelled to ask, Why would a Chicago enforcer be the mastermind of a burglary ring?

Recent indication of on-going interest in tough Tony is the production of a motion picture based on his and Rosenthal's alleged activities in the gaming industry in the late 1970s and 1980s. *Casino,* directed by Martin Scorsese, stars Joe Pesci as Spilotro and Robert De Niro as Rosenthal. Even Oscar Goodman, who represented both Spilotro and Rosenthal in their Black Book hearings, has signed to play himself. Currently in production in Las Vegas, the movie is set for its opening in late 1995, probably just when *The Black Book and the Mob* hits the bookstores.

Even Nevadans who are candidates for political office are fair game for stigmatization on the basis of allegations of association with Spilotro. A Las Vegas radio station aired this political advertisement in October of 1994: "Senator Bryan had a law partner— Oscar Goodman—lawyer to criminal figure Tony 'the Ant' Spilotro. Does that mean Bryan too is lawyer to mob figures?"

Spilotro, however, brings reputability and vitality to some:

those newsmen and columnists who have written about him and law enforcement personnel who were somehow involved. A retired FBI agent was recently interviewed at length about his investigation of Spilotro. The agent was quoted as having spent more than a decade investigating "the Spilotro organization in Las Vegas,"[4] which again raises the question: Why, given all this investigation and wiretapping, was the official record of Anthony Joseph Spilotro so sparse?

Frank Rosenthal also continues to attract the interest of Las Vegas newspapers, which have reported on his sports handicapping radio show broadcast from California, and management of a Boca Raton nightspot. When he recently sued two men for return of a $150,000 cash loan to purchase a North Las Vegas motel, a local editorialist seized upon the opportunity to rehash Rosenthal's earlier days in Las Vegas, including the car bombing and friendship and alleged falling out with Spilotro, and to suggest by implication his continued "presence" in the city. But now the portrayal of Rosenthal is a more evil one, characterizing him as crazy with an "old circle of friends which includes an assortment of psychotic killers and various and sundry knee-crackers."[5]

Chris Petti has been in the news on several occasions, all involving alleged criminal activities. In 1990 in federal court in San Diego, he was found guilty of money laundering, the money allegedly having come from Colombian drug dealers. Within a year, disclosure of FBI wiretaps of his phone calls in the late 1980s, even calls made from pay phones, linked him to the Chicago mob's alleged attempts to become involved in proposed gaming activities on the Rincon Indian Reservation in southern California. The subsequent federal indictment for racketeering and extortion in this case named, along with Petti and seven others, the attorney who defended Petti before the Nevada gaming regulators.[6] And, in 1993, at age 65, Petti was convicted of attempting to infiltrate a planned Indian gaming hall—one which never materialized—and was sentenced to nine-and-one-half years in prison.

William Gene Land, following charges of involvement in an alleged $190,000 card-marking scam at the Lummi Indian casino near Seattle was recently convicted of attempting to defraud in the case.[7] Employees there are said to have removed new decks from the casino and arranged to have them marked and returned to the blackjack tables. Recall that Land was entered into the Nevada Black Book for allegedly marking cards from Las Vegas' Riviera, also for the purpose of cheating at blackjack.[8]

Carl Wesley Thomas, a man who presented some ambiguity for the regulators because he was a trusted casino owner, recently died. He was the victim of a truck accident near his Oregon farm at age 60. A woman was heard to comment upon reading the newspaper coverage of his death that it was unfortunate that the article was prefaced with "Black Book member" rather than his name. By the same token, the first line read: "Carl Wesley Thomas, Sr., a gaming executive whose career crumbled when the FBI caught him teaching mobsters how to skim money from Las Vegas casinos, died Thursday in an Oregon traffic accident."[9] It was just a few years earlier that the application of Carl Wesley Thomas, Jr., for a gaming license in Colorado was threatened by his father's crimes and Black Book membership. Although former commissioner George Swarts commented on that situation to the effect that he "would hate to see the sins of the father fall on the fate of the son,"[10] that is precisely what such denunciation accomplishes, and it is not an unanticipated consequence, we would add.

Suffice it to say that all those Black Book members who have remained in Las Vegas are likely to be under constant surveillance. Frank Masterana, a local character before his 1988 entry, his pony tail now gray, has continued to be seen in sports books on the Strip. In 1991, he left for the Dominican Republic, where bookmaking is legal, with the approval of the U.S. District Court for Nevada. And when the FBI broke up a bookmaking ring in Jamaica in December of 1992, Masterana was said to be one of the 16 arrested at the time. Although said to have violated probation and to have been sentenced to prison for associating with ex-felons, the now 64-year-old Masterana is reported to be back at work taking bets in the Santo Domingo sun.[11]

Among the more recent small-time nominees, even though some occasionally generate news coverage, the coverage only affirms the minimal degree of their threat. Within the last few years, gaming regulators have been successful in apprehending two Black Book members violating the conditions of their exclusion.[12] In April of 1993, gaming control agents located Frank Citro, Jr., sitting in front of a video poker machine at 3:40 in the morning at Sam's Town in Las Vegas. He was booked and charged with the gross misdemeanor of unlawful entry into a gaming establishment, but the case was recently dismissed. Timothy Childs, a convicted slot cheat, was observed playing a gaming machine at Club Cal-Neva in Reno in July of 1992. Childs pled guilty to a misdemeanor charge of trespassing, and after serving 15 days in jail and 120 hours of community service, he reputedly moved to Michigan. And finally, Harold Lyons, another convicted slot cheat, was sentenced to life in prison without the possibility of parole, under a habitual criminal statute, for conviction of drug offenses.[13]

Appendices

Notes

References

Index

Appendix A

Chronology of Important Events and Legislative and Regulatory Acts in Nevada Gaming (1950–1994)

	Events	Legislative and Regulatory Acts
1950–1951	Kefauver committee hearings	
1955	Disclosure of Thunderbird financed by Lansky	Gaming Control Board established
1957	McClellan Senate investigations	
1958	Gangland violence incidents and Teamsters' loans to casinos	
1959		Gaming Control Act; Gaming Commission established
1960		Black Book initiated with entry of 11 men
	Black Book members Caifano and Dragna appeal entry	
1963	Black Book member Giancana visits Sinatra's Cal-Neva Lodge	
1965	Federal convictions of Desert Inn owner Kolod and associates	Kolod and associates briefly entered into Black Book
1966	Arrival of Hughes with purchase of Desert Inn	
1967	U.S. Supreme Court refuses to hear Caifano's appeal	Gaming Control Act revised to provide for notice, hearing, and judicial review in Black Book cases

237

	Events	Legislative and Regulatory Acts
	Federal Task Force on Organized Crime	
1969		Corporate Licensing Act
1970	Hughes's departure from Las Vegas	
1972		Regulation 28 formalizes criteria for entry into Black Book
1974	Glick forms Argent with Teamsters' loans	Governor and board chairman meet with ailing Hughes
1975		Two men entered into Black Book and three nominated
1976	New Jersey approves casino gambling; Hughes dies	Gaming Commission denies Rosenthal licensing
1977	Atlantic City approves casino gambling	
1978	First casino opens in Atlantic City; Spilotro appeals Black Book entry; Federal indictments in Argent case	First public Black Book hearing (Spilotro); Gaming Commission denies Rosenthal licensing second time
1979	Federal convictions for hidden control of Aladdin; Federal indictments for hidden control of Tropicana	Aladdin's license revoked; Argent's orders of registration revoked; Glick's license revoked; Thomas' license revoked; Two men nominated to Black Book
1981	Federal indictments in Tropicana case	

	Events	Legislative and Regulatory Acts
1983	Nevada Supreme Court rules Black Book constitutional; Convictions in Tropicana case; More indictments in Argent case	
1986	Slain bodies of Spilotro and brother found; Convictions in Argent case	
1986–1989		10 persons entered into Black Book
1988	Indian Casino Act (federal)	
1989		Race, color, creed, or national origin cannot be basis for exclusion
1990	Marcus case and allegations of board chairman's involvement	
1990–1994		10 men entered into Black Book and 3 nominated
1991	Pictures of UNLV athletes in hot tub with convicted sports fixer	

Appendix B

Aliases of Nominees and Entries to the Black Book

AGOSTO, Joseph Vincent	"Caesar" Vincenzo DiPaola Pianetti
ALDERISIO, Felix	"Milwaukee Phil"
ALDERMAN, William	"Icepick Willie"
BARR, Douglas Joseph, Jr.	Doug Joe Barr Robert Barr Rocky Barr
BARR, Douglas William	Robert Aston Gene Barr Royce Butler Robert Lee Edwards Donn Pinsonne
BATTAGLIA, John Louis	John Batts John Bats John Bennett John L. Mink
CAIFANO, Marshal	Joe Cafano Marshal Cafano Marshall Califano George Marini Joe Marshal John J. Marshal

Aliases

CAIFANO, Marshal (*continued*)
John Marshall
John Michael Marshall
Joseph Rinaldi
Frank Roberto
Joe Russo
Jack Steffeen

CHILDS, Timothy John
Timothy Brophy
Daniel Robert Childs
Kim Childs
Timothy Jorin Childs
James Cooper
Timothy Singleton

CITRO, Francis, Jr.
"Little Frankie"
Frank Citro

CIVELLA, Carl James
"Corky"
"Cork" Civella
Corky Civella
James Bove
H. Evans

CIVELLA, Nicholas
M. Boyer
Nick Civella

COPPOLA, Michael
"Trigger Mike"
Michael Bruno
John Capolo
John Grosso
Michael Marino
Mike Ross

CORBO, Albert Anthony
Al Carrio
Albert Corbo
Harvey Mittman
Joyce Mittman

CUSUMANO, Joseph Vincent
"Joey"
Joey Cusumano
Joseph London

DELEO, Edward Lawrence
"Fast Eddy"

241

DELUNA, Carl Angelo

"Tuffy"
C. Dogman
Mr. Zoppo

DRAGNA, Louis Tom

Lou Allen
Lou Dragna

GARCIA, Robert L.

Bobby Garcia
Robert Louis Garcia
Louis R. Romero

GIANCANA, Sam

"Mooney" Giancana
Sam Flood
Sam Gencani
Sam Giancaco
Sam Giancano
Sam Giancanno
Sam Gincana
Sam Gincani
Sam Mooney
Sam Wood

GIORDANO, Anthony

unknown

GRZEBIENACY, Motel

Max Jaben

HUMPHREYS, Murray Llewellyn

"the Camel"
M. L. Brunswick
John Burns
Joseph Burns
Mr. Harris
John Humphreys
M. L. Hurley
Dave Ostrund
Alfred Rice

KAOHU, Alvin George

"Ali Baba"

KOLOD, Ruby

unknown

LAND, William Gene

LYONS, Harold Travis

Harold Jarvis Lyons
Harold Lee Lyons
Willis Roebuck Lyons

MANARITE, Samuel Filippo	Springfield Sam
	Sammy Springfield
	Bob Manarite
	Salvatore Manarite
MASTERANA, Frank Joseph	Frank Joseph Masterangelo
	Frank Joseph Masters
MORRIS, Brent Eli	Tom Biago
	Tom Braco
	Tom Brago
	Tom Grago
	Thomas Hubbard
	Walter Hubbard
	Mario Johnson
PERRY, Richard Mark	"the Fixer"
	Alan Cohen
	Richard Cohen
	Richard Alan Cohen
	Ronald Coleman
	Richard Daniels
	Richard A. Daniels
	Richard Perry
	Sam Perry
	Robert Smith
PETTI, Chris George	Chris Poulos
	Christopher Poulos
	Christopher Polous
POLIZZI, Michael Santo	unknown
PULAWA, Wilford Kalaauala	"Brother"
	Nappy Pulawa
RIZZITELLO, Michael Anthony	Mechael Anthony Rizzatello
	Michael Anthony Rizzie
ROSENTHAL, Frank Larry	"Lefty"
	Charles Carpentier
	Frank Carpentier
	Larry Franks
	Frank Grossup
	Frank Larry

ROSENTHAL, Frank Larry (*cont.*)   Larry Rosenthal
            Norman Rosenthal

ST. LAURENT, Anthony Michael, Sr. "the Saint"
            "the Pope"
            Anthony Simone
            Anthony St. Laurent
            Anthony St. Laurant
            Anthony Michael St. Lauren

SICA, Joseph   "Wild Cowboy"
            Joe Lewis
            Joe Russell
            Joe Sica

SPECIALE, Gaspare Anedetto   Jerry Martin
            Jasper Martinson
            Jasper A. Speciale
            Martin Speciale

SPILOTRO, Anthony Joseph   "the Ant"
            Pasquale Peter Spilotro
            Tony Spilotro
            Tony Pasquale Spilotro
            Anthony Stewart
            Anthony Stuart

SPINALE, Dominic   "Dickie Boy"
            Dickie Spinale
            Dominic Rossi
            Roll Star

TAMER, James   George Owen
            John Rouse
            James Occo Tamer
            James Tanner
            George Webb

THOMAS, Carl Wesley   Jimmy Thomas

VACCARO, John Joseph, Jr.   Alan Joseph Champagne

VACCARO, Sandra Kay   Sandra Day Fumagalli
            Sandra Kay Wondra

ZERILLI, Anthony Joseph   unknown

Appendix C

Table C.1. Residence of nominee at time of nomination

	n	%
California	6	13.3
Florida	2	4.4
Hawaii	2	4.4
Illinois	3	6.7
Michigan	1	2.2
Missouri	3	6.7
Nevada		
Las Vegas	18	40.0
Reno–Sparks	2	4.4
Rhode Island	1	2.2
Not known	7	15.6
Total	45	100.0

Note: In this and the following tables, percentages do not always total 100.0 because of rounding.

Table C.2. Birthplace of nominees to the black book

	n	%
Outside continental U.S.		
Canada	1	2.2
Poland	1	2.2
Sicily	2	4.4
Honolulu	2	4.4
Chicago	6	13.3
Kansas City	3	6.7
Other midwestern locations	6	13.3
Canton, Ohio		
Grand Rapids, Michigan		
Detroit, Michigan		
Granite City, Illinois		
Springfield, Missouri		
New York–New Jersey	10	22.2
Other northeastern locations	1	2.2
Pottsville, Pennsylvania		
New England	1	2.2
Providence, Rhode Island		
Los Angeles	2	4.4
Southern states	5	11.1
DeQueen, Arkansas		
Alabama		
Hazard, Kentucky		
New Orleans, Louisiana		
Portsmouth, Virginia		
Unknown	5	11.1
Total	45	100.0

Table C.3. Ethnicity of Black Book nominees and their associates

	Nominees		Associates	
	n	%	n	%
Anglo-Saxon	7	15.6	4	6.4
Italian	28	62.2	39	62.9
Jewish	4	8.9	14	22.6
Hawaiian	2	4.4	0	0.0
Greek	0	0.0	1	1.6
Eastern European	1	2.2	0	0.0
Lebanese	1	2.2	0	0.0
Hispanic	1	2.2	0	0.0
Unknown	1	2.2	4	6.5
Total	45	100.0	62	100.0

Table C.4. Ethnicity of the regulators

	Board		Commission	
	n	%	n	%
Anglo-Saxon	15	75.0	20	74.1
Italian	1	5.0	1	3.7
Jewish	1	5.0	1	3.7
Basque	2	10.0	1	3.7
Hispanic	0	0.0	1	3.7
Black	0	0.0	1	3.7
Unknown	1	5.0	2	7.4
Total	20	100.0	27	100.0

Table C.5. Alleged criminal associations of nominees

	n	%
Associations		
Associate of Black Book member	20	44.4
Associate of organized crime	8	17.8
Organized crime figure	24	53.3
Not mentioned	5	11.1
Total[a]	45	100.0
Syndicate affiliation		
Chicago	10	41.7
Kansas City	5	20.8
Los Angeles	4	16.7
New England	1	4.2
New York	1	4.2
Hawaii	2	8.3
Unknown	1	4.2
Total	24	100.0
Syndicate position		
Boss	7	29.2
Lieutenant	4	16.7
Enforcer	3	12.5
Henchman	1	4.2
Loan shark	4	16.7
Collector	1	4.2
Soldier	1	4.2
Unknown	3	12.5
Total	24	100.0

[a]Within this category the numbers total more than 45 and the percentages total more than 100 because of the multiple classifications of many of the nominees.

Table C.6. Legitimate occupation of nominees

Steel and electronics manufacturer, owner of a country club, and Las Vegas show director	1
Part owner and manager of a casino	2
Owner of a manufacturing company	1
Owner of a construction company	1
Las Vegas show producer	1
Movie line producer	1
Casino entertainment director and TV talk show host	1
Auto retailer	1
Jewelry store manager	1
Sports service owner	2
Plumber's assistant	1
Taxi driver	1
Not known	31
Total	45

Notes

CHAPTER 1. DENUNCIATION AND THE
ILLUSION OF SOCIAL CONTROL

1. Turner 1965: 159–160; Olsen 1976.
2. Nevada Gaming Commission transcripts, June 19, 1986: 6–7 (hereafter cited as "NGC transcripts").
3. Bowers and Titus 1987.
4. Nevada Revised Statutes (as amended in 1985), chapter 463.
5. Nevada Revised Statutes (as amended in 1989), chapter 463.151.4.
6. Morrison 1985a; Koziol 1988.
7. Tobin 1988.
8. Durkheim [1904] 1938; Mead 1918; Garfinkel 1956; Erikson 1966.
9. Gusfield 1967; Galliher and Cross 1983.
10. Erikson 1966; Gusfield 1967; Connor 1972; Inverarity 1976; Davies 1982; Ben-Yehuda 1985, 1990, 1992; Liska 1992.
11. Garfinkel 1956.
12. NGC transcripts, Dec. 2, 1978: 14–16.
13. Edelman 1964; Gusfield 1967; Zurcher et al. 1971; Connor 1972; Chambliss 1975; Spitzer 1975; Inverarity 1976; Swigert and Farrell 1976; Scull 1977; Colvin and Pauley 1983; Ben-Yehuda 1985, 1990, 1992.
14. For explanations of the operation of stereotypes in legal decision making more generally, see Hawkins and Tiedeman 1975; Swigert and Farrell 1977; Lurigio and Carroll 1985; Drass and Spencer 1987; Farrell and Holmes 1991.
15. See Albini 1971; Smith 1975, 1976; Block 1978; Kelly 1978; Albanese 1982.
16. For general explanations of the process, see Emerson 1983; and Farrell and Holmes 1991.
17. See Swigert and Farrell 1977; Farrell and Holmes 1991.

18. See Bodenhausen 1988.
19. See Frey 1986.
20. See Anderson et al. 1980; McCauley et al. 1980.

CHAPTER 2. BABYLON IN THE DESERT

1. O'Dea 1957.
2. Ostrander 1966: 19.
3. O'Dea 1957: 2, 53; Book of Mormon, 2 Nephi 25:6.
4. Book of Mormon, Helaman 15:4, Mormon 5:15, 2 Nephi 5:21.
5. *Doctrine and Covenants* 103: 17; Book of Mormon, 4 Nephi 1:37.
6. Anderson 1942: 334, 420–421; Roberts 1984: 361.
7. Vogliotti 1975: 4.
8. Ostrander 1966: 156.
9. Ostrander 1966: 68, 82.
10. Galliher and Cross 1983: 6.
11. Galliher and Cross 1983: 6; Skolnick 1978: 152, 154; Edwards 1992: 213.
12. *Doctrine and Covenants* 89: 5, 7–9; O'Dea 1957.
13. Anderson 1942: 334; Roberts 1984: 361.
14. See Edwards 1992: 213.
15. Edwards 1992: 213.
16. Wiley and Gottlieb 1982: 199.
17. Skolnick 1978; Elliott 1973.
18. Skolnick 1978.
19. Nevada Gaming Commission and State Gaming Control Board 1989: 7.
20. Skolnick 1978: 215.
21. Vogel 1991: 2B.
22. Skolnick 1978: 215; Findlay 1986: 123.
23. Findlay 1986: 123.
24. Haller 1985: 139; subsequent page references in the text pertain to this source.
25. Findlay 1986: 153.
26. Goodwin 1985; Bowers and Titus 1987.
27. *Evening Review Journal* 1946.
28. Curtis 1981: 65.
29. Ostrander 1966: 217.
30. Vogliotti 1975: 201–202.
31. *Las Vegas Review Journal* 1955.
32. Turner 1965; Curtis 1981; Kefauver Committee Hearings 1951: 91.
33. Reid and Demaris 1964: 151.

34. Nevada Gaming Commission and State Gaming Control Board 1989: 9.

35. Kefauver Committee Hearings 1951: 91; the subsequent page reference in the text pertains to this source.

36. Reid and Demaris 1964: 53; Turner 1965: 65.

37. Reid and Demaris 1964: 54.

38. Vogel 1990a.

39. Bowers and Titus 1987; Findlay 1986: 156; Vogliotti 1975: 202; Reid and Demaris 1964: 66.

40. Ostrander 1966: 218.

41. Reid and Demaris 1964: 70–78; Turner 1965: 109–110.

42. Reid and Demaris 1963: 98–109.

43. Turner 1965: 96–97.

44. Cahill 1976; subsequent page references in the text pertain to this source.

45. Burbank 1992.

46. Goodwin 1985; Bowers and Titus 1987; Nevada Gaming Commission and State Gaming Control Board 1989.

47. Wiley and Gottlieb 1982: 198, 204.

48. Nevada Gaming Control Board transcripts, Nov. 4, 1959, and Apr. 6, 1960 (hereafter cited as "NGCB transcripts").

49. NGCB transcripts, Feb. 2, 1960; NGC transcripts, Feb. 16, 1960.

50. NGC transcripts, Mar. 15, 1960: 16.

51. Turner 1965.

52. NGCB, June 13, 1960.

53. Skolnick 1978.

54. NGCB transcripts, Feb. 2, 1960: 12.

55. NGCB transcripts, May 16, 1960.

56. Reid and Demaris 1964: 128.

57. NGCB transcripts, May 16, 1960: 13; subsequent page references in the text pertain to this source.

58. Kefauver Committee Hearings 1951: 92.

59. NGCB transcripts, May 16, 1960.

60. NGCB transcripts, May 27, 1960; subsequent page references in the text pertain to this source.

61. NGC transcripts, June 1, 1960: 21.

62. Skolnick 1978: 129–130.

63. NGCB transcripts, June 8, 1960.

64. NGCB transcripts, June 8, 1960: 50–64; subsequent page references in the text pertain to this source.

65. Reid and Demaris 1964: 187.

66. NGCB transcripts, Aug. 1960; subsequent page references in the text pertain to this source.

67. Bloom 1960: 21–22.
68. NGCB transcripts, Aug. 1960: 65.
69. Findlay 1986: 157.
70. Vogliotti 1975: 207.
71. Morash 1984: 192.
72. Smith 1975.
73. Turner 1965: 78.
74. Roemer 1990: 324.
75. Associated Press 1978.

CHAPTER 3. GENESIS OF THE BLACK BOOK

1. Bell 1953; Giancana and Giancana 1992.
2. Sion 1987; Bell 1953; Reid and Demaris 1964: 182.
3. Bell 1953; *Las Vegas Review Journal* 1982.
4. *Las Vegas Review Journal* 1982.
5. Kelley 1988; Chambliss 1990; Turner 1965: 162.
6. Kelley 1988; Chambliss 1990; Giancana and Giancana 1992.
7. Olsen 1976: 2–5.
8. Nevada Revised Statutes, chapter 463.145.
9. Olsen 1976: 4.
10. Olsen 1972: 331; Olsen 1976: 2.
11. Olsen 1976: 7; the subsequent page reference in the text pertains to this source.
12. Bowers and Titus 1987; *Las Vegas Review Journal* 1982.
13. Vogliotti 1975: 207.
14. Bowers and Titus 1987.
15. NGC transcripts, June 29, 1961.
16. *Marshall v. Sawyer*, 301 F. 2d.
17. NGCB and NGC transcripts, joint meeting, Dec. 19, 1978: 156–158.
18. Turner 1965: 161–167.
19. Olsen 1972: 371–374.
20. Turner 1965: 165–167.
21. Olsen 1972: 381–382; subsequent page references in the text pertain to this source.
22. *Marshall v. Sawyer*, Civil No. 360, D. Nev., Dec. 1960 and Feb. 13, 1967.
23. *Marshall v. Sawyer*, 365 F. 2d 105.
24. *Marshall v. Sawyer*, 385 U.S. 1006.
25. NGCB transcripts, July 12, 1961: 131–135; subsequent page references in the text pertain to this source.
26. NGCB transcripts, Sept. 8, 1961.

27. Edelman 1964; Galliher and Cross 1983: 125.
28. NGCB transcripts, Feb. 2, 1960: 12.
29. Turner 1965: 134–135; Vogliotti 1975: 201–209; Reid and Demaris 1964: 88.
30. Turner 1965: 135.
31. Kennedy 1965.
32. Vogliotti 1975: 203.
33. *Las Vegas Review Journal* 1982.
34. Vogliotti 1975: 203–209.
35. *Reno Evening Gazette* 1965; Kennedy 1965.
36. *Reno Evening Gazette* 1965.
37. *Las Vegas Review Journal* 1965.
38. *Nevada State Journal* 1965.
39. Turner 1965: 92.
40. Vogliotti 1975: 207–209.

CHAPTER 4. A SAVIOR COMES TO BABYLON

1. Skolnick 1978: 136; Wiley and Gottlieb 1982: 202.
2. NGCB transcripts, Apr. 30, 1968; Curtis 1981: 24; Skolnick 1978: 135.
3. Edwards 1992: 206.
4. Day 1987.
5. Phelan 1976: ix–xvi; subsequent page references in the text pertain to this source.
6. Phelan 1976: 172–174; Skolnick 1978: 139.
7. Vogliotti 1975: 209.
8. Goodwin 1985: 168.
9. Gaming Control Board and Gaming Commission agendas for the 1970s.
10. NGC transcripts, June 21, 1979.
11. NGC transcripts, July 25, 1974: 40; Brill 1978: 232–237.
12. Brill 1978: 232–242; subsequent page references in the text pertain to this source.
13. NGC transcripts, May 26, 1976; Rhodes 1984: 8.
14. Rhodes 1984; Day 1987.
15. *Marshall v. Sawyer,* 365 F. 2d 105.
16. Bowers and Titus 1987.
17. Final Order of Exclusion, Case Nos. 74-13 and 74-14, Jan. 23, 1975.
18. NGC transcripts, Aug. 22, 1974: 8–9; subsequent page references in the text pertain to this source.
19. *Las Vegas Review Journal* 1982.

CHAPTER 5. ENEMIES FROM WITHIN

1. NGC transcripts, Mar. 24, 1977: 2.
2. Journal Wire Services 1981: 1, 5.
3. *Reno Evening Gazette* 1975.
4. NGC transcripts, May 19, 1977: 8.
5. Smith 1992b: 1B.
6. Smith 1992b: 1B.
7. German 1994.
8. *Time* 1977; Goodman 1983a: 1A; Goodman 1983b: 2A.
9. *Time* 1977; Goodman 1983b: 2A.
10. German 1994: 5D.
11. *Time* 1977.
12. Goodman 1983b: 1A, 2A.
13. Goodman 1983c: 4A.
14. Goodman 1983d.
15. Kirby 1978; Goodman 1983e: 1A, 15A.
16. Goodman 1983d: 3A.
17. Goodman 1983e: 15A.
18. Kirby 1978; Morrison 1978a, 1978b, 1978c.
19. Goodman 1983e: 15A.
20. *Las Vegas Review Journal* 1978.
21. NGC transcripts, Dec. 2, 1978; subsequent page references in the text pertain to this source.
22. NGCB transcripts, Jan. 14, 1976.
23. NGCB and NGC transcripts, joint meeting, Dec. 19, 1978: 127.
24. NGCB transcripts, Jan. 14, 1976; subsequent page references in the text pertain to this source.
25. NGC transcripts, Oct. 6, 1978; subsequent page references in the text pertain to this source.
26. NGCB transcripts, Aug. 15, 1979: 120–126.
27. Smith 1992c; Smith 1994a.
28. NGC transcripts, Oct. 6, 1978: 114.
29. NGC transcripts, Nov. 18, 1978.
30. NGCB transcripts, Dec. 6, 1978: 13, 14.
31. NGC and NGCB transcripts, joint meeting, Dec. 19, 1978: 48.
32. NGCB transcripts, Dec. 6, 1978: 12.
33. Brill 1978: 238–241.
34. NGCB and NGC transcripts, joint meeting, Dec. 19, 1978: 121–123; subsequent page references in the text pertain to this source.
35. NGC transcripts, Nov. 30–Dec. 1, 1988: 176; the subsequent page reference in the text pertains to this source.
36. Day 1985.

37. NGC transcripts, Aug. 23, 1979: 4.
38. NGC transcripts, Dec. 17, 1986: 4; subsequent page reference in the text pertains to this source.
39. NGC transcripts, Aug. 23, 1979; subsequent page references in the text pertain to this source.
40. NGC transcripts, Jan. 22, 1987: 67.
41. LaVelle 1987; Stutz 1990a.
42. NGCB transcripts, Mar. 21, 1986: 8.
43. NGC transcripts, Dec. 17, 1986: 19–38; subsequent page references in the text pertain to this source.
44. NGC transcripts, Jan. 22, 1987: 61; the subsequent page reference in the text pertains to this source.
45. NGC transcripts, Dec. 18, 1978: 186.
46. NGC transcripts, Sept. 23, 1977: 153; subsequent page references in the text pertain to this source.
47. NGC transcripts, Nov. 28, 1977: 10, 14, 15.
48. NGC transcripts, Aug. 23, 1979: 92.
49. NGC transcripts, Nov. 28, 1977: 21.
50. Kelley 1979: 1, 12.
51. Griffith 1981.

CHAPTER 6. CONTROL COMES TO BABYLON

1. *Spilotro v. State ex rel. Gaming Commission,* 99 Nev. 187–197; 661 P. 2d 467–470.
2. Bowers and Titus 1987: 320; NGC transcripts, Sept. 21, 1988: 53.
3. NGCB transcripts, Oct. 2, 1986: 318.
4. Hollis 1990.
5. NGCB transcripts, Oct. 2, 1986: 318; Burbank 1992.
6. NGC transcripts, Dec. 17, 1986: 40.
7. NGC transcripts, Dec. 17, 1986: 128.
8. Day 1985.
9. NGC transcripts, Jan. 22, 1987: 39; subsequent page references in the text pertain to this source.
10. NGC transcripts, Dec. 17, 1986: 73–74; subsequent page references in the text pertain to this source.
11. NGC transcripts, Jan. 22, 1987: 6–8; subsequent page references in the text pertain to this source.
12. NGC transcripts, June 21, 1990: 203.
13. NGC transcripts, Nov. 30–Dec. 1, 1988.
14. NGCB transcripts, Mar. 31, 1988: 25–26.
15. NGC transcripts, Oct. 19, 1988.
16. NGC transcripts, Nov. 30–Dec. 1, 1988: 39; subsequent page references in the text pertain to this source.

17. *State of Nevada and State of Nevada Gaming Commission, Appellants, v. Frank Rosenthal, Respondent,* 559 Pacific 2d, 3830, Feb. 3, 1977.

18. NGC transcripts, Nov. 30–Dec. 1, 1988: 137–140; subsequent page references in the text pertain to this source.

19. Bates 1990: 1A.

20. Smith 1990b.

21. Stutz 1990c: 1B.

22. Smith 1990c; Ralston 1990.

CHAPTER 7. TAMER "THE ATYPICAL"

1. NGCB transcripts, July 12, 1978: 2; NGC transcripts, Aug. 26, 1976: 32.

2. NGCB transcripts, Aug. 18, 1976: 122, 123; subsequent page references in the text pertain to this source.

3. NGC transcripts, Sept. 15, 1977: 24.

4. NGCB transcripts, July 12, 1978: 3; subsequent page references in the text pertain to this source.

5. *Marchetti v. United States,* 309 U.S. 39; and *Grosso v. United States,* 390 U.S. 62.

6. NGCB transcripts, July 12, 1978: 38.

7. *United States v. United States Coin and Currency,* 401 U.S. 715.

8. NGCB transcripts, July 12, 1978: 4.

9. NGCB transcripts, Aug. 18, 1976: 121.

10. NGCB transcripts, July 12, 1978: 35–36; subsequent page references in the text pertain to this source.

11. NGC transcripts, Aug. 16, 1978: 3; subsequent page references in the text pertain to this source.

12. NGCB transcripts, Oct. 2, 1986: 301.

13. NGC, emergency order, Mar. 15, 1979.

14. NGC transcripts, Aug. 18, 1988: 49.

15. NGC transcripts, Apr. 24, 1980: 2; subsequent page references in the text pertain to this source.

16. NGCB transcripts, Oct. 2, 1986: 301–302.

17. NGCB transcripts, Mar. 31, 1988: 8–9.

18. NGC transcripts, Aug. 18, 1988: 4; subsequent page references in the text pertain to this source.

19. NGCB transcripts, Aug. 24, 1988: 1–2.

20. NGC transcripts, Sept. 22, 1988: 144; subsequent page references in the text pertain to this source.

CHAPTER 8. RENEWED ZEAL

1. Cressey 1967.

2. Salerno and Tompkins 1969; Roemer 1989, 1990.

3. E.g., Bell 1953; Albini 1971; Moore 1974; Smith 1975, 1976; Pearce 1976; Block 1978, 1983; Kelly 1978; Albanese 1982.

4. For a review see Smith 1975.

5. Cressey 1967, 1969, 1972; Haskell and Yablonsky 1983.

6. Galliher and Cain 1974.

7. NGC transcripts, Apr. 16, 1987; subsequent page references in the text pertain to this source.

8. *People v. Poulos,* CR Action No. 47961, Superior Court of California, County of San Diego, Sept. 12, 1979.

9. NGC transcripts, Apr. 16, 1987: 42–43; subsequent page references in the text pertain to this source.

10. NGCB transcripts, Mar. 31, 1988: 28; subsequent page references in the text pertain to this source.

11. NGC transcripts, July 28, 1988: 6.

12. NGCB transcripts, Mar. 31, 1988: 30, 31.

13. NGCB transcripts, Mar. 31, 1988: 31.

14. NGC transcripts, Nov. 16, 1978: 110; subsequent page references in the text pertain to this source.

15. NGC transcripts, Dec. 15, 1978: 22; subsequent page references in the text pertain to this source.

16. NGCB transcripts, July 21, 1988: 13; subsequent page references in the text pertain to this source.

17. NGC transcripts, Oct. 19, 1988: 4; subsequent page references in the text pertain to this source.

18. NGC transcripts, Dec. 17, 1963; NGCB transcripts, Dec. 8, 1988: 2; subsequent page references in the text pertain to the second source.

19. NGCB transcripts, Mar. 21, 1986: 3–7; NGC transcripts, June 19, 1986: 8–10.

20. NGCB transcripts, Mar. 21, 1986: 4.

21. NGC transcripts, June 19, 1986: 1–46.

22. NGC transcripts, July 12, 1988: 56.

23. NGC transcripts, June 19, 1986: 8–12; subsequent page references in the text pertain to this source.

24. NGC transcripts, Apr. 16, 1987: 17.

25. NGCB transcripts, Oct. 1, 1986: 308.

26. Final Order of Exclusion, Case No. 86–12, Apr. 27, 1987.

27. NGC transcripts, Apr. 16, 1987; subsequent page numbers in the text pertain to this source.

28. NGC transcripts, Mar. 23, 1989: 126.

29. NGCB transcripts, Dec. 8, 1988: 20; subsequent page references in the text pertain to this source.

30. NGC transcripts, Mar. 23, 1989: 126.

31. NGC transcripts, Sept. 21, 1988: 38; subsequent page references in the text pertain to this source.

32. NGCB transcripts, July 21, 1988: 6.
33. NGC transcripts, Sept. 21, 1988: 5; subsequent page references in the text pertain to this source.
34. NGCB transcripts, July 21, 1988: 7, 8.
35. NGC transcripts, Sept. 21, 1988: 40; subsequent page references in the text pertain to this source.

CHAPTER 9. CUSUMANO "THE TYPICAL"

1. Tobin 1988; German 1985; Morrison 1985b.
2. NGC transcripts, June 21, 1990: 297.
3. Morrison 1985b, 1985c.
4. Morrison 1985b; Tobin 1985.
5. Morrison 1985b.
6. Tobin 1985; NGC transcripts, June 21, 1990: 401.
7. NGCB transcripts, Dec. 7, 1989.
8. NGC transcripts, June 21, 1990: 250.
9. NGCB transcripts, Dec. 7, 1989: 581–582.
10. Burbank 1989.
11. NGCB transcripts, Dec. 7, 1989: 584; the subsequent page reference in the text pertains to this source.
12. NGC transcripts, June 21, 1990.
13. Smith 1990a.
14. NGC transcripts, June 21, 1990: 442; subsequent page references in the text pertain to this source.
15. Goodwin and Wise 1989; NGC transcripts, June 21, 1990: 241–242, 245–247, 445–449; subsequent page references in the text pertain to the second source.
16. Goodwin and Wise 1989: 385, 386.
17. NGC transcripts, June 21, 1990: 217–218, 292–293; subsequent page references in the text pertain to this source.
18. Stutz 1990f; Knapp 1990.
19. Burbank 1990.
20. Bates 1991.

CHAPTER 10. CONTEMPORARY MORAL CRISES

1. Morrison 1993a.
2. Smith 1993b.
3. Kirk 1991.
4. Stutz 1990d.
5. Stuz 1990b.
6. Stutz 1990d: 4A; Morrison 1993a: 4B.
7. German 1990a.
8. Smith 1993b.

9. Smith 1990e.
10. Smith 1993b.
11. Stutz and Tobin 1990a.
12. Tobin and Stutz 1990a: 5A.
13. Smith 1990d.
14. Stutz and Tobin 1990b, 1990c; German 1990c.
15. Morrison 1993a.
16. Tobin and Stutz 1990b, quotation from p. 4A.
17. Tobin and Stutz 1990b; Stutz and Tobin 1990d.
18. Tobin and Stutz 1990c; Smith 1990e.
19. Stutz and Tobin 1990d.
20. German 1990a: 1D; German 1990b.
21. Stutz 1990e.
22. German 1990c: 3J.
23. *Las Vegas Review Journal* 1991b.
24. Morrison 1991: 1B.
25. Morrison and Tobin 1991, quotation from p. 1A; the subsequent page number in the text pertains to this source.
26. Morrison 1991.
27. Morrison 1992; Geer 1993a, 1993b, 1993c: 1B.
28. Geer 1993a: 4A.
29. *Las Vegas Review Journal* 1993; quotation from Morrison 1993a: 6B.
30. Palermo 1993b.
31. Pierce 1993: 37.
32. Smith 1991a; *Las Vegas Review Journal* 1991a.
33. Gup 1989: 56; Pierce 1993: 38.
34. Ryan 1992.
35. Smith 1991a; *Las Vegas Review Journal* 1991a.
36. Whaley 1992b: 12A.
37. Hopkins 1991; Lederman 1992: A34.
38. Pierce 1993: 37–38.
39. Tobin 1992a; *Las Vegas Review Journal* 1992a; Vogel 1992a.
40. Tobin 1992a; Whaley 1992a.
41. *Las Vegas Review Journal* 1992b.
42. NGCB transcripts, Apr. 9, 1992: 551–553.
43. Whaley 1992c, 1992b: 3A.
44. Tobin 1992c: 1A.
45. NGC transcripts, Oct. 27–28, 1992: 283–287; subsequent page references in the text pertain to this source.
46. Hill and Looney 1981.
47. NGC transcripts, Oct. 27–28, 1992: 295–297; subsequent page references in the text pertain to this source.

CHAPTER 11. RETURN TO MORALITY

1. NGC transcripts, Nov. 28–29, 1990: 555; subsequent page references in the text pertain to this source.

2. NGCB transcripts, June 7, 1990: 874; the subsequent page reference in the text pertains to this source.

3. NGCB transcripts, June 7, 1990: 876–877; NGC transcripts, Nov. 28–29, 1990: 560; the subsequent page reference in the text pertains to the second source.

4. NGCB transcripts, July 12, 1990: 700–701; NGCB transcripts, June 7, 1990: 875–878.

5. NGC transcripts, Nov. 28–29, 1990: 554–559.

6. Whaley 1993.

7. NGCB transcripts, July 12, 1990: 687–701; Associated Press 1991; Vogel 1992b.

8. NGCB transcripts, July 12, 1990: 688–691; subsequent page references in the text pertain to this source.

9. NGC transcripts, Feb. 27–28, 1991: 206–220; subsequent page references in the text pertain to this source.

10. Vogel 1993, 1992b.

11. NGCB transcripts, Dec. 2, 1993; subsequent page references in the text pertain to this source.

12. NGC transcripts, Feb. 24, 1994: 224, 252.

13. NGCB transcripts, Dec. 6, 1990: 771–773, quotation from p. 771.

14. German 1991.

15. NGCB transcripts, Dec. 6, 1990: 775; subsequent page references in the text pertain to this source.

16. NGC transcripts, Nov. 20, 1991: 483; NGCB transcripts, Dec. 6, 1990: 422, 432; subsequent page references in the text pertain to the second source.

17. Smith 1993c.

18. NGCB transcripts, Dec. 6, 1990: 422–426; subsequent page references in the text pertain to this source.

19. NGC transcripts, Nov. 20, 1991: 487; NGCB transcripts, Dec. 6, 1990: 410; subsequent page references in the text pertain to the second source.

20. NGC transcripts, Nov. 20, 1991: 475; subsequent page references in the text pertain to this source.

21. NGC transcripts, Nov. 20, 1991: 498; Final Order of Exclusion, Case No. 90-20: 4, Dec. 9, 1991; subsequent page references in the text pertain to the first source.

22. NGCB transcripts, Apr. 14, 1993: 159.

23. Smith 1993d.

24. NGC transcripts, Sept. 23, 1993: 222.

25. Tobin 1992b.

26. NGCB transcripts, May 6, 1993: especially p. 234.

27. NGC transcripts, Dec. 16, 1993: 247; subsequent page references in the text pertain to this source.

28. NGC transcripts, Sept. 23, 1993; subsequent page references in the text pertain to this source.

29. NGCB transcripts, May 6, 1993: 224; subsequent page references in the text pertain to this source.

30. Tobin 1992b.

31. NGCB transcripts, Nov. 5, 1993: 125–126.

32. Smith 1991b, 1992a; German 1993; Palermo 1993a.

33. NGC transcripts, Sept. 23, 1993: 233.

34. Tobin 1992b.

35. NGCB transcripts, Oct. 7, 1993: 162–169; NGC transcripts, Mar. 24, 1994: 355–356.

36. NGCB transcripts, Oct. 7, 1993: 164; subsequent page references in the text pertain to this source.

37. NGC transcripts, Mar. 24, 1994.

CHAPTER 12. RIGHTEOUS INDIGNATION AND THE MARK OF CAIN

1. Skolnick 1978: 143.

2. Kefauver Committee Hearings 1951: 91.

3. Skolnick 1978: 152, 154.

4. NGCB transcripts, Oct. 5, 1961: especially p. 23.

5. NGCB transcripts, Aug. 3, 1961: especially pp. 13–15.

6. See Glaser and Strauss 1964.

7. NGC transcripts, Oct. 16, 1987: 9; Apr. 16, 1962; Mar. 20, 1986; Dec. 20, 1990: 274; and Dec. 18, 1977: 58–59.

8. Skolnick 1978: 211.

9. Phelan 1976: 10, 99, 117–119.

10. Nevada Revised Statutes (as amended in 1989), chapter 463.151.4.

11. NGC transcripts, Dec. 2, 1978: 120–121.

12. In addition to obituaries and newspaper accounts, the sources for biographical information on the regulators include: *Capitol's Who's Who for Nevada* (1949); *Nevada the Silver State* (1970); *Biographical Dictionary of the United States Congress 1774–1989* (1989); Dixon 1992; Lee and Wadsworth 1966; Lingenfelter and Gash 1984; Moore 1950; Oxborrow and Fund, n.d.; Patterson et al. 1969; Scrugham 1935.

13. NGC transcripts, Nov. 20, 1991: 475.

14. Turner 1965: 75; Roemer 1990: 324.

EPILOGUE: WHERE ARE THEY NOW?

1. Smith 1994d.
2. Tobin 1991a, 1991b.
3. German 1994.
4. German 1994.
5. Smith 1994b.
6. Associated Press 1990; Lieberman 1991; Cass 1992.
7. *Las Vegas Review Journal* 1994; Smith 1994d.
8. NGC transcripts, Sept. 21, 1988: 38.
9. Morrison 1993b: 1B.
10. Garnaas 1991: 3B.
11. Associated Press 1992; Smith 1992d; Tobin 1992d; Smith 1993a.
12. Burbank 1993.
13. Vogel 1990b.

References

Albanese, Jay S. 1982. "What Lockheed and La Cosa Nostra Have in Common." *Crime and Delinquency* 28: 211–232.

Albini, Joseph L. 1971. *The American Mafia: Genesis of a Legend.* New York: Appleton-Century-Crofts.

Anderson, Craig A., Mark R. Lepper, and Lee Ross. 1980. "Perseverance of Social Theories: The Role of Explanation in the Persistence of Discredited Information." *Journal of Personality and Social Psychology* 39: 1037–1049.

Anderson, Nels. 1942. *Deseret Saints: The Mormon Frontier in Utah.* Chicago: University of Chicago Press.

Associated Press. 1978. "'Moe' Dalitz on California Crime List." *Las Vegas Review Journal,* May 3, 2A.

Associated Press. 1990. "Reputed Mob Figure Convicted in Scheme to Launder Money." *Las Vegas Review Journal,* Oct. 25, 10B.

Associated Press. 1991. "Imprisoned Slot Cheat Placed in Nevada's 'Black Book.'" *Las Vegas Review Journal,* Feb. 28, 6B.

Associated Press. 1992. "Bookmaking Ring Broken Up in Jamaica." *Las Vegas Review Journal,* Dec. 10, 8B.

Balboni, Alan. 1994. *Beyond the Mafia: Italian Americans and the Development of Las Vegas.* Philosophical and Regional Studies Program, Community College of Southern Nevada, Las Vegas.

Bates, Warren. 1990. "Rosenthal Taken from Black Book." *Las Vegas Review Journal,* June 6, 1A, 4A.

Bates, Warren. 1991. "Affidavit Says Lawyer Owes Cusumano Fee." *Las Vegas Review Journal,* Mar. 16, 1B.

Bell, Daniel. 1953. "Crime as an American Way of Life." *Antioch Review* 13: 131–154.

Ben-Yehuda, Nachman. 1985. *Deviance and Moral Boundaries.* Chicago: University of Chicago Press.

Ben-Yehuda, Nachman. 1990. *The Politics and Morality of Deviance.* Albany, New York: SUNY Press.

References

Ben-Yehuda, Nachman. 1992. *Political Assassinations by Jews: A Rhetorical Device for Justice.* Albany, New York: SUNY Press.

Biographical Directory of the United States Congress 1774–1989. 1989. Bicentennial Edition. Washington, D.C.: U.S. Government Printing Office.

Block, Alan A. 1978. "History and the Study of Organized Crime." *Urban Life* 6: 455–474.

Block, Alan A. 1983. *East Side–West Side: Organizing Crime in New York, 1930–1950.* New Brunswick, New Jersey: Transaction Books.

Bloom, Murray Teigh. 1960. "King of the Smugglers." *American Weekly* in the *Los Angeles Examiner,* Feb. 21, 21–22.

Bodenhausen, Galen V. 1988. "Stereotypic Biases in Social Decision Making and Memory." *Journal of Personality and Social Psychology* 55: 726–737.

Bowers, Michael W., and A. Costandina Titus. 1987. "Nevada's Black Book: The Constitutionality of Exclusion Lists in Casino Gaming Regulation." *Whittier Law Review* 9: 313–330.

Brill, Steven. 1978. *The Teamsters.* New York: Simon and Schuster.

Burbank, Jeff. 1989. "New Chapter for 'Black Book.'" *Las Vegas Sun,* Dec. 8.

Burbank, Jeff. 1990. "Cusumano Survives Shooting By Masked Gunman in Garage." *Las Vegas Review Journal,* Oct. 3, 1A, 2A.

Burbank, Jeff. 1992. "Sports Fixer Could Join Black Book." *Las Vegas Review Journal,* Apr. 20, 1B, 2B, 4B.

Burbank, Jeff. 1993. "Gaming Agents Arrest Black Book Member." *Las Vegas Review Journal,* Apr. 7, 1A.

Cahill, Robbins E. 1977. *Recollections of Work in State Politics, Government, Taxation, Gaming Control, Clark County Administration, and the Nevada Resort Association.* University of Nevada, Reno, Oral History Project.

Capitol's Who's Who for Nevada: 1949–1950. 1949. Portland, Oregon: Capitol Publishing Company.

Cass, Connie. 1992. "Nine Linked to Chicago Mob Arraigned." *Las Vegas Review Journal,* Jan. 30, 6B.

Chambliss, William J. 1975. "Functional and Conflict Theories of Crime: The Heritage of Emile Durkheim and Karl Marx." In *Whose Law, What Order?* eds. William J. Chambliss and Milton Mankoff, pp. 1–28. New York: John Wiley and Sons.

Chambliss, William J. 1990. "The State and Organizing Crime." In *Criminal Behavior: Text and Readings in Criminology,* ed. Delos H. Kelly, pp. 367–378. New York: St. Martin's Press.

Colvin, Mark, and John Pauly. 1983. "A Critique of Criminology: Toward an Integrated Structural-Marxist Theory of Delinquency Production." *American Journal of Sociology* 89: 513–551.

References

Conner, Walter D. 1972. "Manufacture of Deviance: The Case of the Soviet Purge, 1936–1938." *American Sociological Review* 37: 403–413.

Cressey, Donald R. 1967. "The Functions and Structure of Criminal Syndicates." In *Task Force Report: Organized Crime,* pp. 25–60, comp. President's Commission on Law Enforcement and Administration of Justice. Washington, D.C.: U.S. Government Printing Office.

Cressey, Donald R. 1969. *Theft of the Nation.* New York: Harper and Row.

Cressey, Donald R. 1972. *Criminal Organization: Its Elementary Forms.* New York: Harper and Row.

Curtis, Stuart. 1981. "Silver Turns to Gold." *Public Gaming Magazine* 8: 19–66.

Dahlberg, Tim. 1979a. "State Says Argent Execs Allowed Slot Machine Scam." *Las Vegas Review Journal,* May 31, 1A, 2A.

Dahlberg, Tim. 1979b. "State Lost 1.1 Million in Argent Scam." *Las Vegas Review Journal,* June 1, 12A.

Davies, Christie. 1982. "Sexual Taboos and Social Boundaries." *American Journal of Sociology* 87: 1032–1063.

Day, Ned. 1985. "Possible Black Book Inclusion Elicits Bitter Reaction." *Las Vegas Review Journal,* July 21.

Day, Ned. 1987. "The Mob on the Run." On "Eyewitness News," Channel 8, Las Vegas, Nevada.

Demaris, Ovid. 1980. *The Last Mafioso.* New York: Times Books.

Dixon, Mead. 1992. *Playing the Cards That Are Dealt.* University of Nevada, Reno, Oral History Program.

Drass, Kriss A., and J. William Spencer. 1987. "Accounting for Presentencing Recommendations: Typologies and Probation Officers' Theory of Office." *Social Problems* 34: 277–293.

Durkheim, Emile. [1904] 1938. *The Rules of Sociological Method,* trans. S. A. Solovay and J. H. Mueller. New York: Macmillan.

Edelman, Murray. 1964. *The Symbolic Uses of Politics.* Urbana: University of Illinois Press.

Edwards, Jerome E. 1992. "The Americanization of Nevada Gambling." *Halcyon* 14: 201–216.

Elliott, Russell R. 1973. *History of Nevada.* Lincoln: University of Nebraska Press.

Emerson, Robert M. 1983. "Holistic Effects in Social Control Decision-Making." *Law and Society Review* 17: 425–455.

Erikson, Kai T. 1966. *Wayward Puritans: A Study in the Sociology of Deviance.* New York: John Wiley and Sons.

Evening Review Journal. 1946. "Sheriff, Local Police to Prevent Hoodlums from Cooling Off Here." Oct. 5, pp. 1–2.

Farrell, Ronald A., and Malcolm D. Holmes. 1991. "The Social and Cognitive Structure of Legal Decision Making." *Sociological Quarterly* 32: 529–542.

Findlay, John M. 1986. *People of Chance.* New York: Oxford University Press.

Frey, Dieter. 1986. "Recent Research on Selective Exposure to Information." In *Advances in Experimental Social Psychology,* Vol. 19, ed. Leonard Berkowitz, pp. 41–80. New York: Academic Press.

Galliher, John F., and James A. Cain. 1974. "Citation Support for the Mafia Myth in Criminology Textbooks." *American Sociologist* 9: 68–74.

Galliher, John F., and John R. Cross. 1983. *Morals Legislation Without Morality: The Case of Nevada.* New Brunswick, New Jersey: Rutgers University Press.

Garfinkel, Harold. 1956. "Conditions of Successful Degradation Ceremonies." *American Journal of Sociology* 61: 420–424.

Garnaas, Steve. 1991. "Casino Owner's Dad Blacklisted." *Denver Post,* Sept. 15, 1B, 3B.

Geer, Carri. 1993a. "Marcus Pleads to Tax Charge." *Las Vegas Review Journal,* Mar. 26, 1A, 4A.

Geer, Carri. 1993b. "LV Bookie's Case Settled." *Las Vegas Review Journal,* Mar. 31, 1B, 4B.

Geer, Carri. 1993c. "Marcus Gets Probation." *Las Vegas Review Journal,* May 13, 1B, 10B.

German, Jeffrey M. 1985. "Inside Story." *Las Vegas Sun,* Mar. 20.

German, Jeffrey M. 1990a. "A Stingman of Notoriety." *Las Vegas Sun,* July 1, 1D, 6D.

German, Jeffrey M. 1990b. "Let's Put the Stingman in the State's Black Book." *Las Vegas Sun,* July 1, 3D.

German, Jeffrey M. 1990c. "State Slow to Resolve Bookmaking Crisis." *Las Vegas Sun,* Dec. 16, 3J.

German, Jeffrey M. 1991. "Ex-felon Citro Battles Black Book Odds." *Las Vegas Sun,* Sept. 22, 3D.

German, Jeffrey M. 1993. "Mob Figures May Enter Black Book." *Las Vegas Sun,* May 2, 3D.

German, Jeffrey M. 1994. "G-Man Retires from Mob Busting." *Las Vegas Sun,* Jan. 23, 1D, 5D.

Giancana, Sam, and Chuck Giancana. 1992. *Double Cross.* New York: Warner Books.

Glaser, Barney G., and Anselm Strauss. 1964. "Awareness Contexts and Social Interaction." *American Sociological Review* 29: 669–679.

Goodman, Michael J. 1983a. "Mobster Rises to Dominate Las Vegas." *Las Vegas Review Journal,* Feb. 22, 1A, 4A, 10A.

Goodman, Michael J. 1983b. "Spilotro Turns His Attention to Las Vegas." *Las Vegas Review Journal,* Feb. 23, 1A, 2A.

Goodman, Michael J. 1983c. "Chicago Killing Puts Spilotro in Spotlight." *Las Vegas Review Journal*, Feb. 24, 1A, 4A.

Goodman, Michael J. 1983d. "Spilotro Moves Up and Around in Vegas." *Las Vegas Review Journal*, Feb. 25, 1A, 3A.

Goodman, Michael J. 1983e. "Gangland Murders Focus FBI Mob Probe on Spilotro." *Las Vegas Review Journal*, Feb. 27, 1A, 15A.

Goodwin, John R. 1985. *Gaming Control Law: The Nevada Model.* Columbus, Ohio: Publishing Horizons, Inc.

Goodwin, Michael, and Naomi Wise. 1989. *On the Edge: The Life and Times of Francis Coppola.* New York: William Morrow and Company, Inc.

Griffith, Martin. 1981. "It Looks Like the Race Might Be Easy for Reid." *Nevada State Journal*, Dec. 6.

Gup, Ted. 1989. "Foul!" *Time*, Apr. 3, pp. 54–60.

Gusfield, Joseph. 1967. "Moral Passage: The Symbolic Process in Public Designations of Deviance." *Social Problems* 15: 175–188.

Haller, Mark. 1985. "Bootleggers as Businessmen: From City Slums to City Builders." In *Law, Alcohol, and Order: Perspectives on National Prohibition*, ed. David E. Kyvig, pp. 139–157. Westport, Connecticut: Greenwood Press.

Haskell, M. R., and Lewis Yablonsky. 1983. *Criminology: Crime and Criminality.* 3rd edition. Boston: Houghton Mifflin.

Hawkins, Richard, and Gary Tiedeman. 1975. *The Creation of Deviance: Interpersonal and Organizational Determinants.* Columbus, Ohio: Merrill.

Hill, Henry, and Douglas S. Looney. 1981. "How I Put the Fix In." *Sports Illustrated*, Feb. 16, pp. 14–21.

Hollis, Ron. 1990. Acting Chief, Special Investigations and Intelligence Division, Gaming Control Board. Interview, June 11, Las Vegas, Nevada.

Hopkins, A. D. 1991. "Photos Tie Rebels to 'the Fixer.'" *Las Vegas Review Journal*, May 26, 1A, 17A.

Inverarity, James. 1976. "Populism and Lynching in Louisiana, 1889–1896: A Test of Erikson's Theory of the Relationship Between Boundary Crises and Repressive Justice." *American Sociological Review* 41: 262–280.

Journal Wire Services. 1981. "Apparent Attempt to Murder Reid Fails." *Nevada State Journal*, July 31.

Kefauver Committee Hearings. 1951. U.S. Senate. *Third Interim Report of the Special Committee to Investigate Organized Crime in Interstate Commerce: A Resolution to Investigate Gambling and Racketeering Activities*, Part 10. Washington, D.C.: U.S. Government Printing Office.

Kelley, Daryl. 1979. "Reid Welcomes Federal Investigation." *Reno Evening Gazette*, Oct. 10.

Kelley, Kitty. 1988. "The Dark Side of Camelot." *People Weekly*, Feb. 29, pp. 106–114.

Kelly, Robert J. 1978. *Organized Crime: A Study in the Production of Knowledge by Law Enforcement Specialists*. Ph.D. dissertation, City University of New York.

Kennedy, Tom. 1965. "Gaming Attorneys Move to Oust 3 from Casinos." *Nevada Appeal*, Apr. 16.

Kirby, Joseph. 1978. "Vegans Target of FBI Raid." *Las Vegas Review Journal*, June 20, 1A.

Kirk, Lisa A. 1991. "Hearing Set on Failed Las Vegas Sting Operation." *Las Vegas Review Journal*, Apr. 5, 2B.

Knapp, George. 1990. "Government Making Life Difficult for Joey." *Las Vegas Review Journal*, Sept. 16.

Koziol, Ronald. 1988. "Reputed Chicago Mob Chief Considered for Black Book." *Las Vegas Review Journal*, Sept. 21.

Las Vegas Review Journal. 1955. "Tax Unit Kept Dark on Lansky." Oct. 11, pp. 1, 3.

Las Vegas Review Journal. 1965. "Dealing with Firm Hands and Nothing Up a Sleeve." Apr. 17.

Las Vegas Review Journal. 1978. "Tony Spilotro May Become Candidate for 'Black Book.' " June 26, 8A.

Las Vegas Review Journal. 1982. "Current Black Book Lists Nine 'Excluded Persons.' " Mar. 7.

Las Vegas Review Journal. 1991a. "Black Book for Perry?" Feb. 26, 4B.

Las Vegas Review Journal. 1991b. "Marcus Case Going Before County Grand Jury in November." Sept. 23, 1B.

Las Vegas Review Journal. 1992a. "Wynn Banned Perry from Mirage." Jan. 1, 2B.

Las Vegas Review Journal. 1992b. "Letter Doesn't Change Facts." Mar. 15, 2C.

Las Vegas Review Journal. 1993. "Del Papa Targets Marcus for Nevada's Black Book." Mar. 31, 4B.

Las Vegas Review Journal. 1994. "Black Book Card Cheat Arrested." Apr. 19, 3B.

LaVelle, Phil. 1987. "Black Book Listing Disputed in Lawsuit." *Las Vegas Review Journal*, July 11.

Lederman, Douglas. 1992. "Business as Usual at Las Vegas: Dramatic, Bitter, Ultimately Ambiguous." *Chronicle of Higher Education* (March 11): A33, A34.

Lee, Ruth, and Sylvia Wadsworth, eds. 1966. *A Century in Meadow Valley: 1864–1964*. Salt Lake City: Deseret News Press.

Lieberman, Paul. 1991. "Wiretaps Show Mob's Ability to Infiltrate Indian Gaming." *Las Vegas Review Journal*, Oct. 20, 9B, 11B.

References

Lingenfelter, Richard E., and Karen Rix Gash. 1984. *The Newspapers of Nevada: A History and Bibliography: 1954–1979.* Reno: University of Nevada Press.

Liska, Allen E., ed. 1992. *Social Threat and Social Control.* Albany, New York: SUNY Press.

Lurigio, Arthur J., and John S. Carroll. 1985. "Probation Officers' Schemata of Offenders: Content, Development, and Impact on Treatment Decisions." *Journal of Personality and Social Psychology* 48: 1122–1126.

McCauley, Clark, Christopher L. Statt, and Mary Segal. 1980. "Stereotyping: From Predjudice to Prediction." *Psychological Bulletin* 87: 195–208.

Mead, George H. 1918. "The Psychology of Punitive Justice." *American Journal of Sociology* 23: 577–602.

Moore, Boyd. 1950. *Nevadans and Nevada.* San Francisco: H. S. Crocker, Inc.

Moore, William H. 1974. *The Kefauver Committee and the Politics of Crime 1950–1952.* Columbia: University of Missouri Press.

Morash, Merry. 1984. "Organized Crime." In *Major Forms of Crime,* ed. Robert F. Meier, pp. 191–220. Newbury Park, California: Sage Publications.

Morrison, Jane Ann. 1978a. "FBI Raid Nets Adult Films, Cash." *Las Vegas Review Journal,* June 23, 1A.

Morrison, Jane Ann. 1978b. "FBI Found Confidential Police Reports in Raid." *Las Vegas Review Journal,* June 24, 1A, 2A.

Morrison, Jane Ann. 1978c. "FBI Lists Final 'Rackets' Warrants." *Las Vegas Review Journal,* June 27, 1A.

Morrison, Jane Ann. 1985a. "Metro Works on Expanding 'Black Book.'" *Las Vegas Review Journal,* Feb. 21, 1B, 3B.

Morrison, Jane Ann. 1985b. "Goodman Fires Salvo in 'Black Book' Battle." *Las Vegas Review Journal,* Mar. 21, 1B, 7B.

Morrison, Jane Ann. 1985c. "Judge Asked to Dismiss 'Black Book' Challenge." *Las Vegas Review Journal,* Apr. 16, 4B.

Morrison, Jane Ann. 1991. "Grand Jury to Sort Out Conflicting Stories in Marcus Case." *Las Vegas Review Journal,* Nov. 17, 1B, 10B, 11B.

Morrison, Jane Ann. 1992. "Marcus Insists Innocence Day Before Arraignment." *Las Vegas Review Journal,* Apr. 9, 6B.

Morrison, Jane Ann. 1993a. "Memos Back Story about Bookie Sting." *Las Vegas Review Journal,* Apr. 18, 1B, 4B, 5B, 6B.

Morrison, Jane Ann. 1993b. "Black Book Member Dies as Truck Flips." *Las Vegas Review Journal,* Nov. 6, 1B, 2B.

Morrison, Jane Ann, and Alan Tobin. 1991. "Ex-Gamer Says He's Scapegoat." *Las Vegas Review Journal,* Oct. 6, 1A, 4A.

References

Nevada Gaming Commission and State Gaming Control Board. 1989. *Gaming Nevada Style.* Carson City, Nevada.

Nevada Gaming Commission transcripts. 1960–1994. Las Vegas, Nevada.

Nevada Gaming Control Board transcripts. 1959–1993. Las Vegas, Nevada.

Nevada State Journal. 1965. "Black Book Ban Lifted on Kolod." May 6.

Nevada the Silver State. 1970. Vol. 2. Carson City, Nevada: Western States Historical Publishers, Inc.

O'Dea, Thomas F. 1957. *The Mormons.* Chicago: University of Chicago Press.

Olsen, Edward A. 1972. *My Careers as a Journalist in Oregon, Idaho, and Nevada, in Nevada Gaming Control, and at the University of Nevada.* University of Nevada, Reno, Oral History Project.

Olsen, Edward A. 1976. "The Black Book Episode—An Exercise in Muscle." In *Sagebrush and Neon,* ed. E. Bushnell, pp. 1–22. Bureau of Governmental Research, University of Nevada, Reno.

Ostrander, Gilman M. 1966. *Nevada: The Great Rotten Borough: 1859–1964.* New York: Alfred A. Knopf.

Oxborrow, Margaret Reid, and Charles Fund, eds. N.d. *White River Valley Then and Now 1889–1980.* Provo, Utah: Melayne Printing Company.

Palermo, Dave. 1993a. "Four Face Nomination to State's Black Book." *Las Vegas Review Journal,* May 6, 1B, 8B.

Palermo, Dave. 1993b. "Call to Nominate Informant into Black Book Rebuffed." *Las Vegas Review Journal,* June 21.

Patterson, Edna B., Louise A. Ulph, and Victor Goodman. 1969. *Nevada's Northeast Frontier.* Sparks, Nevada: Western Printing and Publishing Company.

Pearce, Frank. 1976. *Crimes of the Powerful: Marxism, Crime and Deviance.* London: Pluto Press Limited.

Phelan, James. 1976. *Howard Hughes: The Hidden Years.* New York: Random House.

Pierce, Charles P. 1993. "Jerry Tarkanian Died for our Sins." *Gentlemen's Quarterly* 63 (January): 37–41.

Pileggi, Nicholas. 1986. *Wiseguy: Life in a Mafia Family.* New York: Simon and Schuster.

Ralston, Jon. 1990. "Questions Mount in Wake of Judge's Decision on Rosenthal." *Las Vegas Review Journal,* June 13, 15B.

Reid, Ed, and Ovid Demaris. 1963. *The Green Felt Jungle.* New York: Trident Press.

Reid, Ed, and Ovid Demaris. 1964. *The Green Felt Jungle.* New York: Pocket Books, Inc.

Reno Evening Gazette. 1965. "Vegas Gambler Faces Loss of Club Interests." Apr. 15.

Reno Evening Gazette. 1975. "Frenzied Ambition Has Destroyed Best in Young Harry Reid." May 31.

Rhodes, Robert P. 1984. *Organized Crime: Crime Control vs. Civil Liberties.* New York: Random House.

Roberts, Keith A. 1984. *Religion in Sociological Perspective.* Homewood, Illinois: The Dorsey Press.

Roemer, William F., Jr. 1989. *Roemer: Man Against the Mob.* New York: Donald I. Fine, Inc.

Roemer, William F., Jr. 1990. *War of the Godfathers.* New York: Donald I. Fine, Inc.

Ryan, Bob. 1992. "Personnel Session Minutes Reveal Disturbing Contradictions." *Las Vegas Review Journal,* Oct. 26, 13B.

Salerno, Ralph, and John F. Tompkins. 1969. *The Crime Confederation.* New York: Doubleday.

Scull, Andrew T. 1977. "Madness and Segregative Control: The Rise of the Insane Asylum." *Social Problems* 24: 337–351.

Scrugham, James G., ed. 1935. *Nevada a Narrative of the Conquest of a Frontier Land.* Vol. 2. Chicago: American Historical Society, Inc.

Sion, Michael. 1987. "Infamous Nine Are Banned from Casinos." *San Francisco Chronicle,* Sept. 18.

Skolnick, Jerome H. 1978. *House of Cards.* Boston: Little, Brown.

Smith, Dwight D. 1975. *The Mafia Mystique.* New York: Basic Books.

Smith, Dwight D. 1976. "Mafia: The Prototypical Alien Conspiracy." *Annals of the American Academy of Political and Social Science* 423: 75–88.

Smith, John. 1990a. "Cusumano Fights Being Entered into Nevada's Black Book." *Las Vegas Review Journal,* May 6, 1B, 6B.

Smith, John. 1990b. "Rosenthal Wins a Round, But State's Just Begun This Fight." *Las Vegas Review Journal,* June 6, 1B.

Smith, John. 1990c. "Lefty Wins Bet in Court, But Faces Long Odds in Black Book." *Las Vegas Review Journal,* June 10, 1B.

Smith, John. 1990d. "Blunders, Not Bad Intentions, Led to Gaming Agent's Fall." *Las Vegas Review Journal,* June 22, 1B.

Smith, John. 1990e. "Fat Mat Makes Book under the Protection of His Uncle." *Las Vegas Review Journal,* June 27, 1B.

Smith, John. 1991a. " 'The Fixer' and UNLV Basketball Players Must Never Mix." *Las Vegas Review Journal,* Feb. 17, 1B.

Smith, John. 1991b. "Tough to Tell Sinners from Saints in Muddy Mob Picture." *Las Vegas Review Journal,* Sept 6, 1B.

Smith, John. 1992a. "Not-So-Proper Bostonians Doing Their Thing in Las Vegas." *Las Vegas Review Journal,* Feb. 6, 1B.

Smith, John. 1992b. "Defense Strategy Might Not Have a Ghost of a Chance." *Las Vegas Review Journal*, Mar. 12, 1B.

Smith, John. 1992c. "Longtime Vegas Bookie Goes to Big Betting Parlor in Sky." *Las Vegas Review Journal*, Nov. 26, 1B.

Smith, John. 1992d. "Bookies' Caribbean Cruise Crashes on Reef of Authority." *Las Vegas Review Journal*, Dec. 11, 1B.

Smith, John. 1993a. "Black Book Denizen Going Back to Jail with a Certain Future." *Las Vegas Review Journal*, Mar. 28, 1B.

Smith, John. 1993b. "A Recovering Alcoholic Gets Lucky, and Shakes Nightmare." *Las Vegas Review Journal*, Apr. 1, 1B.

Smith, John. 1993c. "Caesars Out-Muscles Competition: Stars Make Classy Call." *Las Vegas Review Journal*, Apr. 7, 1B.

Smith, John. 1993d. "Nevada Won't Have Any Trouble Fixing This Betting Line." *Las Vegas Review Journal*, Apr. 8, 1B.

Smith, John. 1994a. "Feisty Bookmaker Talked Tough But Was No Real Gangster." *Las Vegas Review Journal*, Feb. 3, 1B.

Smith, John. 1994b. "Old Lefty Rosenthal: He's Still Crazy after All These Years." *Las Vegas Review Journal*, Apr. 8, 1B.

Smith, John. 1994c. "Bookmaking Dinosaur Finds Hassle-Free Island Paradise." *Las Vegas Review Journal*, Sept. 11, 1B.

Smith, John. 1994d. "Mobster's Death Leaves Kansas City Mafia without a Boss." *Las Vegas Review Journal*, Oct. 5, 1B.

Spitzer, Steven. 1975. "Toward a Marxian Theory of Deviance." *Social Problems* 22: 638–651.

Stutz, Howard. 1990a. "Black Book Inductee Ordered to Pay $40,000 in Court Costs." *Las Vegas Review Journal*, Apr. 14.

Stutz, Howard. 1990b. "Agents Raid Unlicensed Sports Book." *Las Vegas Review Journal*, June 5, 2B.

Stutz, Howard. 1990c. "Gamers to Appeal Black Book Ruling on Rosenthal." *Las Vegas Review Journal*, June 7, 1B, 8B.

Stutz, Howard. 1990d. "Bad Judgment Brings Down State Gamer." *Las Vegas Review Journal*, June 17, 1A, 4A.

Stutz, Howard. 1990e. "Grand Jury Sought in Gaming Case." *Las Vegas Review Journal*, July 4, 1B, 3B.

Stutz, Howard. 1990f. "Cusumano Wants Parole Terms Changed." *Las Vegas Review Journal*, Sept. 15, 2B.

Stutz, Howard, and Alan Tobin. 1990a. "Informant's Info Aided Bookmaking Sting." *Las Vegas Review Journal*, June 19, 1A, 4A.

Stutz, Howard, and Alan Tobin. 1990b. "Report: Informant Worked for Gamers, FBI, IRS." *Las Vegas Review Journal*, June 23, 1A, 4A.

Stutz, Howard, and Alan Tobin. 1990c. "Gamers Paid Sting Informant." *Las Vegas Review Journal*, June 24, 1A, 20A.

Stutz, Howard, and Alan Tobin. 1990d. "Miller Asks AG to Expedite Gaming Probe." *Las Vegas Review Journal,* June 26, 1A, 4A.

Swigert, Victoria L., and Ronald A. Farrell. 1976. *Murder, Inequality, and the Law.* Lexington, Massachusetts: Lexington Books D. C. Heath Co.

Swigert, Victoria L., and Ronald A. Farrell. 1977. "Normal Homicides and the Law." *American Sociological Review* 42: 16–32.

Time. 1977. May 16, p. 40.

Tobin, Alan. 1985. "Cusumano Black Book Suit Dismissed." *Las Vegas Sun,* July 9.

Tobin, Alan. 1988. "Convicted Felons among Nominees for Nevada's Black Book." *Las Vegas Review Journal,* June 5.

Tobin, Alan. 1991a. "FDIC Prepared to Take Its Agosto Case to Superior Court." *Las Vegas Review Journal,* Mar. 1, 7D, 12D.

Tobin, Alan. 1991b. "FDIC Wins Ruling in Agosto Case." *Las Vegas Review Journal,* Mar. 9, 9C.

Tobin, Alan. 1992a. "Feds Seek UNLV Data on Perry." *Las Vegas Review Journal,* Jan. 28, 1A, 2A.

Tobin, Alan. 1992b. "Mob-Tainted Vegan May Return to Jail." *Las Vegas Review Journal,* Feb. 26, 1B.

Tobin, Alan. 1992c. "Lawyer Says Perry Might Test 'Book.'" *Las Vegas Review Journal,* July 16, 1A, 15A.

Tobin, Alan. 1992d. "Bookmaker Sought after Jamaica Raids." *Las Vegas Review Journal,* Dec. 11, 6B.

Tobin, Alan, and Howard Stutz. 1990a. "Alleged Illegal Bookmakers Tied to Buffalo Mob." *Las Vegas Review Journal,* June 20, 1A, 5A.

Tobin, Alan, and Howard Stutz. 1990b. "Bible Linked to Gaming Raid." *Las Vegas Review Journal,* June 25, 1A, 4A.

Tobin, Alan, and Howard Stutz. 1990c. "State Probing Marcus Role in Two Arrests." *Las Vegas Review Journal,* June 27, 1A, 18A.

Turner, Wallace. 1965. *Gamblers' Money: The New Force in American Life.* Boston: Houghton Mifflin Company.

Vogel, Ed. 1990a. "First Gaming Regulator Looks Back." *Las Vegas Review Journal,* June 10, 7B.

Vogel, Ed. 1990b. "Court Indicates Habitual Criminal Was Treated Fairly by Las Vegas Judge." *Las Vegas Review Journal,* June 16, 1D.

Vogel, Ed. 1991. "Father of Nevada Gaming Remembered." *Las Vegas Review Journal,* Mar. 18, 1B, 2B.

Vogel, Ed. 1992a. "Black Book Adds Perry 'the Fixer.'" *Las Vegas Review Journal,* Oct. 29, 1A, 5A.

Vogel, Ed. 1992b. "Justices Hear Appeal of a Slot Cheater." *Las Vegas Review Journal,* Dec. 15, 3B.

Vogel, Ed. 1993. "State Supreme Court Rules for Slot Cheater." *Las Vegas Review Journal,* Nov. 25, 2B.

References

Vogliotti, Gabriel R. 1975. *The Girls of Nevada*. Secaucus, New Jersey: The Citadel Press.

Whaley, Sean. 1992a. "Feds Deny Players Part of Probe." *Las Vegas Review Journal*, Mar. 13, 1A, 3A.

Whaley, Sean. 1992b. "Richard Perry Nominated for Black Book." *Las Vegas Review Journal*, Apr. 10, 1A, 3A, 12A.

Whaley, Sean. 1992c. "State Gaming Regulators Seeking Richard Perry." *Las Vegas Review Journal*, May 5, 5B.

Whaley, Sean. 1993. "Barr Nominated to Black Book." *Las Vegas Review Journal*, Oct. 8.

Wiley, Peter, and Robert Gottlieb. 1982. *Empires in the Sun: The Rise of the New American West*. New York: G. P. Putnam's Sons.

Zurcher, Louis A., Jr., R. George Kirkpatrick, Robert G. Cushing, and Charles K. Bowman. 1971. "The Anti-Pornography Campaign: A Symbolic Crusade." *Social Problems* 19: 217–238.

Index

Page numbers in italic refer to the illustrations.

hearings associated with, 6, 7, 9, 13, 46, 61, 69, 74–78, 90, 105–19, 131–37, 143–46, 149–55, 158–59, 164–66, 168–79, 191–93, 195–98, 205–8; evidence used in hearings regarding, 9, 117–18, 121–31, 134–36, 143, 154–55, 164, 168, 172–73, 191–93, 210–11, 223–25; lack of evidence in hearings regarding, 31, 61, 63; history of, 14–15, 31, 39–46, 61–64, 217, 227; ineffectiveness of, against slot cheats, 158–61, 195–96; legal challenges to, 40–46, 141, 161; members of, 8, 31, 61–64, 90, 91, 95, 112, 118, 120, 143, 156, 159, 161, 178, 193, 196, 198, 208, 210, 211, 214; nominees for, 96, 224, 248; only non-unanimous decision in, 162–66; purposes of, 6, 11, 155, 165, 217–18, 227; removals from, 47, 49, 98; selection of individuals for, 5, 14, 62–64, 109, 141–42; self-representation for, 162, 205; stigmatizing effects of, 101, 112, 117, 163, 166, 208, 233; symbolism of, xi, 9–10, 218, 227. *See also* gaming regulation, preferential treatment in
blacklisting, 6
Blaisdel, Henry, 21
Blitzstein, Herbert, 210
Bompensiero, Frank "the Bomp," 146
Bonanno, Joe, 143
bookmaking: illegal, 33–35, 39, 47, 60, 70, 78–83, 114–15, 123, 134, 141, 143, 146–52, 157, 180–87, 206, 209–10, 212, 221; legal, 180, 187–93
bootleggers, 22, 24, 26, 30, 32, 37
Boston, Joey, 84–85
Boston, MA, 22, 209–10, 212
Boston College, 189, 191, 192
bribery, 79, 80, 115
Brill, Steven, 59, 86
Brooklier, Dominick Phillip, 146
Brown, Norman D., *30*
Bryan, Richard, 101, 231
Buffalo, NY, 184
Bunker, Richard, 130

Business Week, 86–87
Bybee, Shannon, 150–51

Caesars Palace (Las Vegas hotel and casino), 57, 63, 152–55, 189, 190
Cahill, Robbins, 26, 28–29
Caifano, Marshal (aka John Marshall), 8, 39–43, 46, 71, 91, 171, 173–74, 230
Caldwell, Billy, 94, 106
California Crime Commission, 146
California Organized Crime Control Commission, 38, 199
Cal-Neva Lodge (Lake Tahoe), 33, 34, 40, 44–45
"capo," 212
Capone, Al, 39
Cardinal, Michelle, *30*
card-marking, 162, 232–33
Carson City, NV, 19, 218
Caruso, Carl, 94, 95
Casablanca Hotel (Miami), 34
Casino (movie), 231
casinos: persons excluded from Nevada, xi; sanctions for, 6; use of Black Book by, 4. *See also* gaming industry; *specific casinos*
Castaways (Las Vegas hotel and casino), 53
Castro, Fidel, 40, 55
Catholics, 223*n*
Central States Southeast and Southwest Conference of Teamsters. *See* Teamsters Union
Chamberlain, James, 145–46
Chessman, Carl, 40
Chiavola, Anthony, Sr., 95
Chicago, IL, 219; Las Vegas residents from, 22, 60, 69–70, 74, 143, 167, 178; organized crime in, 31, 39, 40, 46, 61, 102*n*, 103, 194, 198–208, 224, 228
Chicago Crime Commission, 79, 113, 168, 172–73
Chicago Herald Examiner, 35
Chicago Police Department, 71
Chicago Sun Times, 44
Chicago Tribune, 35